Philosophy of Painting

Bloomsbury Aesthetics

Series Editor: Derek Matravers

The Bloomsbury Aesthetics series looks at the aesthetic questions and issues raised by all major art forms. Stimulating, engaging and accessible, the series offers food for thought not only for students of aesthetics, but also for anyone with an interest in philosophy and the arts.

Philosophy of Painting

Ancient, Modern, Contemporary

Jason Gaiger

BLOOMSBURY ACADEMIC
LONDON · NEW YORK · OXFORD · NEW DELHI · SYDNEY

BLOOMSBURY ACADEMIC
Bloomsbury Publishing Plc
50 Bedford Square, London, WC1B 3DP, UK
1385 Broadway, New York, NY 10018, USA
29 Earlsfort Terrace, Dublin 2, Ireland

BLOOMSBURY, BLOOMSBURY ACADEMIC and the Diana logo are
trademarks of Bloomsbury Publishing Plc

First published in Great Britain 2022

A catalogue record for this book is available from the British Library.

A catalog record for this book is available from the Library of Congress.

ISBN: HB: 978-1-3501-0491-4
        PB: 978-1-3501-0490-7
        ePDF: 978-1-3501-0489-1
        eBook: 978-1-3501-0487-7

Series: Bloomsbury Aesthetics

Typeset by RefineCatch Limited, Bungay, Suffolk
Printed and bound in Great Britain

To find out more about our authors and books visit www.bloomsbury.com
and sign up for our newsletters.

Contents

Illustrations

Colour Plates

Figures

Preface to the Second Edition

This book is a revised and expanded edition of *Aesthetics and Painting*. The main addition is a new chapter on 'Contemporary Painting', but I have made revisions throughout to bring it up to date and to reflect some changes in my own thinking. The structure of the book, which is organized into chapters that follow on from one another both thematically and historically, readily permits the inclusion of a chapter dedicated to contemporary painting. Moreover, the emphasis on painting as a historical practice that guides the latter part of the book seemed incomplete without consideration of more recent developments. I was initially hesitant to write about contemporary art, unsure whether it would be possible to address from a philosophical perspective such a rapidly developing field. I was reminded of Lessing's observation in his *Laocoön* that when La Mettrie had himself depicted as a second Democritus, it proved impossible to capture in paint the fleeting phenomenon of laughter: after repeated viewings his smile turns into a grimace. However, it soon became apparent that the additional chapter afforded an opportunity to deepen the enquiry and to extend it in new directions. I have endeavoured to stay close to the interests and concerns that inform contemporary painting by allowing the chapter to be strongly example-led, while also establishing points of connection that link closely to problems addressed elsewhere within the book. My aim has been to provide a non-conservative defence of contemporary painting, which acknowledges the pressures placed on painting as an art by the emergence of new digital technologies and the expanded field of art practice, while still preserving a place for painting on both sides of the digital divide.

The change of title for the second edition also requires some explanation. Although the term 'aesthetics' is widely used in philosophy to encompass the study of individual art forms, serving as a catch-all description for the philosophy of art as well as the appreciation of nature and everyday objects and activities, it is employed in a different way by artists and critics. In the contemporary art world, aesthetics still tends to be associated with connoisseurship and a restrictive emphasis on the visually rewarding features of artworks. This can be traced, in part, to the use of the term by Clement Greenberg and other modernist critics, with whom it is indelibly associated. The title *Philosophy of Painting: Ancient, Modern, Contemporary* avoids confusion on this issue and it captures more accurately, I believe, the aim and contents of the book. I hope this change will encourage those with a wider interest in painting – who might otherwise be dissuaded – to consider reading it, and that this new edition will prove as enjoyable to read as it was to write.

Acknowledgements

I am grateful to Derek Matravers, the series editor, and to Collen Coalter and Becky Holland at Bloomsbury for the opportunity to publish this new edition. The image costs were supported by research funding from my college, St Edmund Hall, Oxford, and I have gained enormously from the opportunity to share ideas with colleagues and students both in college and at the Ruskin School of Art. I would like to record my thanks to Angela De La Cruz, Katharina Grosse, Wade Guyton, Julie Mehretu, Gerhard Richter and Lynette Yiadom-Boakye for their generosity in allowing me to reproduce their work and for the assistance provided by their galleries. The publication of this book also provides me with an opportunity to express my gratitude to David Davies, Andy Hamilton, Paul Smith and Lambert Wiesing for their guidance, support and intellectual generosity. The book is dedicated to Maggie, Emilia and Edward, who bring new life.

1

Philosophical Questions

The Relevance of Philosophy

Philosophy is said to begin in wonder.[1] But it also begins in perplexity, doubt, curiosity, and a stubborn insistence on asking difficult questions, including questions about the nature and purpose of philosophy itself. This book is a study in philosophy – more precisely, that branch of the discipline that has come to be termed the philosophy of art. It is therefore important to start by asking what, if anything, philosophy can tell us about painting and why painting should be considered an appropriate subject for philosophical enquiry. Although directed at the same underlying issue, these two questions tend in different directions. The first asks whether philosophy can reveal something about painting that might otherwise remain obscure or hidden: in what ways might it deepen our understanding and how does it differ from other forms of writing and thinking about art such as art history and art criticism? The second question asks why philosophers should be interested in painting in the first place. Does painting raise a distinctive set of problems that are not already addressed within other areas of philosophy? And might reflection on these problems cast light on more abstract philosophical concerns?

Painting is a non-discursive art form whose effects are realized through the arrangement of shapes and colours on a material support. A painting does not depend on axioms or chains of inference, nor, even in the most extended sense, can it be said to raise a claim or defend a position. It is therefore far from obvious that a discipline that is primarily concerned with abstract reasoning and logical argument is equipped to provide special insight into a creative practice that operates through images rather than words. Although we might criticize a painting on the grounds of artificiality or insincerity, we cannot assess it in terms of its truth or falsity. Such an approach surely rests on a category mistake. But that we cannot argue *with* a painting does not mean that we cannot argue *about* it. One of the reasons why painting has been a source of enduring fascination to philosophers is that it is irreducible to verbal description. It is not merely that words are inadequate to capture the full visual content of a painting – an idea that finds popular expression in the cliché that 'a picture is worth a thousand words'.

Rather, linguistic description and pictorial representation appear to provide two radically different means of communication and expression.

To describe something through language requires us to place a series of abstract symbols – letters, words, phrases, sentences – in an ordered sequence. As has frequently been noted, neither the symbols themselves nor the order in which they are presented need bear any resemblance to what they stand for or represent. The sentence 'A woman is peeling apples' does not look like a woman peeling apples, nor does the word 'apple' look like an apple. Different languages, of course, have different words for the same objects, so even if we were tempted to look for some common feature, we would also have to find a way of accounting for the differences between the French word *pomme*, the Italian word *mela*, the German word *Apfel*, and so forth. It is therefore widely agreed that the relation between a word and what it represents is fixed by convention rather than the possession of a set of shared characteristics. To understand a language, we need to know not only enough words but also the specific rules that govern their combination into meaningful sequences. By contrast – or at least, so it might first seem – when we look at a representational painting such as Pieter de Hooch's *A Woman Peeling Apples* of c. 1663 (Plate 1) we do not need to possess any such prior knowledge. Unlike a verbal description, the painting provides us with an experience that is similar in certain respects to the experience of looking at the depicted scene – in this case, the sunlit interior of a house in which a seated woman hands a length of apple peel to a waiting child. The intuitive, or pre-philosophical, way of accounting for this is to say that, unlike a sentence, a picture looks like or resembles what it represents.

As we shall see, however, the idea that pictures resemble their subjects is potentially misleading and surprisingly difficult to articulate in a coherent theoretical form. This recognition has led some philosophers to reject our intuitive assumptions and to argue that pictures are, after all, best understood on the model of language. The existence of such conflicting views is testament to the considerable complexity of explaining how pictures work. We can broadly distinguish two different approaches to depiction. The first, perceptualist approach, contends that pictures are to be explained in terms of the psychological effects that they produce in the viewer: to understand the nature of pictorial representation we need to examine the underlying psychological and perceptual processes that allow us to see an apple in a picture of an apple. By contrast, adherents of the symbol-based approach argue that pictures, like language, depend on the correlation of a set of marks with a field of reference, and that pictures are to be analysed as complex symbol systems. More recently, philosophers have sought to produce hybrid theories that combine the strengths of both approaches.

What Ernst Gombrich termed the 'psychology of pictorial representation' in the subtitle to his book *Art and Illusion* in 1960 has proved a rich and fertile field of enquiry.[2] Although Gombrich's ideas are currently out of fashion among art historians, they have been taken up, revised, challenged and extended by analytic philosophers, who have used his work as a starting point to develop their own accounts of the nature of pictorial representation. Remarkably, Gombrich's importance is acknowledged not only by advocates of the perceptualist approach, but also by the principal exponent of the symbol theory of depiction, Nelson Goodman.[3] Gombrich's stated goal in *Art and Illusion* is to 'restore our sense of wonder at man's capacity to conjure up by forms, lines, shades, or colours those mysterious phantoms of visual reality we call "pictures".'[4] How is it that a pattern of marks upon a flat surface is able to provide a convincing representation of a scene or object that is not physically present before us? Are the same perceptual processes at work when we see an object represented in a painting as when we see it in everyday experience? How can something static and two-dimensional succeed in presenting spatial relations or the appearance of movement? What is the role of the viewer's imagination in filling out and completing partially occluded or foreshortened objects? And are there standards of correctness against which different forms of representation can be measured?

These questions are of intrinsic significance and connect in a variety of ways with larger issues in the philosophy of perception. However, it is clear even from this short list that the analysis of pictorial representation intersects with but does not exhaust the philosophical interest of painting. First, not all painting is figurative. The emergence of fully abstract painting in the early years of the twentieth century revealed that painting can dispense with the depiction of recognizable objects, scenes and events without forfeiting its claim on our attention. A central aim of this book is to show that representational content is only one aspect of painting as an art and that equal importance needs to be given to internal or 'configurational' properties, including properties of form and design. Second, although most paintings are pictures, not all pictures are paintings. Stick figures, maps, heads on coins, architectural plans, cartoons, billboard advertisements, newspaper illustrations and computer-generated imagery are all pictures of one sort or another. Despite the high aesthetic value that is traditionally ascribed to painting, its very complexity as an art form and the many different functions it has been made to fulfil make it difficult to accommodate within any single explanatory framework. The more sophisticated or original an artist's work, and the more remote from our everyday concerns, the more recalcitrant it is likely to prove as an example for philosophical analysis.

One response to this problem has been to argue that 'demotic' forms of representation should be taken as fundamental: just as philosophers of language begin by studying basic propositional sentences rather than elaborate verbal conceits or the highly compressed and metaphorical language of poetry, so philosophers who are interested in depiction should start by analysing images that are 'a product of the people rather than the art world'.[5] Only once we have understood these putatively more basic representations will we be in a position to address the greater challenges posed by paintings that are artworks. Although this approach has clear advantages for the construction of a general theory of depiction, it assumes that the communicative and referential function of pictures should be given primacy. As a result, it risks severing philosophical enquiry into painting from the sustaining interests of artists, viewers and critics. Many of the core problems of pictorial representation are studied by other disciplines for quite different purposes. To give just one example, the development of visual recognition software that allows computer programmes to process visual data is frequently modelled on an analysis of information processing in the brain, including the way in which we can read two-dimensional surfaces as containing representations of spatial depth. It is not unusual for there to be an overlap between philosophical enquiry and scientific research, and there is no doubt that philosophy has much to learn from developments in science and technology. However, the isolation of a discrete set of technical problems cannot do justice to the full complexity of the issues that are raised by painting. The claim that 'pictures are at bottom vehicles for the storage, manipulation, and communication of information' may hold true as the basis for a general theory of visual representation, but it is tendentious when extended to works of art, for it relegates aesthetic considerations to secondary status.[6]

The Practice of Painting

In a panel discussion held in 1952 on the subject of 'Aesthetics and the Artist', the American painter Barnett Newman made an observation that has passed into the folklore of twentieth-century art. Responding to Susanne Langer's suggestion that the research she and her colleagues were carrying out in aesthetics might be of interest to contemporary artists, he replied: 'I have never met an ornithologist who ever thought that ornithology is for the birds.'[7] Newman's remark captures in witty and memorable form the view that the philosophy of art is external to what it describes and thus has no real significance for artists, who are motivated by different interests and concerns.

This claim needs to be assessed on its own terms, independently of the circumstances in which it was voiced. However, it is worth noting that at the same time as he was developing his characteristic 'signature style' of vertical stripes against a coloured ground, which he first explored in his painting *Onement I* (1948, Museum of Modern Art, New York), Newman was also writing and publishing essays in avant-garde periodicals.[8] His theoretical reflections on topics such as 'primitivism' and the concept of the sublime do not provide a rationale for his work at this time, but they do suggest that his search for a type of painting that was appropriate to the age in which he lived was not carried out in isolation from ideas about the place and purpose of art. Indeed, writing and thinking about art seems to have played an important role in his recognition that *Onement I* constituted a significant breakthrough rather than a failed experiment.[9]

Newman is not the only artist to have suggested that philosophy is irrelevant to art. Wyndham Lewis told the critic and philosopher T. E. Hulme, 'I do it, and you say it.' More brutally, Picasso once retorted to someone who was trying to explain his work: 'Don't speak to the driver!'[10] What lies behind these remarks is the belief that the artist is one step ahead of the philosopher, who frequently arrives too late on the scene and whose efforts at comprehension never quite live up to the originality and excitement of the creative process. The opposing point of view – that without philosophy to interpret it art remains 'mute' – is forcefully expressed by the German philosopher Theodor W. Adorno in his book *Aesthetic Theory*, which was published posthumously in 1970.[11] Adorno's position is difficult to summarize without distortion, but his central idea is that since the meaning of an artwork is necessarily indeterminate, it requires philosophy to disclose its full significance. Unlike, for example, a propositional sentence, whose content is intended to be directly communicable, a work of art does not explicitly declare its meaning. It is this very indeterminacy that makes art different from – and potentially richer than – conceptual thought. According to Adorno, philosophy has need of art since art expresses something that cannot be fully captured through rational argument. However, without interpretation by philosophy – that is to say, without critical reflection upon its meaning and significance – art remains incomplete. The two therefore stand in a reciprocal relation in which each is dependent on the other.

The problem with both approaches – represented, on the one hand, by Newman's dismissive attitude towards philosophy and, on the other, by Adorno's insistence on its indispensability – is that they rely on a forced opposition between theory and practice in which philosophy and painting are treated as fully distinct forms of activity. The relation between painting and philosophy cannot be reduced to that between 'doing' and 'saying', as if painting were an unreflective process carried out by individuals who are unaware of the significance of their work. The French expression *bête comme un peintre*, which means 'stupid as a painter', or more literally, 'a beast or dumb creature like a painter', reminds us that painters were once derided as mere craftsmen or skilled labourers, whose trade depended on the physical activity of mixing and applying paint. The artist Marcel Duchamp, who is perhaps best known for having 'abandoned painting' in favour of presenting found objects as works of art – including the notorious act of exhibiting an upside-down urinal in his *Fountain* of 1917 – claimed to have been motivated by a desire to get away from this conception of the artist. Rejecting what he described as the merely 'retinal' satisfactions of oil painting, he sought to produce works of art that were addressed to the mind rather than to the senses.[12] Duchamp's belief that painting had become obsolete led him to explore new forms of artistic activity, but the opposition between art as a mere craft or technical skill and art as a vehicle for the presentation of ideas goes back to some of the oldest disputes about painting.

Rather than accepting these divisions at face value, we should acknowledge that painting and philosophy are independently valuable modes of enquiry. Newman is perhaps unusual in having published theoretical essays at the same time as producing major works of art, but advanced art practice has always been characterized by a high degree of critical self-reflection. There have, of course, been 'learned' painters, such as the seventeenth-century French artist Nicolas Poussin, who was praised by his contemporaries for his erudition and classical knowledge. And there are other examples of artists such as Newman who have written in a highly insightful – and sometimes highly misleading – way about the ideas behind their work. However, most artists have expressed their thoughts about art through the practice of painting. Painting has its own internal complexity, a complexity that is largely worked out in and through painting itself rather than by means of manifestos and statements about art, even though these are sometimes produced alongside it. It is this internal complexity that philosophy needs to address, and there is therefore a moment of truth in Adorno's observation that without interpretation artworks remain silent.

While the writings of artists are clearly important, they do not provide an infallible guide to understanding their work. Even if we set aside those cases – more common than one might think – in which the artist sets out deliberately to mislead or to provoke the reader, there remains a considerable gap between the artist's self-understanding and the kind of explanation that is provided by philosophy. This can be seen by considering the analogous case of moral action. If we want to understand why someone acted in a certain way, it makes sense to enquire into her motives and to consider what may have led her to behave in the way she did. However, we do not thereby assume that because someone engages in moral deliberation, she is able to provide a fully developed theory of moral action or to give a rationally defensible explanation of the meaning of terms such as 'justice' and 'responsibility'. Philosophy asks questions that are both more general and more abstract than the ones we wrestle with in everyday life. Precisely because of its distance from concrete decision-making, it can investigate the implicit assumptions that sometimes guide our actions without our being aware of them. It also aims at a degree of clarity in the use of concepts and the presentation of arguments that would be otherwise be hard to sustain. Similarly, even though artistic activity involves a wide range of practical and theoretical decision-making, artists are not necessarily in a privileged position to address the distinctively philosophical issues that are raised by their work. The questions that philosophers ask touch upon but do not always coincide with the questions addressed by artists. One of the challenges in writing about painting is to remain sufficiently attentive to the specific goals that have motivated artists at different historical periods while at the same time addressing fundamental questions that pertain not just to this or that artist's work but to painting as such.

The real provocation behind Newman's remark lies in the suggestion that art has nothing to learn from philosophy. Most of us would, I think, be willing to agree that moral philosophy can help us to clarify our moral intuitions and that critical reflection on our most basic ethical commitments is an important and worthwhile activity, even if it does not necessarily make us better human beings. (Few moral philosophers would hold themselves up as paragons of moral virtue even though they spend much of their working lives thinking about the subject.) Similarly, we do not need to share Adorno's view that art is somehow incomplete without philosophy to recognize that philosophy has a valuable role to play in elucidating the nature and purpose of art. The idea that art is beholden to philosophy is itself, perhaps, based on the mistaken assumption that philosophy has a prescriptive rather than a merely explanatory role. Philosophy of art, in its modern guise at least, does not aim to provide a set of rules or instructions that can serve as a guide for artistic practice. Nor does it offer a set of principles for judgment that can enable us to evaluate the relative merits of different works of art. It is therefore to be distinguished from both art criticism and connoisseurship, though it may contribute to both. The distinction between a descriptive and a normative theory of art has not always proved easy to sustain. Nonetheless, it is important to distinguish between these two goals. Whereas a normative theory seeks to *justify* a particular type of artistic practice or a particular set of aesthetic preferences, a descriptive theory seeks to *explain* these phenomena, either by showing how they come about or by analysing their constitutive elements.

A Preliminary Definition

If asked to give a typical example of a painting, most readers of this book would probably choose a work that falls under the category of easel painting: a work that is executed on a portable support such as wood, paper or canvas. Since it is not bound to a specific location, an easel painting can be framed and transported, as well as traded, bought and sold. This type of painting is mentioned by Pliny the Elder in his *Natural History*, which dates from the first century AD, but evidence of its existence goes back even further to the ancient Egyptians. From the thirteenth century onwards, easel painting gradually rose in importance and, in the West at least, it is what most of us now think of under the rubric of painting as an art. The rise to prominence of easel painting is closely connected to the emergence of the idea of aesthetic autonomy: the view that art is intrinsically valuable and that it is, or should be, free of any determinate social function. The very portability of an easel painting – its physical independence from the place at which it was made – allows it to be treated as a discrete object of attention. A painting that is made to be hung on a wall can be moved from room to room, or from building to building, without this changing the work itself. It therefore seems natural to us to assume that the internal relations between the various parts of a painting are more important than the external relations that connect it to a particular site. To see that this was not always the case, we need to remind ourselves that an altarpiece would have been painted for a particular church, that a portrait of a monarch or high court official would have been designed for display where it could convey a sense of the individual's power and prestige, and that prior to modern technology a mosaic or fresco would have been physically inseparable from the wall, floor or ceiling of the building of which it formed a part.[13]

The dominance of easel painting can lead us to overlook the plurality of functions that painting has traditionally fulfilled and to assume that the meanings we attribute to the practice of painting are timeless rather than socially and historically conditioned. Despite the unprecedented availability in museums and through reproduction of many thousands of years of art belonging to a wide diversity of cultures and traditions, painting remains elusive and enigmatic. Once we become aware of the variety of circumstances in which paintings have been produced and the range of purposes for which they have been made – ceremonial, religious, decorative, commemorative, etc. – we are forced to question the assumption that a single concept can be used to accommodate such divergent practices. Some philosophers hold that any systematic study of the arts must rest on the firm foundations of definition and classification. Others have countered that the attempt to identify universal and necessary conditions for a practice such as art, which is not only socially and historically variable, but, by its very nature, subject to revision and transformation, is both fruitless and potentially misleading.[14] Without attempting to offer a strict definition of painting – an achievement that would potentially impede rather than further our enquiries – a provisional investigation into the meaning of the term and the range of objects that it can be taken to designate is helpful if we are to grasp what is distinctive to painting as an art.

One of the earliest myths about the origins of painting is related by Pliny the Elder in his *Natural History*.[15] There he tells how a 'Corinthian maid', despairing at the prospect of her lover's imminent departure, drew the outline of his face on a wall by tracing the shadow thrown from a lamp. Fanciful as this story may be, it already contains the basic elements needed for an account of painting: the purposive marking of a surface through direct bodily movement to create a visual image. Let us consider each of these elements in turn. I have described the making of marks as purposive to distinguish painting from naturally occurring shapes and patterns. It is possible for us to see the striations of a rock face or the stains left by water on a wall as resembling the outline of a face, but we would not normally be prepared to describe these fortuitous configurations as paintings. (I will discuss the reasons for this in Chapter 3.) Second, painting requires the modification of a surface through the making of marks. This part of the description helps to distinguish painting from other art forms such as music and architecture. As we shall see, however, there are many ways in which a surface can be marked or modified and for this reason I have deliberately kept the terms broad. Third, the observation that the marks are made through direct bodily movement provides a way of distinguishing the humanly constructed character of painting from merely mechanical or natural processes. One way of thinking about this is to note that Pliny locates the origin of painting not in the shadow cast by the lamp, but in the drawing of the shadow by the maid. If this is right, then, we need to rule out not only the temporary images created by optical devices such as the camera obscura, but also the more permanent record provided by photography, film and digital media. Finally, I have described the marks as resulting in a visual image to distinguish painting from writing, which can also be characterized as the purposive marking of a surface through direct bodily movement. This part of the description also serves to exclude non-artistic forms of painting, such as painting a wall or a chair where the goal is to protect the object and perhaps to make it more beautiful, but not to create a pattern of marks that has a discernible meaning.

The fluid yet more or less viscous substance that we term paint is normally put on with a brush, but it can also be worked with a palette knife or, as in the case of the late Titian, applied directly with the fingers. Oil paint can be built up in thick layers so that it is encrusted on the surface. A striking example is provided by Rembrandt's *Man with a Golden Helmet* (c. 1650/5, Gemäldegalerie, Berlin) in which the gleaming surface of the soldier's headpiece is built up out of layers of pigment that stand proud of the rest of the canvas. At the other extreme, twentieth-century colour field painters such as Morris Louis used heavily thinned oil paint to soak into and stain unsized and unprimed duck-weave canvas, a technique that was first employed by Helen Frankenthaler in *Mountains and Sea* (1952, National Gallery of Art, Washington D.C.). This method of applying paint so that it is absorbed into and becomes one with the surface rather than sitting on top of it is also used in watercolour and in fresco, in which pigment is applied directly onto wet lime or gypsum plaster. Paint can also be sprayed, dripped or thrown, as in Jackson Pollock's all-over drip and splatter paintings, which required laying the canvas flat on the floor rather than propping it up on an easel. (For an example, see Plate 16: *Silver over Black, White, Yellow and Red*, 1948.) Different types of paint such as oil, enamel, acrylic and watercolour have different properties, as do different types of support such as paper, oak, copper and plaster. While most painting involves the use of variously coloured pigments, some techniques limit the palette to monochrome. Examples include grisaille, which is restricted to various shades of grey, and sepia, which employs the warm range of browns that can be derived from cuttlefish ink.

The account of painting that I have derived from Pliny's story of the Corinthian maid – the purposive marking of a surface through direct bodily movement to create a meaningful visual image – is too loose to serve as a strict philosophical definition. With sufficient determination it is possible to find examples of paintings that it fails to cover. Thus, for example, Damien Hirst's 'spin paintings' rely on the centrifugal force created by a revolving table to create randomly coloured circles. The deliberate cultivation of chance effects is intended to undermine the connection between the finished work and what I have termed the purposive marking of its surface. It is also possible to find examples of visual images that meet the requirements I have identified but which do not aspire to aesthetic interest. A good example would be the illustrations that accompany the instructions for flat-pack furniture. Nonetheless, this provisional attempt to identify the defining features of painting does provide a useful way of thinking about what distinguishes a painting from other objects and artefacts. It helps us to see that although the term painting is frequently used in a restrictive sense to refer to works of art made using oil paint, acrylic, gouache, ink or some other semi-liquid medium, the specific substance through which the marks are made does not play a determining role. If this is right, then we may need to expand the scope of our enquiry to include a broader class of objects.

Support for this suggestion can be given by considering the example of mosaic, an ancient method of creating images and decorative designs that has been used for over five thousand years. A mosaic is constructed by embedding small, uniformly shaped pieces called tesserae into a mortar or cement base. Tesserae can be made from a wide range of natural and man-made materials, including stone, shells, terracotta and glass. Plate 2 shows a mosaic dating from the second century BC that was found in the Villa of Cicero at Pompeii, but which has been relocated to the National Archaeological Museum in Naples. Signed by Dioskourides of Samos, it is thought to show a scene from a Roman comedy play in which the stage is occupied by a group of masked street musicians. The work is sufficiently detailed that anyone who is interested in ancient theatre or music making can learn a great deal about Roman costumes and instruments. What lifts it into the realm of artistic rather than merely historical interest is the vivid impression of life and movement, and the way in which the masked figures are individualized through their actions and postures. These are not mere ciphers, but players and dancers, whose weighted bodies cast shadows on the stage and who interact with one another in a remarkably convincing and life-like representation of a vanished world. Part of our admiration for the work surely consists in the felt contrast between the laborious and time-consuming process of its construction and the freedom and liveliness of the resulting image. However, the fact that it has been made by cementing coloured pieces of stone rather than applying dabs of paint has little bearing on its status as a work of art. Despite the difference in the manner of its execution, this mosaic surely deserves consideration under the rubric of painting.

The English language lacks a suitable generic term that groups together all and only these art forms that meet the basic requirements that I have identified for painting. The term 'visual arts' is too broad, since it is normally taken to include sculpture, film and architecture. The same problem arises with the term 'graphic arts', which derives from the Greek word for writing (*graphē*) and embraces calligraphy and typography as well as painting and drawing. The term 'pictorial arts' suffers from the opposite problem insofar as it gives undue weight to picturing or figurative representation. I therefore propose to go against conventional linguistic usage by employing the term 'painting' to describe a wide range of different methods of making images and abstract designs, including not only drawing, etching, engraving, lithography and other forms of printmaking, but also mosaic, intarsia (inlaid wood), embroidery, tapestry and collage. This is standard practice among philosophers who take the nature of pictorial representation to be central to the philosophy of painting, but it reopens the question, treated somewhat summarily at the start of this section, as to whether photography should be included in the present enquiry. There I suggested that since painting is a product of direct bodily movement, we could rule out photography, film, digital media, and other forms of image-making that depend upon mechanical or automated processes. However, the distinction between human agency and automation starts to break down when we consider the role played in photography by the artist's choice of the subject matter, viewpoint, exposure, and so forth, together with the possibilities for subsequent manipulation of the resulting image, whether this be a photographic plate in the darkroom, or a pixelated image uploaded onto a computer. Although photography depends upon causal processes in a way that painting does not, human decision-making and intervention also play a crucial role.[16]

I should therefore concede from the outset that the decision not to make photography central to the present enquiry is, in part, a matter of convenience. Photography, film and digital media raise several distinct philosophical questions that require independent consideration. Since painting predates the invention of photography by several millennia, many of the core issues concerning, say, the nature of pictorial representation or the relation between surface and subject, can be addressed without considering the impact of modern technologies of visual imaging. The richness and complexity of these questions provides ample material for the present study without extending the enquiry further. Nonetheless, the development of painting from the mid-nineteenth century onwards has partially been shaped by its relation to photography and to this extent photography does form part of the subject matter of this book.[17] It is arguable, for example, that photography's ability to fulfil many of the traditional functions of painting played a key role in the turn toward abstraction in the early twentieth century. I return to these issues in Chapter 6, which also examines how artists such as Gerhard Richter have responded to the success and ubiquity of the photographic image by incorporating elements of photography into the practice of painting. The concluding chapter addresses the prevalence of digital image-making and the pressures that are placed on contemporary painting by the seemingly limitless capacity for storing, manipulating and distributing visual information that is provided by new technologies of reproduction. However, the focus is on painting as it has come to terms with photography and digital media rather than on photography and digital media as independent forms of art.

Two Requirements

I would like to conclude these preliminary remarks by establishing two requirements on a theory of painting. These play an important role in what follows since many of the rival theories of painting that I discuss in this book, while helping to illuminate key features of painting as an art, fail to satisfy one or both. The first requirement, which bears on the relation between the marks that make up the surface of a painting and what those marks are taken to stand for or represent, is widely acknowledged among philosophers working in the analytic tradition. However, the second requirement, which bears on the historicality of painting, has received less attention and is potentially more controversial. I shall offer a brief account of these requirements here, but their full significance will emerge in the course of the book.

To view a painting as a work of art is to attend both to what can be seen in the painting – what it depicts or shows – and to the structure and organization of the painting itself. Whereas mimetic theories give primacy to a painting's representational content, formalist theories give primacy to its design or composition, treating features such as line, shape and colour as independently significant pictorial elements. In their strong versions, both theories fail to acknowledge that the marks on the surface of the canvas and what those marks are taken to represent stand in a relation of reciprocal tension and enhancement. The attentive viewer responds not only to the subject or content of the painting and to its painted surface but also to the way in which the one is sustained in and through the other. It is a requirement on a theory of painting that it acknowledge the complexity of this relation and that it be able to account for the interaction of both representational and configurational elements in a single, dynamic experience.

Painting is an historical practice, in which artists respond to the work of other artists, as well as to wider social and cultural developments. We cannot therefore examine a painting in isolation as if its full meaning were somehow distilled into its visible properties, which simply await sufficient scrutiny to disclose their significance. Our responses to art are tractable in relation to external knowledge and information. Without some attempt to identify the differences between the culture in which a painting was produced and the governing assumptions of our own, we run the risk of imposing our own prejudices and assumptions. However, the task of historical recuperation is potentially endless since it requires not only that we seek to make intelligible other cultures that are temporally and geographically remote from our own, but also that we try to reconstruct the complex motivations that may have guided the work of individual artists. To what extent is philosophy bound by the results of historical scholarship? And how are we to understand the differences in approach that distinguish philosophy of art from art history? Such questions are easier to raise than to answer. Philosophy cannot hope to match the depth of historical knowledge that art history is able to provide, but it is enormously to its benefit to be able to draw on the information that specialist studies make available. The demand for historical understanding raises the spectre of relativism: the abandonment of a unified theory of painting in favour of a merely additive account of a plurality of different practices. Philosophers are understandably anxious to identify a coherent set of problems that are amenable to analysis and to avoid the fragmentation that results from the piecemeal study of individual cases. Nonetheless, questions concerning art's historical character cannot be treated as marginal or secondary to the philosophy of painting. The distinction between the philosophy of art and the philosophy of art history – a curiously cumbersome designation that equates reflection on art's changing character with reflection on the academic discipline that describes those changes – leads us into a *mise en abyme*, in which the conjunction of art and history is endlessly deferred.

The second requirement on a theory of painting, then, is that it sustain the connection between painting and historical knowledge. At a minimum, this means opening the field of investigation to include what Michael Podro terms the 'changing pressures and possibilities of pictorial imagining'.[18] This is vital, I would argue, not only for understanding the art of the past, but also for understanding the specific conditions under which painting is practised today. The strategy that I pursue in this book is to start out from debates that are internal to philosophy and then to show that these debates can be opened to broader social and historical considerations. The earlier chapters are primarily analytic in orientation insofar as they are concerned with the most basic features of pictorial representation. This is particularly important in steering a way through the highly involved debates on seeing-in and denotation, and it allows for a gradual increase in complexity as the book progresses. Over the course of the book, the account of painting is deepened and extended to include questions concerning the historical development of art and the role of historical explanation. Such questions are particularly germane to the period extending from the late nineteenth to the mid-twentieth century, which saw the emergence of an historically self-conscious avant-garde. However, they are also directly relevant to the period extending from the 1960s through to the present day, for the very status and value of painting as an art has been challenged by the emergence of new visual technologies and alternative forms of art practice. Some theorists have argued that contemporary art is separated from the past by a kind of break or caesura, brought about – or, more persuasively, brought to cognizance – by the conceptual art movement of the 1960s, which rejected the idea that the artist is constrained to work within a specific medium such as painting or sculpture. This view is reinforced by an increasingly internationalized museum culture that privileges installation, video and performance over traditional forms of making. The final chapter of this book challenges some of the assumptions underpinning this account and offers a non-conservative defence of contemporary painting that acknowledges the pressures that arise from the changed cultural and historical circumstances under which artists work today. A philosophical investigation of contemporary painting therefore seems timely, and I hope that the arguments presented here can contribute to these wider debates.

2

A Window onto the World

Art and Imitation

When the French art theorist Roger de Piles, writing at the end of the seventeenth century, defined painting as 'an art, which by means of drawing and colour imitates on a flat surface all visible objects', he could confidently claim that 'this is how all those who have spoken of painting have defined it and no one has yet found it necessary to alter this definition'.[1] By contrast, contemporary philosophers have been less sanguine about the success of this definition, finding it easy to show that any attempt to define painting in terms of imitation is prey to counterexamples. If the purpose of a definition is to identify all and only those objects that belong to a particular category or class, the definition fails since the class of things that are paintings and the class of things that are imitations are not coextensive: an abstract painting is still a painting even if it does not imitate 'visible objects'. As George Dickie has pointed out, a successful definition needs to specify two conditions rather than one, each of which is necessary and both of which are jointly sufficient.[2] Although the definition of art as imitation goes back to the ancient Greeks, its compliance class is too broad for it to serve any useful purpose: a definition that stipulates just one condition posits a relation of identity between two different terms and so is unable to pick out the relevant set of objects.

Contrary to the convictions of some analytic philosophers, this piece of philosophical good housekeeping does not carry us very far. Rather than clarifying the connection between art and imitation, it renders the relation between them deeply mysterious. Dickie goes on to argue that:

> for over two thousand years . . . the view that art is imitation was around in a thoughtless kind of way as a slogan definition. The persistence of this implausible theory was due to a lack of interest in the philosophy of art; philosophers just never bothered to examine the view.[3]

Dickie's suggestion is more implausible than the view it purports to replace. It is highly unlikely that a definition of art would have remained in circulation for so long, simply because philosophers never got round to demonstrating its inadequacy. Instead, we should ask what purpose or function the definition was intended to fulfil. For someone writing in the seventeenth century, with its comparatively secure terms of reference, there would have been little point in providing a means of identifying all and only those things that can be categorized as paintings. I would like to suggest that de Piles's remarks are best understood as specifying the central end or goal of painting, and thus as fulfilling an elucidatory function. While this conception of art is open to challenge, it is not inherently confused. Rather than rejecting de Piles's definition, we can use it as starting point to investigate why the concept of imitation has played such a central role in the theory and practice of painting. Only once we have understood the different ways in which the concept has been employed will we be able to assess its usefulness for philosophers working today.

Delight in painting's capacity to represent the visible world has been an enduring feature of writing about art from the earliest recorded documents in ancient Greece through until the present day. The highest praise that the Greeks could bestow upon a work of art was to call it lifelike, and numerous stories have come down to us from antiquity that celebrate the painter's ability to create a convincing likeness. Perhaps the best known of these tells of a competition between the Greek painters Parrhasius and Zeuxis. This is how the story is recounted by Pliny is his *Natural History*:

> Parrhasius entered into a pictorial contest with Zeuxis, who represented some grapes, painted so naturally that birds flew towards the spot where the picture was exhibited. Parrhasius, on the other hand, exhibited a curtain, drawn with such singular truthfulness, that Zeuxis, elated with the judgment that had been passed upon his work by the birds, haughtily demanded that the curtain should be drawn aside to let the picture be seen. Upon finding his mistake, with a great degree of ingenuous candour he admitted that he had been surpassed, for whereas he himself had only deceived the birds, Parrhasius had deceived him, an artist.[4]

This story is no doubt as fanciful as that of the Corinthian maid, but it does succeed in capturing the ancients' admiration for what Xenophon terms 'the appearance of life'.[5] The *Greek Anthology*, a collection of epigrams put together from various sources, contains innumerable hymns of praise for artworks, many of which contain the stock phrase that a painting or a statue 'lacks only breath' or seems as if it is 'about to move'.[6]

Lifelikeness or truth to nature also served as one of the principal measures of artistic value in the Renaissance. Alberti, whose ideas will be explored later in this chapter, observes that painting 'possesses a truly divine power' since it can 'make the absent present' and 'represent the dead to the living many centuries later'.[7] The reader of Vasari's *Lives of the Artists*, published in the mid-sixteenth century, cannot fail to be struck by the importance he attaches to the realism with which painters can depict folds of drapery, the soft down of skin and hair, the glistening of a tear or the gleam of a weapon. Echoing the terms of praise that had been used by the ancients, he extols Leonardo da Vinci for having 'painted figures that moved and breathed'.[8] In his famous description of the *Mona Lisa* he declares that her mouth 'appeared to be living flesh rather than paint' and that 'looking closely at the pit of her throat one could swear that the pulses were beating'.[9] Vasari claims that the rebirth or 'renaissance' of painting began with Giotto's introduction of the practice of drawing from life, which enabled him to make 'a decisive break with the crude traditional Byzantine style', and that the progress of art to the state of 'complete perfection' reached in his own day has been achieved by learning to 'exactly reproduce the truth of nature'.[10] Near the start of his 'Life of Masaccio' he offers in passing, and without according it any great weight, a definition of painting that is virtually identical to that provided by de Piles: 'painting is simply the imitation of all the living things of nature, with their colours and design just as they are in life'.[11] He concludes that 'the best painters follow nature as closely as possible' and that those artists are most worthy of esteem who produce work that is 'living, realistic, and natural'.[12]

Vasari's criticisms of Byzantine painting, which he condemns for its stiffness and artificiality, as well as for 'absurdities' such as feet pointing downwards, sharp hands and the absence of shadows, alert us to the fact that verisimilitude or truth to appearances has not always been given primacy.[13] Vasari was unwilling to recognize that the features of earlier religious painting that he decries arose not from ineptitude, as he frequently claims, but from a different understanding of the role and purpose of art. As we shall see, the assumptions behind Vasari's account of artistic progress have been challenged by later philosophers and historians. However, the underlying conception of painting as an art of imitation is so central to the development of Western art that it cannot be reduced to the views of any specific individual, no matter how influential their writings may have been. In later chapters of this book, I will consider alternatives to the theory of imitation and examine the reasons why avant-garde artists working in the late nineteenth and early twentieth centuries came to reject the goal of 'truth to nature'. George Braque's pithy observation that 'One must not imitate what one wishes to create' betrays his impatience with the inherited concept of imitation, which came to be associated with a slavish adherence to external appearances.[14] For artists such as Braque, a new frame of reference was needed if due weight was to be given to the conceptual and constructive dimension of artistic activity. It goes without saying, however, that the polemics of the avant-garde provide a highly unreliable guide to the art they sought to replace.

Vasari's *Lives* has a strong normative component. Not only does he promote the work of certain artists over others, but he also identifies the exact imitation of nature as a goal that artists ought to pursue if they are to produce work of the highest quality. The great store that earlier writers placed on art as imitation – even to the point of deceiving the viewer – is difficult for us to appreciate today when modern technologies such as film and digital photography provide us with a seemingly effortless superfluity of visual images. Nonetheless, when we look closely at specific examples, there remains something compelling about the way in which artists have succeeded in using the limited means of coloured pigment upon a flat surface to represent not only the three-dimensionality of objects and spatial relations but also the most subtle textures and effects of light. Velázquez's *The Waterseller of Seville* of c. 1618–22 (Plate 3), begun when he was just 19 years old, seems to have been intended as a demonstration piece to display his technical accomplishments as an artist. The painting shows a young boy receiving a glass of water from a street vendor, something that would have been a commonplace sight in the artist's native Seville. The two principal figures, whose hands meet on the stem of the glass, are curiously pensive and withdrawn, as if absorbed in thought. The solitary onlooker remains a shadowy presence in the background. The absence of dramatic action leaves the viewer free to take in details such as the rough cloth of the vendor's cloak and his crumpled shirt. Rather than being caught up in a narrative or asked to imagine the thoughts and feelings of the represented figures, the viewer is invited to participate in a moment of suspended calm in which everyday objects gain in prominence through the stillness of the depicted scene.

Velázquez clearly relished the challenge of using paint to convey the shape and texture of different types of objects. The large water jug in the foreground appears to push out of the picture plane into the space of the viewer, its rounded body contrasting with the dimpled surface of the small pitcher on the table behind. Such is the level of detail that we can make out the striations where it has been turned on the wheel and the slight unevenness with which it has been thrown. Beads of water glisten on its surface and there are marks left behind where these have run down its side. The irregular shape of the pitcher allows Velázquez to explore the subtle interplay of protrusion and recession. However, perhaps the greatest opportunity for virtuosity is provided by the glass of water, for here Velázquez has not only represented the transparent sides of the glass, but he has also depicted the transparency of the water that it contains, a double effect that is emphasized by the presence of a fig that can be seen at the bottom of the glass.

Painting's uncanny ability to capture the most subtle visual effects has persuaded many art theorists that there is an especially close relation between painting and imitation. The connection certainly seems stronger than for arts such as music and architecture. Although music can imitate bird song or the rhythm of a march, and architecture sometimes incorporates natural forms, such as branches or flowers, these are marginal cases. On the other hand, imitation clearly plays an important role in art forms such as sculpture and literature. This suggests that it is not imitation as such that is distinctive to painting, but the specific means that are at its disposal. But what does it mean to describe one thing as an imitation of another?

One of the principal obstacles to grasping what is meant by the concept of imitation as it relates to painting arises from the confusion between an imitation and what we might term a copy or a replica. Although a painting can imitate the look of an object, such as a jug, a curtain or a bunch of grapes, it does not reproduce its physical properties. This, according to the story, is what confounded the birds when they sought to peck at the grapes and Zeuxis when he tried to pull back the curtain. The earliest formulation of the distinction is to be found in Plato's dialogue *Cratylus*, where Plato draws attention to the difference between an image of an object, such as a painter makes by imitating its outward form and colour, and a second instance of the object itself. In the dialogue, Socrates points out to Cratylus that if a god were to create another person identical to Cratylus, with his same features, body, inward organization, soul and mind, then we would have to say that there were two Cratyluses. However, when a painter makes a picture of Cratylus, we do not have another Cratylus but rather an image or a representation. Socrates concludes that 'images are very far from having qualities which are the exact counterpart of the realities that they represent' and that for this reason 'we must find some other principle of truth in images'.[15] Plato's metaphysical commitments lead him to cast doubt on the reliability of images, which, on his account, are less real than the objects they represent. I shall return to Plato's critique of art as a mere appearance or semblance when I discuss his indictment of painting and the other 'imitative arts' in the *Republic*. However, it should already be clear that an account of painting as an art of imitation cannot be based exclusively on the likeness between a painting and its subject. It must also identify and explain those 'qualities' that belong to the painting but not to what it represents. This is the aim that I will pursue in the rest of this chapter.

Alberti's *On Painting*

I want to start by considering a key text of Renaissance art theory, Alberti's *On Painting*, whose composition in 1435 is widely recognized as marking the point of transition from medieval workshop practices to the modern humanistic conception of painting. Alberti originally wrote the treatise in Latin, but he also produced an Italian version the following year, which he dedicated to the Florentine architect Brunelleschi. In the Dedication he expresses his regret that none of the classical treatises on painting has survived and that so many of the artworks described by authors such as Pliny have been lost or destroyed. However, he also affirms his belief that painting is once again returning to its former greatness and that in the hands of contemporaries such as Masaccio it is beginning to rival the achievements of the ancients. While he frequently refers to Greek and Roman literary sources, his aim is not to reconstruct the views of his predecessors but to offer a new, systematic theory of painting grounded in the most recent advances of geometry and mathematics. The treatise is divided into three books, which move progressively from a theoretical discussion of painting through to its practical and pedagogical application:

> The first, which is entirely mathematical, shows how this noble and beautiful art arises from roots within Nature herself. The second puts the art into the hands of the artist, distinguishes its parts and explains them all. The third instructs the artist how he may and should attain complete mastery and understanding of the art of painting.[16]

Unlike the authors of medieval workshop manuals, Alberti locates the rudiments of painting not in practical skills involving knowledge of pigments and the preparation of surfaces, but in a correct understanding of how the world reveals itself to sight. By starting out from geometry and mathematics, he seeks to substantiate his claim that painting requires expert knowledge of the sciences as well as of human character and action, and thus deserves to be ranked among the liberal arts.

On Painting contains the earliest written presentation of a theory of linear perspective. Although artists had been painting objects in perspective prior to Alberti's treatise, they seem to have relied on intuition and empirical judgment rather than following scientifically grounded procedures: techniques for representing certain types of objects were passed down between artists, but this knowledge was largely acquired through trial and error. What Alberti offers for the first time is a systematic theory of perspective construction based on mathematical principles. Drawing on both medieval optics and Euclidean geometry, he starts out from a simplified analysis of visual perception according to which rays of light travel in straight lines from the surfaces of objects to the eye, thereby forming a visual cone or pyramid. Alberti's principal innovation is to suggest that the picture plane should be conceived as an imaginary intersection that cuts through the pyramid of light. What this means can quickly be grasped by looking at Figure 2.1, which is taken from an eighteenth-century textbook on perspective. The illustration shows a viewer, a rather bulky painted panel, and a three-dimensional object – a cube. The lettered vectors represent rays of light as they travel from the surfaces of the cube through the painting to the viewer's eye. By tracing the points at which the light rays pass through the plane of the painting, it is possible to make an accurate representation of the visual appearance of the cube as it is seen from a particular standpoint.

Objects will appear to be larger or smaller depending upon their distance from the eye, but because they remain proportional to one another within the visual pyramid, they can be scaled relative to the viewer. Lines that are perpendicular to the imaginary picture plane will appear to converge on a 'centric point' or vanishing point. Since Alberti identifies the stationary eye as

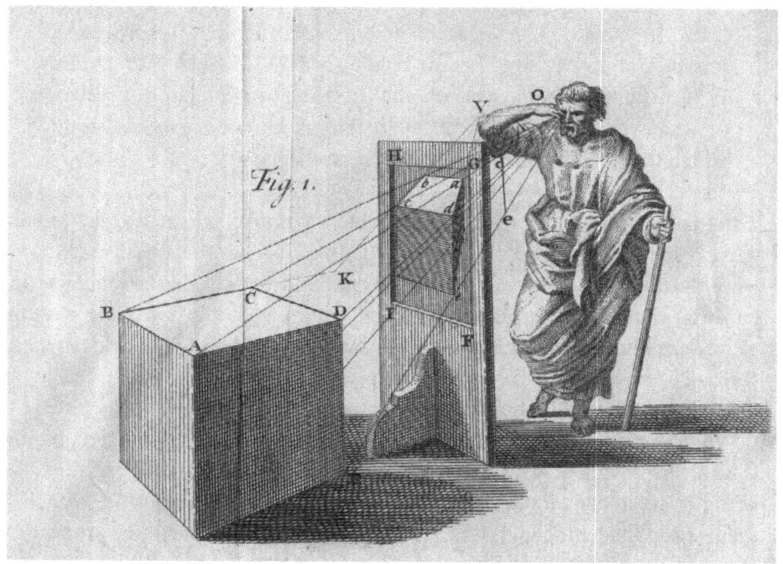

Figure 2.1 The visual cone, illustration from Brook Taylor, *New Principles of Linear Perspective*, London, 1715.

the fixed centre at which the rays of light meet, he is obliged to discount both the binocularity of vision and the mobility of the viewer. His theory does not therefore accurately characterize the physiology of vision. Nonetheless, his account of the way light passes through an imaginary rectangle to the viewer's eye provides a highly effective means of describing the requirements of planar projection. We are to conceive the picture plane as a surface suspended between the viewer and the external world on which the artist fixes the visual appearances of objects with lines and colours. This proposal is fully consistent with the idea, expounded by later writers such as Vasari, that artists should seek to provide an exact imitation of the way things appear to sight.

The important point that I want to emphasize here is that Alberti's account of the geometry of vision does not seem to allow for any variation between the image that is produced by the painter on the rectangle of the canvas and the virtual rectangle that lies at the intersection of the 'rays of light'. In the second part of the treatise, in which he turns to the practical task of constructing a picture, he makes a telling analogy between the surface of a painting and a window onto the world:

> Up to now we have explained everything related to the power of sight and the understanding of the intersection. But as it is relevant to know, not simply what the intersection is and what it consists in, but also how it can be constructed, we must now explain the art of expressing the intersection in painting. Let me tell you what I do when I am painting. First of all, on the surface on which I am going to paint, I draw a rectangle of whatever size I want, which I regard as an open window through which the subject to be painted is to be seen.[17]

This analogy vividly captures the idea that a painting is 'transparent' to what it represents: just as we look through a window to the world outside, so we look through a painting to the objects and figures that are depicted. A painting that fulfilled this requirement would not only meet the demand of verisimilitude or truth to nature, but it would also provide an exact counterpart to our normal perception of objects as this is described in the first part of the treatise.

For the modern reader, the central difficulty presented by Alberti's treatise is how this thoroughly naturalistic conception of painting is to be reconciled with his insistence on the importance of 'composition' (*compositio*), which he defines as 'that procedure in painting whereby the parts are composed together in a picture'.[18] It may well be, as Thomas Puttfarken has argued, that Alberti's theory of composition has more to do with the integrity of the representation of bodies on a two-dimensional surface than with modern theories of pictorial composition.[19] However, when read in conjunction with his claim that the 'great work of the painter is the "historia" (*istoria*)', the ordering of figures in a dramatic narrative that can communicate the attitudes and feelings of the participants, it is clear that he is concerned with effects that are produced by the internal ordering of the constituent elements of the painting.[20] Much of the second book of the treatise is taken up with a discussion of topics such as proportion, harmony, variety and decorum. Alberti expresses his disapproval of 'those painters who, in their desire to appear rich or to leave no space empty, follow no system of composition (*nullam sequuntur compositionem*), but scatter everything about in random confusion with the result that their "historia" does not appear to be doing anything but merely to be in a turmoil'.[21] These properly aesthetic considerations presuppose a meaningful distinction between the artwork as something that has its own internal structure and the arbitrary framing of a view from a window. If the artist is to 'hold the eyes of the learned and unlearned spectator for a long while with a certain sense of pleasure and emotion', as Alberti requires, he cannot base his work simply on the accurate representation of a section through the visual pyramid of normal vision.[22] Instead, he must consider questions of pictorial structure and unity, ordering the parts to achieve an effect that guides the responses of the viewer.

There is, then, an unresolved tension between the conception of painting that is presupposed by Alberti's theory of perspective construction and the conception of painting that is presupposed by his theory of 'historia'. Since the resolution of this tension bears directly on the claim that painting is an art of imitation, it may be useful to stand back from Alberti's text and to consider the differences between them in a more abstract way. Let us call the first conception of painting P^1 and the second P^2:

P^1 A painting that is produced in accordance with the geometrical method of perspective construction provides an equivalent using marks and colours on a flat surface of an orthogonal slice through the pyramid of light that reaches the eye.

P^2 A painting that is produced in accordance with the requirements of 'historia' is structured by the artist to create pictorial unity and to maximize its effect upon the viewer.

Whereas P^1 is compatible with the belief that a painting is like a window, a transparent rectangle that arbitrarily crops a view of the visible world, P^2 identifies a painting as a composition, something that is ordered by the artist to fulfil a specific purpose. According to P^1 the framing edge is extrinsic to what is contained within it; but according to P^2 it marks the boundary between the real world and the pictorial world, to which a different set of principles apply. On this conception, the pictorial world is discontinuous with the real world – that is to say, the world as it presents itself to normal vision. This remains the case even if the artist has striven to arrive at the greatest possible verisimilitude in the representation of individual figures and objects and their spatial relations.

The difference between P^1 and P^2 also has important consequences for our understanding of the distinctive kinds of interest that a painting has for the viewer. According to P^1, a painting is simply a means of recreating on a flat surface a cross section of the pyramid of light that would have reached our eyes from the viewed objects. As the window analogy indicates, the painted surface is 'transparent' – that is, it is not something of interest in its own right. This suggests that the viewer should look through or past the surface of the painting and its framing edge to the depicted scene. According to P^2, however, a painting is purposively structured by the artist, both to create pictorial unity and to bring about certain effects. This suggests that the viewer should also direct her attention to the way in which the artist has ordered the constituent elements of the painting. To view a painting as a composition is no longer to see it as a window onto the world, rather it is to identify it as a purposeful ordering of parts that is governed by its own laws and principles. This is reflected in Alberti's use of terms such as proportion, harmony, variety and decorum. Whereas P^1 assumes that the viewer looks at a painting as if it were continuous with ordinary experience, P^2 acknowledges that the viewer brings a different set of expectations to a painting, some of which are specifically pictorial.

We can examine the tension between these two conceptions of painting – and the ways in which artists working within the naturalist tradition of Italian Renaissance art were able to exploit this tension for aesthetic effect – by considering a painting that Giovanni Bellini made in 1505 for an altarpiece in the church of San Zaccaria in Venice: *Virgin and Child Enthroned with Saints* (Plate 4). This late work, still in its original location, displays full mastery of the Albertian system of perspective construction, but it uses these techniques to reveal an imaginary higher realm in which the seated Virgin and Child are accompanied by an angel playing music and four saints, depicted as deep in thought. The ornamented columns and the upper section of the framing arch are repeated inside the pictorial space, creating visual continuity between the physical architecture of the building and the imaginary architectural elements that are depicted in the painting. The sense of continuity between the real world and the pictorial world is further reinforced by the scale of the painting, which, at over 4 metres high, allows Bellini to render the figures life-size. In the dim light of the church, we are invited to imagine a celestial scene in which the figures are vividly present, occupying the same physical space as ourselves. Nonetheless, I believe it would be wrong to conclude that we are meant to be deceived into believing that the Virgin and saints are present in the church. Each of the figures is depicted as self-contained and inviolable, as if in acknowledgment that beings such as these do not belong to the mundane world. The painting is unmistakeably a 'composition', which has been constructed with the needs of the viewer in mind. The symmetrical organization of the four saints around the central motif of the seated Virgin and their arrangement in bands parallel to the picture plane create a sense of internal lawfulness that establishes a clear visual relationship between the constituent parts. The frontality of the composition is 'addressed' to the prospective spectator, from whose standpoint in front of the altarpiece the painting is intended to be seen.

I suggested at the end of the previous section that an account of painting as an art of imitation cannot be based exclusively on the likeness between a painting and its subject but must also identify and explain those 'qualities' that belong to a painting but not to what it represents. Another way of formulating this question is to ask: how does a painting differ from what it is a painting of? The foregoing discussion has shown that although Alberti characterizes painting as a window onto the world, he also identifies several *sui generis* features that distinguish a painting from an arbitrary view through a window. These features can broadly be gathered under the heading of 'composition' and point to an awareness of the way in which the constituent elements of a painting are selected and ordered to bring about certain effects in the viewer. The concept of pictorial order is incompatible with the idea of painting as a direct 'copy' of reality since it establishes conditions on painting that do not apply to everyday experience. In the final part of this chapter, I shall return to Alberti's *On Painting* to show that, despite his attempt to ground the art of painting in the knowledge provided by geometry and mathematics, he succeeds in providing a positive account of painting's reliance on sensory experience. First, however, I want to consider the opposing view, which received its definitive articulation in Plato's critique of art as a mere semblance of reality. By identifying the reasons for Plato's notorious attack on the 'imitative' arts, we can prepare the ground for a positive re-evaluation of painting as an art of appearance.

Plato's Theory of Mimesis

I have already discussed Plato's argument, put forward in the dialogue *Cratylus*, that since a painting represents only the outward form and colour of an object, it cannot be characterized as a simple copy or counterpart, and that we therefore need to find 'some other principle of truth in images'.[23] I now want to consider in more detail his account of the nature of artistic representation, focusing on his theory of mimesis. The ancient Greek word *mimēsis* is a polysemic term, whose correct translation remains a source of considerable debate. Its origins have been traced back to the practice of 'miming' a person's character and movements and hence to the 'mime' as a form of dramatic performance, though this is still a matter of controversy.[24] The difficulty of finding a single English equivalent arises from its usage in a variety of different contexts, not all of which refer to works of art. This problem is compounded by the lack of a single Greek term for our modern concept of art. As has frequently been noted, the Greek word *technē*, which is standardly translated as 'art', has a much broader meaning. It was used to describe any human skill or accomplishment, and thus encompassed not only those things that we would categorize as art – such as poetry, painting, sculpture, music and architecture – but also crafts and skills such as shoemaking and horse riding.[25] It seems that Plato was the first to identify the concept of mimesis as the key to explaining the distinguishing features of painting and the other 'imitative arts', among which he includes drama and music. Near the start of book 10 of the *Republic*, Socrates asks his interlocutor, Glaucon, 'Could you tell me in general what imitation (*mimēsis*) is?'[26] In the ensuing discussion, Socrates seeks to answer this question with special reference to art. Plato's use of the term 'mimesis' decisively shaped subsequent attempts to understand the distinctive character of art, and it continues to inform the ideas of philosophers working today. Nonetheless, the problems of translating both *technē* and *mimēsis* need to be borne in mind as we proceed, since Plato's distinctions do not always map neatly onto our own.

The claim that there is a 'principle of truth' that applies to images is puzzling and we are entitled to ask what Plato might mean by this suggestion. His basic thought seems to be that truth consists in a relation of correspondence or *homoisosis* between two things: something is a true or accurate representation if it is identical to what it stands for or represents in every respect. However, this conception of truth as correspondence is greatly complicated by Plato's theory of ideas, according to which the material objects that are presented to our senses are themselves imperfect instances or copies of pre-existing ideas or forms (*eidē*). This results in a threefold or tripartite distinction between ideas, material objects and representations, including both works of art and natural images, such as a reflection in a lake. In the *Republic* Plato elucidates the difference between these levels of reality by using the example of a couch or bed. Through his spokesperson Socrates he observes that although a carpenter makes the physical object that we term a couch, he does not make the 'idea' of a couch – the underlying form or concept that guides his actions and that is shared with other couches. According to Plato's metaphysics, it is the idea or form that should be considered the 'real couch', whereas the couch that is made by the carpenter is 'only a dim adumbration in comparison with reality'.[27] If an artist makes a painting of a couch, he produces something that is at yet a further remove, a mere copy of a copy, or what Plato terms a 'product three removes from nature'.[28] Whereas the craftsman is guided by the *idea* of a couch, the painter imitates the *appearance* of a couch, depicting it as it is seen from a certain viewpoint, such as from the front or from the side. Plato concludes that since painting is not directed at 'reality as it is' (i.e. the underlying form or idea) but at 'appearance as it appears', it possesses a lesser degree of truth.[29]

Anyone who does not endorse Plato's view that the highest level of reality is the level of forms or ideas is unlikely to be persuaded by this argument. His position rests on the claim that both material objects and artistic representations of material objects can be ranked in terms of their greater or lesser proximity to an abstract concept or idea – an idea, moreover, that can never be fully known. Even if we concede that a painter represents a couch as it is revealed to sight, and hence its 'superficial appearance', which varies according to the viewpoint from which it is seen, rather than its unchanging essence or 'form', nothing constrains us to privilege conceptual knowledge over sensory experience. Unless we are already committed to the belief that the idea of an object is somehow more real than any of its material manifestations, we are not required to accept the conclusion that the representation of the visible appearance of an object belongs to a lower order of reality.

Fortunately, Plato also offers a second argument in support of his claim that 'mimetic art is far removed from the truth'. Whereas his first arguments rests on the identification of a hierarchy of different levels of reality – idea, material object and representation – the second argument rests on the identification of a hierarchy of skills belonging, respectively, to the user, the maker and the imitator of an object. The two hierarchies are not directly correlated with each other, but in each case artistic representation is situated at the lowest level. Plato develops the second argument by considering the example of an artist who paints the reins and bit that are used to guide a horse. Once again, he begins by observing that whereas the artist merely makes an image or a representation of these objects, it is the craftsman who makes the actual reins and bit. This time, however, his argument turns on the type of knowledge that is required in each case. Plato maintains that since the artist only imitates the external appearance of the reins and bit, it is the maker rather than the imitator who has proper knowledge of their 'quality', by which he means knowledge of how they can be designed most effectively to guide a horse. The knowledge of a craftsman, while superior to that of an artist, is surpassed in turn by the knowledge of a rider who uses the reins and bit, for the craftsman is expected to adapt the work he produces in accordance with the rider's report of how well he has achieved the desired end. Plato maintains that since an artist can paint reins and bit without any knowledge of their use in controlling a horse, 'the imitator knows nothing worth mentioning of the things he imitates.' He concludes that 'imitation is a form of play, not to be taken seriously' and that it does not draw on or provide 'genuine knowledge' (*epistemē*).[30]

Unlike the argument from different levels of reality, this argument does not require prior acceptance of Plato's theory of ideas – it stands or falls independently of his larger metaphysical commitments. One evident weakness is that some of the distinctions on which the argument rests are artificial: nothing precludes an artist from also being a horseman or a craftsman, and thus from having practical knowledge of the things that he represents. Plato is right to point out, however, that a painter does not *need* expert knowledge of how reins and a bit function to make an accurate representation. If knowledge of this sort were essential to pictorial representation, painters would only be able to depict things that they also had experience of making or using. It therefore seems to be correct to say that painters are primarily concerned with the visual appearance of objects and that they do not normally draw on practical knowledge in the same way as actual makers of objects or those who use them. But this can only be used as an argument against painting if we accept that the value of painting is closely linked to practical knowledge. An alternative strategy, which Plato does not consider, is to investigate whether painting has its own distinctive contribution to make, a contribution that cannot be assimilated to other forms of knowledge.

Plato's third argument against painting is that it exploits a 'confusion . . . in our souls.'[31] He singles out the technique of *skiagraphia*, or shadow painting, for censure, claiming that it 'falls nothing short of witchcraft.'[32] *Skiagraphia*, similar to what today we term 'chiaroscuro' – the blending of light and dark tones to model the reflection of light on three-dimensional objects – is thought to have been introduced during Plato's youth by the Athenian painter Apollodorus, and was thus a comparatively recent discovery. When combined with established techniques such as foreshortening, it resulted in a more convincing representation of volume and depth, allowing figures and objects to appear to stand forth from the ground on which they were depicted. Plato argues that if we trust the deliverance of our senses rather than reason, we can easily be taken in by such illusions. Citing familiar examples such as the way a stick appears to be bent when viewed through water, he maintains that the senses provide an unreliable guide to objective reality. The path to true knowledge is to be found in practices such as measuring, weighing and numbering, which are carried out by that part of the soul that reasons and calculates. By contrast, painting is addressed to the lower faculties of the mind and trades in deceptive semblances.

Although Plato develops these criticisms in relation to painting, his real target is tragic poetry, which carried great prestige in Athenian society. By associating poetry with the deception and trickery of painting, he aims to discredit its authority as a source of knowledge. His strategy is to show that tragic poetry also appeals to the inferior – or non-rational – part of the soul insofar as it arouses our emotions and inhibits our capacity for rational self-control. He claims that when we respond to a poem or a play, we are ruled by our feelings instead of ruling over them as we should through the exercise of reason and that 'after feeding fat the emotion of pity there, it is not easy to restrain it in our own sufferings'.[33] The poet is 'the counterpart of the painter, for he resembles him in that his creations are inferior in respect of reality, and … his appeal is to the inferior part of the soul'.[34] With these observations in place, Plato moves quickly to his conclusion that since art 'stimulates and fosters [the lower] element in the soul, and by strengthening it tends to destroy the rational part', we are justified in excluding artists from the ideal state or, at the very least, subjecting their work to censorship.[35]

Plato's unflinching condemnation of mimetic art as 'an inferior thing cohabiting with an inferior and engendering inferior offspring' needs to be understood in the context of the overall aim of the *Republic*, which is to prescribe the type of education that should be given to the guardians of an ideal state in order to ensure that they are fit to rule.[36] His primary concern is to demonstrate the deceptive character of art, both as a source of knowledge and as a guide to right action, and hence its potentially corrupting effect on those who have not yet arrived at true philosophical understanding. Although Plato's theory of art is clearly intended to subserve a broader political purpose, it can be assessed independently of the conclusions that he draws from it. I will therefore conclude this discussion by identifying what I believe are the two principal weaknesses of Plato's account of art as imitation. To do so, I want to turn to another of the dialogues that contains a substantial discussion of the concept of mimesis: the *Sophist*. Here, too, the passages that are devoted to art also serve a larger purpose in that Plato's goal is to show that sophistry, like art, substitutes the making of semblances for the pursuit of knowledge and that its claims to truth are a mere 'shadow play of words'.[37]

Whereas the discussion of art in the *Republic* is framed by the question 'what is imitation?', the discussion in the *Sophist* is framed by the question 'what is an image?'. In answering this question, Plato repeats an argument already familiar to us from the dialogue *Cratylus*. Although it makes sense to say that an image is 'another thing of the same sort, copied from the real thing', when we investigate what is meant by the phrase 'of the same sort' it becomes clear that an image is not simply another instance of the object. An image has 'some sort of existence', but it combines the real and the unreal together in a 'perplexing way'.[38] Plato divides the art of making images into two kinds. The first, which he terms the making of a 'likeness' (*eikon*), involves producing an image that corresponds to the size, shape and colour of the original. This, however, is not what artists do, since rather than employing the real proportions of an object they change its dimensions in order make their work appear beautiful – by which he means both pleasing to the viewer and optically consistent. As an example, he draws attention to the way in which painters and sculptors, when they are producing a colossal figure, will increase the size of its upper parts so that it doesn't appear to diminish as it recedes. Plato terms this form of image-making, which he describes as '"appearing" or "seeming" without really "being"', the making of a 'semblance' (*phantasma*).[39] In a much-quoted phrase, he claims that just as nature produces semblances in the form of shadows, dreams, reflections and mirror images, so the artist who makes a painting of a house rather than building an actual house produces 'a man-made dream for waking eyes'.[40]

In drawing the distinction between a 'likeness' and a 'semblance' Plato recognizes that an artistic image or representation differs in important respects from what it represents. Whereas a perfect copy would be identical to the original, a painting or sculpture contains an ineliminable moment of non-identity or difference.[41] The concept of mimesis – although frequently rendered as imitation – cannot be understood in terms of a simple doubling or mirroring of the original. The question at issue is how this moment of difference is to be characterized. As we have seen, Plato's search for the 'principle of truth' that applies to images is guided by the belief that truth resides in the correspondence or identity between two things. As a result, he interprets the non-identity between an artwork and its model in nature as a misrepresentation: an imitation is always less than the thing that it imitates.

We can make this clear to ourselves by recalling the distinction between P^1 and P^2 that I introduced in the previous section. Plato's recognition that an artistic image is a 'semblance' of reality rather than a 'likeness' prevents him from falling into the mistake of treating a painting as if it were a window onto the world. He is therefore able to reject the assumptions behind P^1. However, his theory of truth as correspondence leads him to give an entirely negative account of the differences between a painting and its subject. P^2 requires that we acknowledge a work of art as a 'composition', an internally structured whole in which the parts are selected and ordered by the artist to meet the demands of pictorial unity and to achieve a desired effect upon the viewer. Whereas on Plato's account a representational painting always falls short of its model in nature, P[2] points to the existence of *sui generis* features that help to explain the distinctive interest and value that we attach to art.

The second main weakness of Plato's theory of mimesis as it relates to painting can be traced back to his idealism and to his corresponding distrust of sensory experience. As we have seen, Plato claims that the highest level of reality lies in the universal forms or ideas that underlie appearances, rather than in the material world that is presented to our senses. Since painters represent things as they are revealed to sight, they are not concerned with things as they really are but as they appear, and so remain at the level of opinion and confusion. At best, painting, like the other mimetic arts, can be described as a form of play or diversion, whose purpose is to give pleasure to the viewer by creating a semblance of reality.[42] More typically, in the *Republic* and some of the other dialogues, Plato emphasizes the deceptive character of art, insisting that its effects are potentially harmful and corrupting.

Ideal Form and Sensory Knowledge

Readers of Plato have long been struck by the contradiction between his negative view of art and the degree of artistry, imagination and creativity that characterizes his own writings. What, after all, are the dialogues if not dramatic exchanges in which different individuals are given voice? And how is Plato's vivid use of metaphor and analogy – not to mention his frequent recourse to myths and stories to explain his ideas – to be reconciled with his insistence on the power of art to corrupt and to deceive? These reflections have inevitably led to a search for passages in other dialogues that reveal a more sympathetic understanding of art. Thus, for example, Plato's observation in the dialogue *Ion* that poets are only able to compose when they are 'inspired' by a divine power might be taken to prefigure the modern concept of artistic genius. However, when this passage is read in context it becomes clear that Plato is drawing attention to the lack of critical reflection that accompanies inspiration: although the poet is 'a light and winged thing', he is 'beside himself, and reason is longer in him'.[43] A more subtle, and more complex, strategy has been to focus on Plato's account of beauty as a path to higher knowledge in dialogues such as *Phaedrus* and the *Symposium*. In a famous speech in the *Symposium*, Diotima argues that we can ascend from a love of human beauty to an appreciation of the beauty of human institutions and finally to an appreciation of 'pure beauty' or beauty as it is 'in itself', distinct from its mundane or merely individual manifestations.[44] From here it is but a short step to the claim that the beauty of works of art can serve as a guide to the beauty of the ideal forms, and that artists should strive to represent not the shifting world of appearances but the eternal and immutable forms themselves.

A large stumbling block lies in the way of this interpretation. For not only does Plato neglect to accord any role to art in the ascent to 'pure beauty', but he also expressly denies that artists can represent or be guided by ideal forms. In book 10 of the *Republic*, he raises the question, 'To which is painting directed in every case, to the imitation of reality as it is or of appearance as it appears? Is it an imitation of a phantasm or of the truth?'[45] As we have seen, his unequivocal answer is that painting belongs to the realm of appearances and that it leads us away from rather than towards true knowledge. Nonetheless, Plato's theory of ideas, heavily mediated through the writings of Plotinus, was refashioned by later philosophers and art theorists, who promoted the contrary view that through divine inspiration artists are granted direct access to the realm of ideal forms. This formed an important current of thought in the Renaissance and was a mainstay of academic classicism throughout the late seventeenth and eighteenth centuries. Discoveries of important works of antique sculpture helped to reinforce this view, and it was widely held that the greatness of classical art derived from its realization of an ideal of perfection.[46] Aspiring artists were enjoined to correct nature and to overcome the 'imperfections' that might inhere in any one individual by comparing and synthesizing several different examples. This approach is given a typically robust formulation by Joshua Reynolds in his *Discourses on Art*, who claims that 'long, laborious comparison should be the first study of the painter, who aims at the greatest style':

> By this means, he acquires a just idea of beautiful forms; he corrects nature by herself, her imperfect state by her more perfect. His eye being enabled to distinguish the accidental deficiencies, excrescences, and deformities of things, from their general figures, he makes out an abstract idea of their forms more perfect than any one original; and what may seem a paradox, he learns to design naturally by drawing his figures unlike to any one object. This idea of the perfect state of nature, which the Artist calls the Ideal Beauty, is the great leading principle, by which works of genius are conducted.[47]

An early version of this argument is found in the third book of *On Painting*, in which Alberti recounts a story about the Greek painter Zeuxis that had been passed down in different forms by both Cicero and Pliny. When Zeuxis was asked to produce a painting of the mythical figure of Helen for a temple at Croton, 'he chose from all the youth of the city five outstandingly beautiful girls, so that he might represent in his painting whatever feature of feminine beauty was most praiseworthy in each of them'.[48] Contrasting Zeuxis' work with that of the painter Demetrius, who 'failed to obtain the highest praise because he was more devoted to representing the likeness of things than to beauty', Alberti concludes that Zeuxis 'acted wisely': 'excellent parts should be selected from the most beautiful bodies' since 'the merits of beauty are not all to be found in one place, but are dispersed here and there in many'.[49] The construction of an ideal type is not, of course, the same as being guided by the Platonic form or idea, which, according to Plato at least, is not so easily come by. Nonetheless, Alberti does not seem to have identified any conflict between his insistence on the accurate representation of the observable world through linear perspective in book 1 and his endorsement of the theory of ideal beauty in book 3. He takes it as given that unless the artist can provide a convincing representation of three-dimensional forms and non-planar spatial relations his work will appear awkward and unbalanced to the viewer. However, it does not follow from this that the artist should simply copy what lies before him. As we have seen, Alberti's theory of 'composition' requires that the painter submit his material to principles of visual ordering that are not found in nature. While the claim that the artist should improve nature by selecting and combining parts from different individuals takes this argument a step further, it is not inconsistent with his basic position.

Although a case can be made for Alberti's support for the theory of ideal form, I believe that the main impetus of his thought tends in the opposing direction and that the real interest of *On Painting* resides in its positive re-evaluation of painting's reliance on sensory knowledge. Like Plato, Alberti identifies a close link between painting as a specifically visual mode of representation and the realm of 'appearances', but – unburdened by Plato's metaphysical commitments – he recognizes that this is what gives painting its special interest and value. To see how he arrives at this position, we need to return to the distinction between mathematics and painting with which the treatise begins. The argument of book 1 is obscured by Alberti's insistence in the dedication to Brunelleschi that its contents are 'entirely mathematical'. This suggests that the abstract knowledge provided by mathematics provides the foundation on which the treatise is based, and that the role of the subsequent books is to show how this knowledge can be 'applied' to the art of painting. However, in the main body of the text Alberti makes it clear that mathematics and painting have different objects: whereas mathematicians 'measure the shapes and forms of things in the mind alone and divorced entirely from matter', the painter 'strives to represent only the things that are seen'.[50]

What Alberti means by this is revealed by his discussion of points and lines. For the mathematician, point and lines are abstractions: a point is something that is indivisible into parts and a line is something that can be divided along its length but not along its breadth. The painter, however, works not with mathematical concepts but with physical marks. Rather than divorcing form from matter, the painter is concerned with matter's visible form. The same argument applies to the treatment of surfaces. According to Alberti, the surface of an object can be defined as 'the outer limit of a body which is recognised not by depth but by width and length, and also by its properties'.[51] Considered in abstraction from the standpoint of a specific observer, the properties of a surface such as its outer edge and its local colour are fixed. They cannot be altered without altering the object itself. However, when seen from a particular viewpoint and under specific conditions of light, not only the apparent size but also the outline and the colour of an object are subject to change. Thus, for example, a round coin seen from the side will have the shape of an ellipse and bright colours will appear darker when placed in the shade. Alberti observes: 'These matters are related to the power of vision; for with a change of position surfaces will appear larger, or of a completely different outline from before, or diminished in colour; all of which we judge by sight.'[52] Although the appearance of an object changes in accordance with the conditions of light and the position from which it is viewed, these changes are not arbitrary. Viewed from the side rather than above, a coin will always take on the shape of an ellipse, just as the part of a surface that is in shade will always appear darker than the part that is exposed to direct light.

Whereas mathematics and geometry are exclusively concerned with the permanent qualities that inhere in the object itself, painting is also concerned with the impermanent qualities that change relative to the standpoint of the observer. The artist must understand these changes and learn to employ the appropriate methods for representing the visible world through the medium of paint. Although the painter draws on the knowledge provided by mathematics and geometry, he does so in the service of depicting appearances, of things as they are seen. In contrast to Plato, who argues that we should use the intellectual knowledge provided by our rational faculties to correct the deception of the senses, Alberti seeks to bring sensory knowledge into the domain of science. However, rather than privileging the realm of concepts and abstract ideas over the realm of appearances, he recognizes that painting has its own, unique claim on our attention – a claim that derives, at least in part, from its rootedness in sensory experience.

3

Surface and Subject

Two Forms of Awareness

One effect of a picture that shows someone absorbed in the act of looking is to draw attention to the viewer's own activity of looking. Adolph Menzel's *Lady with Opera Glasses* (Plate 5) depicts a woman at the theatre gazing intently at something that we cannot see. But what do we see when we look at Menzel's drawing? There are two different ways to answer this question, both of which are correct but insufficient on their own. The first is to insist, somewhat obtusely, that what we see is a small rectangular piece of paper overlain with coloured chalk – a flat surface marked with a configuration of lines and shapes. We can describe the difference between the unmarked cinnamon-coloured paper that serves as the ground and those areas where the grain has been used to hold traces of chalk. We can also describe the direction, density and pattern of the marks, perhaps focusing on the contrast between the opaque patches of red and the lighter, transparent touches of white, or the hatching where two sets of lines cross each other. We can look at these lines and marks *as* lines and marks, for that is what they are, perhaps even recognizing in them traces of the movement of the artist's hand, whose variations of pressure and direction have given rise to pronounced differences in weight and texture. We can do all this, however, without referring to the content of the drawing – that is, without saying what those marks and lines are taken to represent.

The second way of answering the question is to observe, with equal justification, that what we see when we look at *Lady with Opera Glasses* is a picture of a seated woman looking through a pair of binoculars. We can make out the red shapes of the seat backs, the white dress that covers her back and shoulders, the jutting shape of the binoculars, and even the parting in her hair. We can also describe the position from which we view her – looking down from above and at an angle – and note that this prevents us from seeing her left arm and her face. There is much, of course, that is not shown. We are aware, for example, both of the isolation of the figure from her surroundings and of the incompletion of the lower part of her body. Just as the woman focuses her attention on what can be seen through the binoculars, so the artist has focused his attention on the seated woman to the exclusion of whatever – or whoever – else he might have been able to see in the theatre. Rather than interpreting this omission as evidence that the work is unfinished, we recognize it as continuous with the saliency of looking. We see what the artist saw, or, at least, what the artist retained in his memory, as is indicated by the German word *Erinn*[*erung*], which is written across the bottom left-hand corner.

The loose handling of *Lady with Opera Glasses* makes it comparatively easy to distinguish between these two forms of awareness: our awareness of the marked surface as a configuration of lines and shapes and our awareness of that surface as a representation of a woman holding a pair of binoculars. Both seem to be necessary to pictorial perception. For unless you were aware that you were looking at a marked surface, you would not be aware that you were looking at a picture; and unless the experience of looking at the picture is in some way like the experience of looking at its subject, you would not be aware of what it represents.[1] Once we have made this distinction, the question inevitably arises as to how these two ways of seeing the picture are related to one another: how does our visual awareness of the drawing as a physical object with a discrete set of properties enter into or inform our awareness of its representational content? Do we alternate between seeing the marked surface and seeing the subject of the picture? Or do we hold the two together in our mind as part of a single composite experience? What enables us to see a pattern of marks as a representation of a woman with binoculars? And how does the experience of seeing someone (or something) in a picture differ from the experience of seeing someone (or something) actually before us?

Current philosophical discussion of these questions takes its starting point from the work of Ernst Gombrich, who, more than anyone else, succeeded in revitalizing interest in the relation between visual perception and pictorial representation. Gombrich trained as an art historian in Vienna at a time when the disciplinary boundaries between philosophy, psychology and art history were not firmly in place. In a groundbreaking series of books and articles from the 1930s through until his death in 2001, he carried out a wide-ranging interdisciplinary investigation into the historical development of art that brought together cognitive psychology, philosophical aesthetics and detailed historical research. Gombrich's own illusion theory of pictorial perception has found few supporters, but many of the core arguments that he brings to bear in its favour have been taken up by others, often in markedly conflicting ways. As we saw in Chapter 1, both the two main rival strategies for explaining the distinctive nature of visual representation derive inspiration from his work. Whereas the perceptualist approach is grounded in his account of the psychological effects that pictures bring about in the mind of the viewer, the symbol-based approach draws on his analysis of the role of conventions in different representational systems. I shall examine the perceptualist approach in this chapter, reserving discussion of the symbol-based approach – and the possible unification of the two in a 'hybrid' theory – until Chapter 4.

The reason why Gombrich's ideas have proved so fertile, or so I shall argue, is that he succeeded in demonstrating the inadequacy of narrowly mimetic theories of art without producing a satisfactory alternative. By challenging the underlying assumptions that had dominated thought on the topic since the time of Plato, he revealed the need for a new explanatory framework. However, the clarity and effectiveness of his arguments removed what common ground had previously been shared and opened the way for a range of competing positions. The fiercest debates have focused on whether, as Gombrich claims, recognition of the subjectivity of vision still allows for 'objective standards of representational accuracy' or whether we are forced to accept the relativist conclusion that no system of representation is able to represent reality any more accurately than another.[2] I shall return to these disputes in the next chapter. First, I want to examine the presuppositions behind Gombrich's illusion theory of pictorial perception and to show how this theory arises out of his root-and-branch rejection of the concept of mimesis.

Sustaining Illusion

The title of Gombrich's book, *Art and Illusion: A Study in the Psychology of Pictorial Representation* (1960), forewarns the reader that its scope extends beyond the Western canon of art to include a wide assortment of pictures and images – including not only posters, signs and advertisements, but also the optical illusions that are employed by psychologists to analyse visual perception. Gombrich's use of the term 'illusion' also points back to a much earlier tradition of enquiry, finding an important counterpart in Plato's characterization of art as a 'semblance' or 'phantasm'.[3] Whereas Plato criticizes mimetic art as a practice of deception that is directed at the 'lower part of the soul', Gombrich's avowed goal is to 'recapture the thrill and shock which the first illusionist images must have caused when shown on the stage or on the walls of Greek houses'.[4] He acknowledges that realistic representation is now an everyday achievement, mastered by the skilled amateur and the professional designer alike – 'even the crude coloured renderings we find on a box of breakfast cereal would have made Giotto's contemporaries gasp' – but he contends that the simultaneous 'victory and vulgarisation of representational skills' presents an obstacle to understanding the nature of visual representation.[5] The very facility with which these skills are deployed prevents us from recognizing that they were achieved only through a lengthy process of study and investigation. Because we stand at the end of this process, it is easy for us to assume that these hard-won techniques have always been available and that anyone who seeks to record what she sees by making marks on a surface will follow the same self-evident rules of representation. Gombrich pursues two separate lines of thought to break the hold of this assumption: the first is captured in his claim that the artist 'cannot transcribe what he sees; he can only translate it into the terms of his medium'; the second is captured in his oft-repeated slogan that 'making comes before matching'.[6] Let us consider each of these ideas in turn.

The materials out of which art is made become a medium when they are used in the service of representation.[7] A line of chalk can be used to represent the outline of a shoulder, a row of tesserae to represent the edge of a stage, and a transparent glaze of paint the bead of water on a jug. But the medium also imposes constraints upon the artist. The coarse lines made by a piece of chalk permit the artist to explore a different range of effects from the thin lines of a pencil, just as the blending of oil-based pigments allows the painter to evoke subtleties of tone that must elude even the most patient mosaicist. Once we are aware of these differences, we find ourselves hard-pressed to say which offers the more faithful representation of nature. For the world as it reveals itself to sight no more looks like a soft residue of chalk than it does a hard line of graphite. The difference between the painter's brushstroke and the mosaicist's pieces of stone is a difference of degree rather than of kind. The artist cannot duplicate what she sees with the resources of her medium since – apart from some very rare exceptions such as the use of gold leaf to represent gold – the medium and what it is used to represent are radically dissimilar. The world we see extends in depth, alters its colour with the modification of light, and is animated with motion, but a picture offers us only a static two-dimensional surface marked with pigment.[8] How, then, are we to explain the fact that some pictures can provide us with visual experiences similar to those that would be provided by the depicted scene were we actually to see it? In other words, how is it that pictures can generate the 'illusion' of seeing something that is not actually there?

In raising this question, Gombrich returns to a problem with which Plato had wrestled in the dialogues. Plato had already acknowledged that 'images are very far from having qualities which are the exact counterpart of the realities that they represent' and that we must therefore seek 'some other principle of truth in images'.[9] The innovative character of Gombrich's solution is achieved through a pivotal transformation in the terms in which the problem is addressed. Instead of enquiring whether a work of art 'looks like' or resembles its model in nature – and hence whether it offers a more or less accurate copy of the original – he focuses on the type of *response* that each can elicit. Rather than comparing art with nature, he compares the different psychological effects that the two produce in the mind of the viewer. Although a static two-dimensional surface does not share the same physical properties as the three-dimensional moving world, it can nonetheless be made to trigger the same perceptual responses. Since these responses are largely involuntary, they can be directed and manipulated by providing the appropriate visual cues. Recalling Alberti's famous analogy, Gombrich contends that:

> What may make a painting like a distant view through a window is not the fact that the two can be as indistinguishable as a facsimile from the original: it is the similarity between the mental activities both can arouse.[10]

Artists do not learn to 'copy' what they see: they discover ways of mobilizing the viewer's recognitional responses through the resources of their medium. This can only be achieved by experimenting with different pictorial effects and observing their effect on the viewer. However, once successful techniques such as occlusion, diminution, foreshortening and shading have been developed, they can be deployed by other artists. Deploying a vivid metaphor, Gombrich claims that the history of art 'may be described as the forging of the master keys for opening the mysterious locks of our senses to which only nature herself originally held the key'.[11] We have no direct access to the inner mechanism, but once artists have learned to spring the lock, this knowledge can be passed from generation to generation.

A picture that is intended to offer an accurate representation of a particular scene or object can be tested against experience and modified accordingly. But since a picture is not a direct copy of nature, the artist must start out with some basic design or motif that can serve as a basis for investigation. 'Making' comes before 'matching' in the sense that artists are only able to discover whether certain techniques will elicit the appropriate response through a process of trial and error. Historical studies of various different kinds of art – from humble woodblock prints to the most ambitious Renaissance altarpiece – have shown that artists frequently rely on existing forms and compositional structures that were derived from the work of earlier artists.[12] In emphasizing the extent to which 'the familiar will always remain the likely starting point for the rendering of the unfamiliar', Gombrich's goal is not merely to show that artists learn from each other as well as from their own experience: he seeks to undermine the misleading assumption that the process of artistic creation begins with direct visual observation, which is then 'transcribed' as a visual representation.[13] The information that reaches us through our senses is so abundant and so varied that we must first impose a means of selection and organization. There is no perception without conception: seeing and knowing are inextricably bound up with one another through the 'expectations' that structure experience. 'Making' therefore comes before 'matching' in the sense that pictorial representation depends on a prior conceptual schema through which the artist can seize hold of, and give order to, the flux of experience. Gombrich concludes: 'All art originates in the human mind, in our reactions to the world rather than in the visible world itself, and it is precisely because all art is "conceptual" that all representations are recognisable by their style.'[14]

The interplay of schema and correction is likened by Gombrich to the role played by hypothesis and evidence in the development of scientific knowledge. Once artists have set themselves the task of producing a convincing representation of the visible world, they can test the effectiveness of a particular design or schema against the deliverances of the senses and use the results to develop ever more effective means of triggering the relevant responses. The evolution of naturalism as this took place first in ancient Greece and then in the Renaissance should be understood as the progressive 'conquest of appearances' through a process of making and matching.[15] As Gombrich acknowledges, the question begged by this account is why some cultures but not others have pursued the goal of producing 'life-like' images in the sense in which he uses this term. One of the central aims of *Art and Illusion* is to explain why 'different ages and different nations have represented the visible world in such different ways'.[16] There are two components of Gombrich's answer that are directly relevant to our present concerns. The first is his claim that what counts as artistic progress is closely tied to the purpose or function that art is intended to fulfil. During the Byzantine period, for example, the emphasis on didactic clarity resulted in images that were clearly legible. However, there was no requirement that the artist provide a plausible representation of three-dimensional space or that the figures be placed in coherent spatial relations with one another. Instead, 'the sacred event was told in clear and simple hieroglyphs which make us understand rather than visualize it'.[17] Similarly, Gombrich argues that the rise of naturalism in Renaissance art should be traced back not to some generalized goal of imitating nature as accurately as possible, but to 'a specific demand for the plausible narration of sacred events'. The very success with which artists such as Giotto were able to satisfy this requirement allowed viewers to ask questions such as 'What does this onlooker feel?'; 'What sort of fabric is his cloak?'; 'Why does he throw no shadow?'[18] These questions – together with the corresponding technical interest in the representation of appearances – became relevant only when pictures were treated not as emblems or symbols but as vivid representations of biblical scenes as they might have been perceived by an eyewitness.

The second component of Gombrich's answer is to be found in his claim that the development of ancient Greek and Renaissance art is distinguished from that of other historical periods by the 'admixture of science'.[19] By this he means not merely that artists were able to draw on – and in some cases contribute to – related fields of enquiry, such as anatomy, optics and projective geometry, but that investigation into the underlying mechanisms through which artists could produce a realistic image was carried out in a scientific spirit. The work of Renaissance artists such as Alberti and Brunelleschi clearly fits this model, but Gombrich also includes later artists such as John Constable, who were scientific in their method rather than in their training. Citing Constable's remark that 'Painting is a science and should be pursued as an inquiry into the laws of nature', Gombrich concludes: 'In the Western tradition, painting has indeed been pursued as a science. All the works of this tradition that we see displayed in our great collections apply discoveries that are the result of ceaseless experimentation.'[20]

Though this account has many virtues, it remains unmistakeably Whiggish. Gombrich too readily assimilates the problem 'why representation should have a history' to the problem 'why it should have taken mankind so long to arrive at a plausible rendering of visual effects that create the illusion of life-likeness'.[21] He thereby overlooks, or downplays, the genuine diversity of visual art that has been produced in different cultures and at different historical periods in favour of a single, unified narrative that culminates in the development of fully-fledged naturalism. Even with the confines of the specific European tradition on which Gombrich focuses, it is far from clear that naturalism has been the main or even a primary goal that artists have pursued. It is only on the implausible assumption that the artists he discusses shared the same set of motivations and that they were attempting to find a solution to a problem that they all formulated in the same way that his theory of 'making and matching' can fulfil a satisfactory explanatory role.

I shall return to these issues in Chapter 5, in which I investigate in more detail Gombrich's claims concerning the historical development of art. However, even this brief discussion allows us to see that Gombrich's account of pictorial representation is severely circumscribed. His illusion theory of pictorial perception is primarily concerned with naturalistic works of art in which the artist creates a convincing illusion of reality by activating the mechanisms of sight.[22] The artist, like the scientist or conjuror, is identified as an 'experienced manipulator', who 'has been able to find out how to predict and trigger certain non-veridical visual experiences through the arousal of visual sensations'.[23] It follows from Gombrich's equation of naturalism with the pursuit of illusionistic effects that the complete 'conquest of appearances' would be a painting that the viewer was unable to distinguish from reality: so effectively would the artist be able to simulate the clues that we rely on in ordinary vision that the viewer's experience of the painting would be indistinguishable from her experience of the scene or object that it depicts. Gombrich concedes that this could only be achieved, if at all, under highly artificial conditions, such as requiring the viewer to look through two boxes with peepholes, one of which opens onto the painting and the other onto a reconstruction of the motif.[24] Without such devices, including the imposition of strictly controlled lighting conditions, the viewer's illusion that she is looking at a real scene would be dispelled by her awareness of the picture's framing edge and the wall or table against which it is displayed. Moreover, if she were allowed to move around, she would notice that, unlike in the real world, the objects in the picture do not change their perspective profiles relative to the viewpoint of the observer. (You can confirm this for yourself by looking at Plate 4, Bellini's *Virgin and Child Enthroned with Saints*, and noting how when you move your head to the right, everything else in your field of vision shifts, but the figures in the painting retain the same outline shape and stay in the same spatial relations.)

Some philosophers have argued that these considerations provide sufficient grounds to reject Gombrich's position. Goodman, for example, argues that:

> deception under such nonstandard conditions is no test of realism; for with enough staging, even the most unrealistic picture can deceive. Deception counts less as a method of realism than as evidence of magicianship, and is a highly atypical mishap. In looking at the most realistic picture, I seldom suppose that I can reach into the distance, slice the tomato, or beat the drum.[25]

Gombrich's response to this objection is to insist that it is the eye not the mind that the painter sets out to deceive, and that being taken in by an illusion is not the same as holding a false belief. We do not need to believe that we are looking at the seated Virgin to have a visual experience as of the scene depicted. The core of Gombrich's illusion theory of pictorial perception resides in the claim that 'certain perceptual configurations can "trigger" specific reactions' and that these reactions are beyond our volitional control.[26] This, in turn, is buttressed by the much stronger claim that although we can alternate between attending to the marks on the surface of a picture and experiencing it as a realistic depiction, we cannot do both at once. Gombrich concludes that it is not possible for the viewer simultaneously to view the painting as a configuration of lines and marks and to see what those lines and marks represent, for as soon as we direct our attention to the painting as a physical object that possesses its own material reality, the illusion that the artist has so carefully crafted will disappear.[27]

Ambiguity and Pictorial Representation

The drawing that is reproduced as Figure 3.1 has proved a remarkably fertile stimulus for philosophers. It first appeared in the German satirical magazine *Fliegende Blätter* in 1892, but discussion of its significance, among philosophers at least, dates from Ludwig Wittgenstein's inclusion of a simplified line-drawing version in his *Philosophical Investigations*, which was published posthumously in 1953. The German original carries the inscription, 'Which animals are most like each other?' and is labelled at the bottom 'Rabbit and Duck'. The drawing is an example of an ambiguous or reversible figure. If you allow your interpretation of the drawing to be guided by the idea of a rabbit, the image resolves itself into a rabbit's head facing to the right (as you

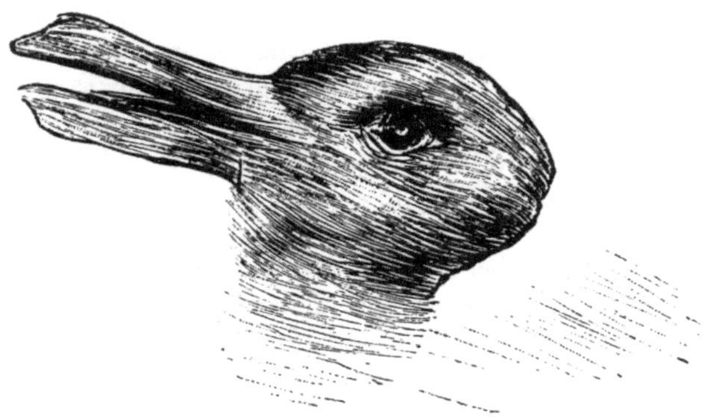

Figure 3.1. Rabbit-Duck (*Kaninchen und Ente*), illustration from *Fliegende Blätter*, 23 October 1892.

look at the picture), with two protruding ears sticking out behind; however, if you allow yourself to be guided by the thought of a duck, the image resolves itself into a duck's head with its bill pointing to the left. When we move from seeing the drawing as a rabbit to seeing it as a duck, the drawing itself does not change, but we see it differently. Wittgenstein calls this kind of change in the way of seeing something 'noticing an aspect'.[28] He is interested in characterizing the change that takes place when we see the drawing first one way, then another, at least in part, because it provides a means of showing that concepts play a role in perceptual experience.[29] We do not have a prior, purely visual experience that we interpret in two different ways. Rather, interpretation enters or informs the way in which we see the object: 'we *see* it as we *interpret* it.'[30] This line of thought is also central to the argument of *Art and Illusion*, but Gombrich has another reason for giving such prominence to the rabbit-duck drawing, which, he claims, is 'the key to the whole problem of image reading'.[31]

Like Wittgenstein, Gombrich employs the rabbit-duck drawing to elucidate the role of projection in visual experience. Throughout the book he emphasizes the 'beholder's share' in interpreting an image: successful representation depends upon the viewer's ability to make connections and to draw on the store of patterns and images that she holds in her mind.[32] By showing that one and the same set of marks can be read in two different ways he is able to undermine the claim that there is a one-to-one correspondence between the distribution of marks on a flat surface and the scene or object those marks are intended to depict. However, the rabbit-duck drawing also fulfils a second and more problematic function in Gombrich's theory of pictorial perception. As well as using the drawing to explore the 'flexibility' of our interpretations, he also uses it to demonstrate what he terms their 'exclusiveness'.[33] He points out that if we attend carefully to what happens when we look at the drawing, we can observe the shift between seeing it as a depiction of a rabbit and seeing it a depiction of a duck, but no amount of effort will allow us to sustain both readings at the same time. We can train ourselves to oscillate between the two with increasing rapidity, and we can hold in mind or remember the rabbit while we see the duck, but we cannot see the drawing simultaneously as both a rabbit and as a duck. Gombrich concludes that 'though we may be intellectually aware of the fact that any given experience *must* be an illusion, we cannot strictly speaking, watch ourselves having an illusion'.[34]

The very simplicity of the drawing makes perspicuous something that we normally overlook: the impossibility of direct visual awareness of the ambiguity through which an illusion is sustained. Although this demonstration is undeniably effective, few readers are likely to be convinced that a simple trick drawing can enable us to understand what happens when we look at a work of art. For this reason, Gombrich adduces a second example, taken from the writings of Kenneth Clark, in which the art historian describes his attempt to 'stalk' the illusion created by Velásquez's painting *Las Meniñas* [The Maids of Honour] (Plate 6). This is how Clark himself recounts his struggle to discover the mysterious process by which the artist has succeed in transforming 'appearances into paint':

> one cannot look for long at *Las Meniñas* without wanting to find out how it is done ... I would start from as far away as I could, when the illusion was complete, and come gradually nearer, until suddenly what had been a hand, and a ribbon, and a piece of velvet, dissolved into a salad of beautiful brush strokes. I thought I might learn something if I could catch the moment at which this transformation took place, but it proved to be as elusive as the moment between waking and sleeping.[35]

The experience that Clark describes is one with which every gallery visitor is familiar. It can be recalled, perhaps, by looking at the detail reproduced in Plate 7, which shows the hands of Maria Augustina Sarmiento as she holds out a small red jug, or *bucaro*, on a silver tray to the Infanta Margarita Maria. Curious as to how the artist has succeeded in conveying the shimmer of light on the metal surface of the tray, the texture and pattern of the Infanta's dress, or the intricate design of her brooch, we approach the painting ever more closely only to discover that all we can see are patches and marks. To prevent the image from breaking up into its constituent elements we are forced to retreat further back. At a certain point, the marks resolve into a meaningful shape, but then the image regains its hold on us, and we find ourselves once again in the position from which we started out.

Taken together, the presentation of these two examples appears to offer strong evidence in support of Gombrich's argument for the 'inherent ambiguity of all images'.[36] As we have seen, the illusion theory of pictorial perception issues in the claim that it is impossible for the viewer both to attend to the marked surface and to enter into the illusion that it sustains. To see something as a picture is to be aware either of the depicted content or of the lines and shapes out of which the picture is made. We can alternate between these two different forms of awareness, but we cannot simultaneously be aware of the marked surface as a configuration of lines and shapes and be aware of what that surface represents. The first of Gombrich's examples is intended to show that we are unable directly to experience the visual ambiguity on which illusion depends, while the second is intended to establish the relevance of this simplified demonstration to the experience of looking at works of art. Despite the initial persuasiveness of this strategy, further consideration reveals that there are important differences between the two examples and that neither singly nor jointly can they bear the weight that Gombrich places upon them.

Let us start with the rabbit-duck figure. There are two separate problems here. First, as several readers have pointed out, Gombrich misidentifies the source of the picture's ambiguity.[37] The viewer, who sees the drawing first as a rabbit and then as a duck, changes from one interpretation to another. But this is not the same as the change from seeing the drawing as a set of marks to seeing it as an image. The drawing is ambiguous in respect of its representational content not in respect of the relation between surface and subject. Gombrich incorrectly assumes that the disjunction rabbit/duck corresponds to the disjunction surface/subject. The slippage from the one to the other is made explicit when he claims that 'instead of playing "rabbit or duck" [artists] had to invent the game of "canvas or nature", played with a configuration of coloured earth which – at a distance at least – might result in illusion'.[38] Gombrich's argument for the impossibility of sustaining simultaneous attention to both the surface and the subject rests on a false analogy: to see the drawing either as a rabbit or as a duck is not analogous to seeing it either as an illusion or as a set of marks. Equally problematic is his failure to acknowledge that the rabbit-duck drawing possesses a special characteristic that is not necessarily shared by other representations.[39] As a reversible or bistable figure, the drawing allows of two mutually exclusive interpretations. Since we cannot hold two incompatible interpretations at one and the same time, we are obliged to switch from the one to the other. However, nothing that Gombrich has said shows that we cannot concurrently sustain different interpretations. A separate argument is needed to show that our awareness of the marks used to make a picture is incompatible with our awareness of its representational content.

Few viewers experience any difficulty perceiving the rabbit-duck figure at one and the same time as a drawing – that is to say, as a pattern of marks on a flat surface and as an image. However, it could be argued that in the case of more complex representations, such as Velásquez's *Las Meniñas*, we are unable to sustain this dual awareness. This would seem to be the appropriate conclusion to draw from Clark's account of his inability to capture the moment at which the 'salad' of brushstrokes transforms itself into a convincing representation of a hand, a ribbon or a piece of velvet. To see that the example does not license this conclusion, we need to examine more closely the nature of the experience that Clark describes. By his own admission, Clark sets out to discover the secret behind Velásquez's painting. He does so by going right up to the picture's surface until all he can see are individual strokes of paint.

But from this distance he can no longer view the painting as it is meant to be viewed. There is an optimum distance for viewing a painting or a drawing – a distance that varies from work to work. If we stand too far away, we are unable to make out sufficient detail; if we approach too close, all we see are marks and patches. As is the case with any complex unity, the whole cannot be grasped by isolating its individual parts. Adorno describes this phenomenon with characteristic flair:

> When artworks are viewed under the closest scrutiny, the most objectivated paintings metamorphose into a swarming mass and texts splinter into words. As soon as one imagines having a firm grasp on the details of an artwork, it dissolves into the indeterminate and the undifferentiated … Under micrological study, the particular – the artwork's vital element – is volatilized; its concretion vanishes.[40]

Just as a painting can be dissolved back into a welter of brushstrokes, so a novel can be reduced to words, or a piece of music to a sequence of sounds. Clark's attempt to 'stalk' the illusion of *Las Meniñas* reveals how hard it is to isolate and objectify the transformation of paint into appearances. But it does not allow us to draw conclusions about what takes place under normal viewing conditions, when the painting is viewed from the appropriate distance.

The most powerful objection to Gombrich's theory of pictorial perception is that it misdescribes what takes place when we look at a representational painting under normal viewing conditions. Even before an artwork as large and ambitious as Velásquez's *Las Meniñas* we do not experience the illusion of looking at an actual scene. This is not merely due to the complex structure of the painting, with its three different centres of focus, or the insistent gaze of the figures, some of whom look out of the picture towards the projected spectator. Nor can it be attributed to the prosaic fact that we have no first-hand experience of the court of King Phillip II and so are unlikely to enter the illusion that we are seeing the Infanta Margarita and her maids of honour. Any possibility that we might overlook the work's constructed character is forestalled by the inclusion of the artist himself, brush in hand, at work on a painting whose content is hidden from our view. Velásquez also leaves the viewer uncertain whether the framed image of the king and queen on the rear wall is a reflection in a mirror or a painted portrait, creating an irresolvable visual ambiguity at the centre of the painting. The artist's intentions have been variously interpreted, but there is a broad consensus that the painting thematizes the uncertainties of visual representation and that it is intended to make the viewer aware of the exigencies of looking.[41] It is therefore curious that Gombrich elects to employ this of all paintings in support of his illusion theory of pictorial perception. However, since he takes his cue from Clark, we should, perhaps, focus our attention not on the complex structure of the image as a whole but on the depiction of a single figure, such as the Infanta Margarita. If Gombrich is right, we should be forced to oscillate between seeing the young princess and seeing the painted surface as an assemblage of marks, but nothing prevents us from seeing both the marks on the surface and what those marks represent. Unless we were able to sustain simultaneous awareness of the subject of the painting and the way in which the artist has employed the resources at his disposal, we would be unable, for example, to admire the facility with which Velásquez uses thick slabs of colour to capture the elaborate finery of the infanta's dress and the splendour of her brooch, or the way in which he uses the dense medium of oil paint to fulfil the seemingly impossible task of depicting the pale gold of her hair.

I started this chapter by drawing a distinction between two different forms of awareness: our awareness of the marked surface as a configuration of lines and marks and our awareness of that surface as a representation of something that is not physically present. We are now able to see that these two forms of awareness are not only mutually compatible but – in certain cases at least – mutually sustaining: far from excluding one another, our awareness of the lines and marks *as* lines and marks and our awareness of what those marks represent can come together in a single composite experience. This can be confirmed by returning once again to Menzel's *Lady with Opera Glasses*. Consider, for example, the way in which we can follow the direction of a line as it is drawn across the paper while at the same time becoming aware of the way in which that line circumscribes the outline of a shoulder or the curved back of a chair. Rather than switching from the one to the other, we look for continuities between the subject of the picture and the shapes and patterns formed by the lines and marks, whose variations in texture, direction and density take on meaning once recruited in the service of representation. The most cursory indications of light and shade or the partial outline of an object can elicit recognition even as we remain aware that we are actively engaged in filling out and completing highly abbreviated visual clues. We see the hatching of black lines both as chalk marks that have been drawn in different directions and as a suggestion of shadow. So adept are we at these transitions that we can look through the white chalk to the surface of the paper while also seeing this as a means of representing the woman's back as it is revealed through the material of her dress. Even the parts of the paper that have been left unmarked by the artist serve both as a flat undifferentiated surface and as means of suggesting spatial depth. Far from being troubled by the incompletion of the figure and her surroundings, we remain aware that at a certain point the drawing simply stops. What gives the picture its sense of rightness is the correspondence between the selectivity that is imposed by the procedure of drawing, which omits and emphasizes in accordance with the work's own internal structure and order, and the selectivity of vision itself, which isolates and gives prominence to certain features of the visual field.

Representational Seeing

Richard Wollheim's account of 'seeing-in' is widely recognized as the most robust and philosophically sophisticated defence of the view that simultaneous awareness of the subject and the surface of a painting is not merely consistent with, but essential to, pictorial experience. Wollheim's theory evolved over time, and he presented it in different versions, but its basic lineaments remained largely consistent. From his inaugural lecture 'On Drawing an Object' through to his book *Painting as an Art*, where it forms part of a broader and more comprehensive theory of pictorial representation, he sought to provide a coherent philosophical analysis of 'the strange duality – of seeing the marked surface, and of seeing something in the surface – which [he calls] *twofoldness*'.[42]

Wollheim pursues two different strategies, both of which are designed to show that the visual experience of looking at a picture has a distinctive phenomenology that is irreducible to other forms of experience. The first strategy, which he adopts in *Art and its Objects*, is to examine the most basic form of pictorial representation – the making of a single mark upon a blank canvas – to show that what he terms 'representational seeing' can be distinguished from 'straightforward perception'.[43] Drawing on a teaching strategy employed by the abstract painter Hans Hofmann, Wollheim observes that a black mark placed on white canvas will appear to sit in front of the surface, while a blue mark will appear to sit behind it. To see the black as in front of the white surface or the blue as behind it is to see something other than their physical properties: the relation 'behind' and 'in front of' need not correspond to the physical relation between the mark and the surface. Wollheim contends that these examples 'give us in elementary form the notion of what it is to see something as a representation, or for something to have representational properties'.[44] The minimum requirement for representational seeing – and thus for successful visual representation – is the recognition of figure–ground relations. The viewer who identifies a mark or shape as lying in front of or behind the surface on which it sits sees not only a flat, patterned surface but also the non-planar spatial relations that belong to the 'virtual' space of the picture. (Even a page of printed text, such as the one you are now reading, can be viewed representationally. If you abstract from the meaning of the words and view the text as a set of black marks against a white ground, the dark shapes of the letters will appear to float in front of the surface of the paper.) Representation is therefore to be distinguished from figuration: the depiction of recognizable objects, scenes or persons. All that representation requires 'is that we see in the marked surface things three-dimensionally related'.[45]

One important consequence of this approach is that it extends the notion of representational seeing to include abstract as well as figurative painting. Wollheim gives as an example Hofmann's *Pompeii* (1959, Tate Gallery, London), a large abstract painting that exploits the push-and-pull effect created by the juxtaposition of differently coloured rectangles against a variegated ground. By finely tuning the saturation and intensity of the colours, Hofmann creates a dynamic relation between the different areas of the painting, which appear to press forward or to recede within a shallow pictorial space. Despite the absence of figurative content, this painting therefore satisfies Wollheim's minimum requirement for representational seeing, since it 'manifestly ... requires that we see some planes of colour in front of other planes, or that we see something in the surface'.[46] For the moment, I want to leave open the question whether *all* abstract paintings are representational in Wollheim's sense of the term or whether some non-figurative paintings do not allow for representational seeing. The answer to this question bears directly on his claim that twofoldness is essential to the experience of a picture. To see why this is the case, we need to examine the relevant sections of *Painting as an Art* in which he both elaborates and refines the thesis that representational seeing requires simultaneous awareness of the surface and the subject of a painting.

In *Painting as an Art* Wollheim adopts an alternative expositional strategy. This time he starts out not from a single mark on a blank canvas but from a special kind of perceptual experience, which, he claims, is both logically and historically prior to representation: the experience of seeing something, such as a fighting horseman or the figure of a boy, in a wall stained by damp or in rough and uneven stones. He characterizes 'seeing-in' as follows:

> Seeing-in is a distinct kind of perception, and it is triggered off by the presence within the field of vision of a differentiated surface ... when seeing-in occurs, two things happen: I am visually aware of the surface I look at, and I discern something standing out in front of, or (in certain cases) receding behind, something else.[47]

Seeing-in is logically prior to representation since it can take place when looking at surfaces or objects, such as clouds or rocky crags, that are not representations. However, Wollheim also maintains that 'seeing-in is prior to representation historically in that surely our remotest ancestors engaged in these exercises long before they thought to decorate their caves with images of the animals they hunted'.[48] These two levels of description, the logical and the historical, are both operative in Wollheim's claim that pictorial representation 'arrives' when someone purposively marks a surface with the intention that others are able to see something in it – such as, for example, a bison or a seated woman. Wollheim concludes that representation imposes on seeing-in something that it otherwise lacks: a 'standard of correctness and incorrectness'.[49] Unlike the generic capacity for seeing-in, there is a right and wrong way of seeing a representation, and this is 'set – set for each painting – by the intentions of the artist in so far as they are fulfilled'.[50]

Wollheim's claim that there is a correct way of seeing a representation, and that this is determined by the intentions of the artist, can only properly be understood in the context of his theory of the 'spectator in the picture', according to which the artist is not only an agent, who alters and corrects her work to her own satisfaction, but at the same time and as part of this process, also adopts the role of an imaginary spectator, whose responses she both anticipates and seeks to direct. To see a painting correctly, the viewer must occupy the position of the imagined spectator: he must see it as the artist intended it to be seen. As Wollheim explains:

> On this account, what a painting means rests upon the experience induced in an adequately sensitive, adequately informed, spectator by looking at the surface of the painting as the intentions of the artist led him to mark it. The marked surface must be the conduit along which the mental state of the artist makes itself felt within the mind of the spectator if the result is to be that the spectator grasps the meaning of the picture.[51]

Fortunately, Wollheim's theory of representational seeing does not depend upon this controversial argument. All he needs to establish is the difference between an open-ended process of seeing-in, akin to reverie and free association, in which there are no constraints on interpretation, and the type of looking appropriate to painting, in which the viewer takes into account 'the traditions, usages and purposes of the painter'.[52] Thus, for example, the knowledge that *Pompeii* is a work by a major abstract artist might count as a reason not to identify the rectangles of colour as a visual representation of the facade of a building. But there is no single correct way to see the painting, whose dynamic pictorial relations are set in motion rather than strictly controlled by the intentions of the artist. Even in the case of a figurative painting, such as Velásquez's *Las Meniñas*, the meaning of the work cannot simply be identified with, or reduced to, the intentions of the artist. Someone who failed to recognize that the marks isolated in Plate 7 represent, inter alia, a pair of hands, a red jug and an elaborate brooch could be said to have failed to see the painting correctly, but this minimal level of identificatory accuracy is only one component of the viewer's understanding of the meaning of the work.

The strategy that Wollheim pursues in *Painting as an Art* is potentially misleading insofar as it is designed to establish a close link between intention and pictorial content that is not entailed by the theory of twofoldness. However, he also makes an important refinement to the theory that helps to clarify the difference between his position and Gombrich's illusion theory of pictorial perception. In *Art and its Objects* Wollheim characterizes twofoldness in terms of the viewer's simultaneous awareness of two different phenomena: the surface of the picture and the representation of pictorial depth. He thereby simply inverts Gombrich's claim that the viewer's awareness of the picture's material surface and her awareness of what that surface represents are mutually effacing. But in *Painting as an Art* he abandons the underlying dichotomy of 'nature or canvas' by reconceiving twofoldness as two different aspects of one and the same experience. The first of these is the recognitional aspect: the viewer's awareness of what is represented, the content or subject of the picture. The second is the configurational aspect: the viewer's awareness of the design properties of the picture, including its shape or format, the visibility and disposition of the marks on the surface, the relative contrasts between light and dark, and, in the case of figurative painting, the viewpoint from which the subject is represented. Although these two aspects are 'distinguishable', they are also 'inseparable':

> They are two aspects of a single experience, they are not two experiences. They are neither two separate simultaneous experiences, which I somehow hold in the mind at once, nor two separate alternating experiences, between which I oscillate – though it is true that each aspect of the single experience is capable of being described as analogous to a separate experience.[53]

Wollheim's analysis of the distinctive phenomenology of the experience of looking at a picture is intended to rectify one of the central weaknesses of the illusion theory of pictorial perception: its inability to characterize what takes place when we look at a picture under normal viewing conditions. By showing that representational seeing allows the viewer to attend both to what is represented and to the way in which it is represented, he aims to provide a more satisfactory account of pictorial recognition.

The theory of twofoldness is also intended to make good a second major defect of the illusion theory of pictorial perception: its failure to accommodate the distinctive pleasure and interest that we derive from looking at pictures. In his review of *Art and Illusion*, which appeared in 1961, shortly after the book was first published, Wollheim observed that Gombrich's conception of naturalism is not only 'false to our ordinary attitude to paintings', it also 'conceals or distorts the kind of admiration we feel for them'.[54] Unless twofoldness were possible, or so Wollheim argues, we would be unable to recognize 'a characteristic virtue that we find and admire in great representational painting: in Titian, in Vermeer, in Manet we are led to marvel endlessly at the way in which a line or brushstroke or expanse of colour is exploited to render effects or to establish analogies that can only be identified representationally'.[55] The pleasure of looking at a painting or drawing derives at least in part from the interplay of recognitional and configurational aspects: we are concerned not merely with what is depicted but with the way in which the artist has represented it.[56] Although it is theoretically possible to recognize the 'how' of depiction by alternating attention between the marked surface and the picture's content or subject matter, this would make admiration of the artistry of depiction external to pictorial recognition.[57] One of the great strengths of Wollheim's account is that it shows how aesthetic appreciation is sustained in and through the act of looking.

Strong Twofoldness

What I have identified as a major strength of Wollheim's theory also leaves it exposed to a potential objection. Dominic Lopes claims that Wollheim 'invalidly generalizes from what is required of one class of pictures to all pictures: [his theory] takes art pictures – indeed, art pictures of a particular "painterly" style – as paradigmatic'.[58] Similarly, Jerrold Levinson argues:

Plausibly *not* all seeing-in or registering of pictorial content is aesthetic in character, or even informed by the awareness of pictures as pictures; for instance, that directed to or had in connection with postcards, passport photos, magazine illustrations, comic strips, television shows, or movies. Thus, any view that builds aesthetic character, or even awareness of pictures as pictures, directly into seeing-in would seem to have something amiss.[59]

In its simplest form, the objection is that although twofoldness may be essential for the *aesthetic appreciation* of a picture, it is not essential for the *experience* of a picture.[60] If sound, this objection would undermine a central feature of Wollheim's account. For although he initially couches the twofoldness thesis in permissive terms, he is committed to the view that twofoldness is a necessary condition of seeing something as a representation: 'if I look at a representation as a representation, then it is not just permitted to, but required of, me that I attend simultaneously to object and medium.'[61]

Considering Wollheim's attempt to make good the shortcomings of the illusion theory of pictorial perception, it is ironic that criticism of his position has tended to focus on his account of *trompe l'oeil* paintings – that is, paintings that are designed to 'trick the eye' using illusionistic devices. However, given Wollheim's residual indebtedness to Gombrich's perceptualist starting point, it is, perhaps, unsurprising that existence of pictorial 'illusions' creates difficulties for the theory of twofoldness. Like Gombrich, Wollheim maintains that when we look at a painting 'visions of things not present . . . come about through looking at things present'.[62] Indeed, Wollheim's distinction between 'straightforward perception', defined as 'the capacity of perceiving things present to the senses', and 'representational seeing', which 'allows us to have perceptual experiences of things that are not present to the senses', is intended to capture in its most elementary form the contrast between reality and appearance that Gombrich describes as the indispensable tool of naturalistic art.[63] The core of the theory of twofoldness is contained in the claim that the viewer is simultaneously aware both of the marked surface and of what that surface represents. However, in *Painting as an Art* Wollheim concedes that the experience of looking at a *trompe l'oeil* painting is *not* characterized by twofoldness, since, if successful, it will forestall the viewer's efforts to focus on the marks out of which it is made. Wollheim claims that *trompe l'oeil* paintings, such as those produced by the French artist Leroy de Barde (Plate 8), are 'non-representational . . . because they do not invoke, indeed they repel, attention to the marked surface'.[64] He also contends that although most abstract paintings have their own internal pictorial space, some are intended to be seen merely as a pattern arrayed across a two-dimensional plane, and that when perceived correctly – that is, when perceived in conformity with the artist's intentions – an abstract painting of this type fails to count as a representation for the complementary reason: the viewer see the marks arranged on the surface, but she does not have an awareness of depth.

These concessions severely weaken Wollheim's position. It seems that it is only by putting forward the counter-intuitive claim that two widely recognized genres of painting are non-representational that he can establish the claim that twofoldness is essential to the experience of pictures. Moreover, his argument risks being trapped in a vicious circle: twofoldness cannot be used to explain pictorial representation without begging the question, for he has already defined what it is to be a picture in terms of the experience of twofoldness. The problem that these two cases generate for Wollheim's account has led some philosophers to argue that he has no option but to abandon both the strong twofoldness thesis – the claim that twofoldness is essential to the experience of pictures – and the claim that looking at pictures requires the exercise of the special perceptual capacity that he terms 'seeing-in'.[65] The most trenchant advocate of this position is Lopes, who argues: 'Some pictures, *contra* Gombrich, are experienced simultaneously as designed surfaces and as of their subjects; other pictures, *contra* Wollheim, preclude twofoldness.'[66] In place of Wollheim's strong twofoldness, he advocates what he terms 'weak twofoldness': the claim that twofoldness is merely consistent with the experience of pictures. Twofoldness is a property that is possessed by some pictures but not by others:

> Pictures might be thought of as arranged along a spectrum, at one end of which lie *trompe l'oeil* pictures … at some intermediate point lie pictures which afford one kind of experience or the other, but not simultaneously … At the other extreme lie pictures typical experiences of which are simultaneously experiences of their subjects and experiences of flat, pigmented surfaces … Experiences of these pictures may properly be described as twofold.[67]

Whereas Wollheim's account purportedly privileges 'art pictures' over demotic forms of representation, Lopes maintains that his spectrum view can accommodate the full range of pictures, from anatomy textbook illustrations to family snapshots: while aesthetic appreciation of 'painterly' works of art might require the experience of twofoldness, this is neither a necessary, nor a desirable, feature of other kinds of pictorial representation.

Should we accept this conclusion? Lopes's claim that it is possible to reconcile Wollheim's approach with the illusion theory of pictorial perception is initially attractive, and the suggestion that twofoldness is for the most part restricted to artworks rather than illustrations does not appear too damaging given that Wollheim is explicitly concerned with painting as an art. I shall argue, however, that to sever the connection between representational seeing and the experience of looking at a picture is to abandon Wollheim's project rather than to delimit its scope. The spectrum theory of pictorial perception, in which twofoldness is located at one pole and illusionism at the other, identifies twofoldness as a feature that inheres in, or is elicited by, certain types of pictures. Wollheim himself appears to endorse this view when he claims that *trompe l'oeil* paintings and some abstract paintings are not characterized by twofoldness and so are non-representational. I believe that this concession is mistaken and that a robust defence of strong twofoldness can be mounted only by showing that the thesis identifies a non-empirical condition on the possibility of seeing a picture *as* a picture. Unless the viewer exercises the special perceptual capacity that Wollheim terms 'representational seeing', she will not see a picture as a picture, but only a pattern of marks on a surface or – in the case of a *trompe l'oeil* painting – an illusion of something that is not actually present to the senses. There are numerous empirical conditions that must also be satisfied, such as standing sufficiently close to the picture to be able to make out its content, or the presence of a light source that is powerful enough to illuminate its surface. However, the experience of twofoldness possesses a different, presuppositional status insofar as it is a conceptually necessary condition of the possibility of experiencing a picture as a picture.

What I mean by this can best be explained by re-examining the two cases that – according to Wollheim – are not covered by the twofold thesis: *trompe l'oeil* paintings and abstract paintings that are experienced as surface designs. Citing Ruskin's observation that *trompe l'oeil* invariably 'has some means of proving at the same time that it is an illusion', John Hyman has persuasively argued that enjoyment of the skill and virtuosity of this genre of painting depends on the viewer's recognition that she is looking at a depiction rather than, say, a set of shallow boxes containing stuffed birds.[68] The viewer who is genuinely taken in by the illusion does not see the painting as a painting: she is fooled into believing that she sees a real collection of ornithological specimens. The viewer who makes this mistake is no different to the birds who are supposed to have pecked at Zeuxis' painting believing that the grapes were real. To see the picture as a picture, she must not only recognize what is represented; she must also be aware that it is a representation – and this requires some awareness, however minimal, of its configurational features. This argument is not restricted to the genre of *trompe l'oeil* for, as Goodman has pointed out, under the right circumstances 'even the most unrealistic picture can deceive'.[69] Rather than serving as a limit case, marking the point at which the twofoldness is no longer applicable, *trompe l'oeil* helps us to identify a specific kind of failure or breakdown of representational seeing that can, in principle, take place in relation to any picture whatsoever.

The opposite, but complementary failure to engage in representational seeing occurs when someone sees a painting as a marked surface without this eliciting any recognition of content, including pictorial depth. Here, too, Wollheim erroneously identifies this generic possibility with a specific *type* of painting, which he classifies as non-representational. If a single mark placed on a blank canvas allows for representational seeing, then a fortiori, an abstract painting that contains one or more marks can be viewed as containing non-planar spatial relations. To see a picture as a picture – rather than as mere surface design or configurational pattern – the viewer must see something in the design, even if what she sees meets only the minimal requirement of pictorial depth. Lopes maintains that Wollheim invalidly takes 'painterly' art pictures as paradigmatic and that what he terms 'pictorial design features' – including 'marks, directions, boundaries, contours, shapes, colours, hues' – are just as prevalent in 'demotic' pictures.[70] It is true that when we look at works of art we tend to pay special attention to their design properties, rather than simply extracting whatever informational content they may contain, but nothing prevents us from focusing our attention on the design properties of demotic pictures – and perhaps, too, submitting them to a specifically aesthetic mode of contemplation.

In the case of abstract paintings that do not appear to contain any informational content, the complementary danger arises that they might be viewed merely as decorative designs. When Kandinsky produced his first fully abstract paintings sometime around 1911, he was worried that they might be seen as 'works having the appearance of geometrical ornament, which would – to put it crudely – be like a tie or a carpet'.[71] The pioneers of abstract art, including Mondrian and Malevich as well as Kandinsky, were acutely aware that their claim to have produced work that could be experienced as significant depended upon maintaining continuity with the tradition of easel painting. If non-objective art was to hold the interest of the viewer and to satisfy the demand for new forms of complexity and simplification, it had to be viewed as a picture rather than as a pleasing decorative pattern. In the absence of recognizable imagery, the establishment of spatial depth provided a means of securing the status of abstract painting and of ensuring that the viewer bring relevant expectations of meaning or at least meaningfulness. What I have termed 'strong twofoldness' allows for the possibility that a fully abstract painting can meet these requirements even if the risks of failure are higher.

Some of the difficulties addressed here can be resolved by drawing a distinction between two different forms or levels of engagement that might be considered essential to pictorial experience. Bence Nanay has identified an ambiguity in Wollheim's use of the term 'awareness' to characterize the phenomenon of seeing-in. On the first interpretation, the claim Wollheim seeks to defend is: 'We *consciously attend* both to the depicted object and to some properties of the depicted surface'. However, on the second interpretation, he defends only the weaker claim: 'We *perceptually represent* both the depicted object and some properties of the picture surface (while we may or may not attend to them).'[72] Nanay maintains that Wollheim did not clearly distinguish between these two claims and that this has led to considerable confusion about the scope of his account of twofoldness.[73] It can plausibly be argued that whereas it is a necessary feature of seeing-in that we perceptually represent both the depicted object and some properties of the picture surface, nothing compels us to accept the stronger claim that we must consciously attend to both the depicted object and to some properties of the surface. The advantage of this approach is that is allows Wollheim's account of twofoldness to accommodate the full spectrum of depiction – including cases such as looking at advertisements and other demotic images in which our conscious attention is focused exclusively on the represented content – while also granting that it has special purchase on those kinds of depiction, predominantly but not exclusively art pictures, that reward detailed attention to their surface properties. It is, perhaps, only in relation to painting (in the broad sense in which that term is employed here) that we need to trace the 'thread of recognition' that connects the viewer's awareness of the materiality of the medium with her awareness of the depicted subject, but Wollheim's theory of seeing-in helps us to understand how these two forms of awareness can interact and reciprocally transform one another in pictorial experience.[74]

4

Resemblance and Denotation

Pictorial Signs

In an interview published in 1961 Daniel-Henry Kahnweiler, the Parisian art dealer who had represented Braque and Picasso in the pre-war years, declared: 'absolutely fundamental . . . to the comprehension of Cubism and of what, for me, is a truly modern art [is] the fact that painting is a form of writing (*écriture*)'. He then went on to explain in more detail what this puzzling assertion might mean:

> A woman in a painting is not a woman; she is a group of signs that I read as 'woman'. When one writes on a sheet of paper 'f-e-m-m-e', someone who knows French and knows how to read will read not only the word '*femme*', but he will see, so to speak, a woman. The same is true of paintings; there is no difference. Fundamentally, painting has never been a mirror of the external world, nor has it ever been similar to photography, it has been a creation of signs, which were always read correctly by contemporaries, after a certain apprenticeship, of course. Well, the Cubists created signs that were unquestionably new, and this is what made it so difficult to read their paintings for such a long time.[1]

The claim that painting is a form of writing is exposed to an obvious rejoinder: we must first learn the meaning of the word *femme* if we are to grasp what it stands for or represents, but there does not seem to be any comparable learning process required to see what is represented in an unfamiliar picture. Whereas someone who does not know Dutch and German would not be able to understand the original titles of de Hooch's *De Appelen van een van de Vrouw Schil* (Plate 1) and Menzel's *Dame mit Opernglas* (Plate 5), no such impediment stands in the way of recognizing that both pictures represent a woman. We do not have to read a picture: we simply look and see.

This objection is not as conclusive as it first appears. Kahnweiler acknowledges the ease with which viewers can interpret certain pictorial signs, but he suggests that this is a matter of enculturation. Once we have undergone the necessary 'apprenticeship', we have no difficulty apprehending a painting produced in accordance with a specific system. Although nearly two hundred years separate Menzel's drawing from de Hooch's painting, both pictures employ the same basic techniques of pictorial representation. The development of Cubism, or so Kahnweiler and others have argued, represents a radical break with the conventions for depicting objects and non-planar spatial relations that were established during the Renaissance. Most viewers still experience considerable difficulty identifying the subject of Braque's painting of 1911–12, *The Portuguese* (Plate 9). Even among specialists, there is disagreement as to what it represents. For a long time, the stencilled letters 'D BAL' at the top right-hand corner were interpreted as a fragment of a poster advertising a dance hall ('[GRAN]D BAL'). However, the assumption that the setting of the painting is a café has been challenged by the discovery of a letter from Braque to Kahnweiler in which he describes a painting of 'an Italian emigrant standing on a bridge of a boat with the harbour in the background'.[2] The dense overlapping planes and the partial or contradictory character of the visual clues make it difficult to assign determinate pictorial sense to the different parts of the painting. Does the figure hold a guitar diagonally from his body or is it horizontal as the angle of the strings suggests? Should the rope-like marks under the lettering be interpreted as a curtain tie, such as might be found in a café, or as a heavy ship's rope tied to a bollard? What representational function, if any, is fulfilled by the shoals of brushstrokes that float free of any confining shape or boundary? And how are we to interpret the letters and numbers that are stencilled onto the surface of the painting? Are they a device for drawing attention to the relation between the picture plane and the physical surface of the painting – thereby emphasizing the painting's two-dimensionality – or should they be read illusionistically as fragments of a poster affixed to a wall in the background?

Kahnweiler's observation that Braque and Picasso invented new pictorial signs provides one way of accounting for the difficulty of deciphering Cubist paintings – though more, of course, needs to be said about the nature of these signs and how Cubism differs from other forms of representation. I shall return to this issue at the end of this chapter when I consider the viability of recent semiotic – or sign-based – interpretations of Cubism. The suggestion that Braque and Picasso discovered the 'principle of semiological arbitrariness' and that they showed how this could be used to construct a non-mimetic system of pictorial representation deserves independent consideration.[3] First, however, I want to examine the more radical claim that *all* painting is a creation of signs. In the passage cited above, Kahnweiler argues that Cubism differs from earlier forms of art not in its deployment of signs but in the unfamiliarity of the signs it uses. The incorporation of features such as parallel lines for the strings of the guitar and fragments of the outline shape of the figure's arm and face might be taken to provide a means of orientation for the viewer who is not yet conversant with Cubism. But these remnants of the Renaissance system of representation turn out to be just another set of signs that no more provide a mirror of reality than do the words and numbers that are written across the picture's surface. Just as the shallow, interlocking planes of Cubist pictorial space both suggest and contradict the illusion of spatial depth, so the use of a restricted vocabulary of rectilinear and curvilinear forms allows the same set of marks to be read in multiple ways. A circle can stand for both a glass and a bottle, while the arc of the figure's shoulder might also stand for the back of a chair or the hull of a ship. The insistent materiality of the painted surface, with its individuated brushstrokes and loose grid-like structure, defeats any attempt to treat the painting as transparently opening on to the space it depicts. If Kahnweiler is right, then the complexity of Cubist painting, with its multiple terms of reference and its incorporation of letters and numbers alongside illusionistic details, helps us to recognize something that had been obscured by the quest for verisimilitude: we must learn how to interpret a painting just as we must learn how to understand a language. To identify painting as a form of writing, as Kahnweiler proposes, is to hold that pictorial signs, like words, are conventional and that their reference is established not through natural likeness or similarity but through human cultural practice.

The distinction between what belongs to nature (*physis*) and what is a matter of convention or agreement (*thesis*) can be traced back to Plato's dialogue *Cratylus* in which the participants discuss whether names are 'natural and not conventional', as Cratylus proposes, or whether, as Hermogenes contends, 'there is no name given to anything by nature; all is convention and the habit of the users'.[4] The clearest and best-known attempt to distinguish between 'natural' and 'conventional' signs is to be found in a treatise written in the fourth century AD by the theologian St Augustine of Hippo.[5] Augustine defines a sign as 'a thing which, over and above the impression it makes on the senses, causes something else to come into the mind as a consequence of itself'.[6] He then precedes to distinguish between two types of sign. A natural sign (*signa naturalia*) stands in a causal or intrinsic relation to what it signifies. Thus, for example, the track left by an animal is a sign that it has passed by. The sign is caused by the imprint that the weight of the animal's body leaves in soft ground and its shape or form is determined by the anatomy of the animal's foot. By contrast, a conventional sign (*signa data*), such as the word 'fox', does not possess any intrinsic connection to the animal it represents. Augustine concludes that in order to understand a conventional sign we need to know what it is intended to signify: conventional signs 'are those which living beings mutually exchange for the purpose of showing, as well as they can, the feelings of their minds, or their perceptions, or their thoughts'.[7] Unlike a natural sign, a conventional sign neither resembles nor possesses any direct casual connection to what it represents; its meaning depends on human custom and contrivance.

Closer scrutiny shows that Augustine conflates two different types of relation that a natural sign can have to its referent. Whereas some natural signs – such as the imprint of an animal's foot – look like or resemble in certain respects what they represent, others stand in a causal connection without this resulting in any physical likeness. Smoke, for example, is a sign of fire although there is no visual correspondence between the smoke and the flames beneath it. Similarly, spots can be a sign of measles or a knock on the door a sign that someone is outside. In order to capture these differences, the American philosopher Charles Sanders Peirce proposed a tripartite division of signs into icons, indices and symbols.[8] The first two types of signs correspond to what Augustine terms a 'natural sign'. An *Icon* represents in virtue of its 'similarity' to its referent: 'Anything whatever … is an Icon of anything, in so far as it is like that thing, and used as a sign of it.'[9] A picture, for example, is an icon according to Peirce since it resembles what it represents.[10] By contrast, an indexical sign is linked to its object by what Peirce terms a 'dynamical connection': 'An *Index* is a sign which refers to the Object that it denotes by virtue of being really affected by that Object.'[11] Thus, for example, a weathercock is an index of the direction of the wind because the wind causes it to point in a specific direction, and a low barometer reading is an index of a low-pressure weather system because the height of the mercury in the gauge is determined by the level of pressure in the air. Peirce's third type of sign, which he terms a 'symbol', corresponds to Augustine's category of a conventional sign: 'A *Symbol* is a sign which refers to the Object that it denotes by virtue of a law, usually an association of general ideas, which operates to cause the Symbol to be interpreted as referring to that Object.'[12] Peirce claims: 'All words, sentences, books, and other conventional signs are Symbols.'[13] Unlike icons and indices, a symbol is connected to its referent only through habit or agreement among those who use it. For this reason, it requires a law or rule that allows it to be interpreted.

Although Peirce presents the tripartite schema of icon, index and symbol as an analysis of different kinds of signs, it is best understood as describing different sign functions, for, as he acknowledges, the same sign can stand in more than one relation to its referent. If we return once again to the example of a track left by an animal, we can see that a footprint is both an index and an icon: the weight of the animal causes the mark, but the mark also resembles the shape of the animal's foot. Some conventional signs also have iconic or indexical constituents. The familiar Woolmark sign is a symbol, since we need to know the convention or rule that allows it to stand as a guarantee of a garment's fibre content and quality, but it also functions iconically by representing the interwoven strands characteristic of wool fibres. Similarly, a painting or a drawing is also an index since the individual marks are caused by the movement of the artist's hand and thus function as a sign of the artist's activity.

The analysis of sign functions allows for the possibility that the referent of a sign can be established in more than one way, and that the same sign can have more than one referent. Thus, for example, the figure on the right-hand side of Bellini's San Zaccaria altarpiece (Plate 4) is an iconic sign of a man reading a book; however, in accordance with the conventions of Christian art, it is also a symbol of St Gerome, who translated the Bible into Latin. To interpret the sign as an iconic representation of a man reading a book, we need to be able to recognize its likeness or similarity to what it represents; but to interpret the sign as a symbolic representation of St Gerome we need to know the code established by the Christian Church that allows saints to be identified through the possession of specific attributes, such as a book, a key, a transverse cross, and so forth. Peirce does not investigate the question in any detail, but he appears to have upheld the traditional view that whereas words and other symbols are based on conventions, and thus require knowledge of the rule governing the relation between the sign and its referent, no prior knowledge is needed to interpret an iconic sign. Contrasting icons with indexes, he claims: 'The icon has no dynamical connection with the object it represents; it simply happens that its qualities resemble those of that object, and excite analogous sensations in the mind for which it is a likeness.'[14]

Peirce's analysis of different sign functions has been taken up by advocates of a semiotic, or sign-based, approach to the study of visual culture. However, some adherents of this approach have rejected what they see as the residual, perceptualist elements in Peirce's account and have sought to show that pictorial meaning, like language, is conventional through and through. Norman Bryson, for example, maintains that the ability to identify what is represented in a painting 'presupposes competence within social, that is socially constructed, codes of recognition.'[15] He rejects the idea that depiction can be explained in terms of the psychological and physiological responses of the individual viewer, arguing that 'the crucial difference between term "perception" and the term "recognition" is that the latter is *social*':

It takes one person to experience a sensation, it takes (at least) two to recognise a sign. And when people look at a representational painting and recognise what they see, their recognition does not unfold in the

solitary recesses of the sensorium but through their activation of codes
of recognition that are learnt by interaction with others, in the acquisition
of human culture.[16]

The advantage of the semiotic approach – at least according to its proponents
– is that it opens to analysis the social and political dimension of painting
that is excluded by perceptualism. As Rosalind Krauss, another exponent of
the semiotic approach, has argued:

> the impulse toward structural linguistics t is not the drive for a method
> for unpacking a style or a painting, for decoding it, so to speak, but is
> instead motivated by a wider consideration about the nature of
> representation. That wider consideration is one of total resistance to a
> realist or reflectionist view of art, namely, the idea that the painting or
> the text is a reflection of the reality around it, that reality enters the work
> of art with the directness of the image striking the mirror.[17]

Salutary as this goal might be, it is far from clear that semiotics offers the only
alternative to a reflectionist view of art. As we saw in Chapter 2, even those
philosophers who defend a resemblance account of depiction recognize that
since a visual representation is not a replica or copy of what it represents, a
painting must be understood in terms of its difference as well as its similarity
to what it represents. Moreover, Gombrich, whose work Bryson identifies as
'the climax of the "Perceptualist" tradition', explicitly rejects the idea that
painting can be understood as a copy of reality.[18] Here we need only recall
core features of his account such as the selectivity of vision, the limits of
likeness imposed by the medium, the importance of the beholder's share, and
the interplay of schema and correction.

The real difference between perceptualism and semiotics lies in the role
that is accorded to conventions in pictorial representation. Defenders of the
perceptualist approach such as Gombrich and Wollheim claim that pictorial
recognition depends on perceptual mechanisms that are natural rather than
social: pictures stimulate responses in the viewer that are at least partially
conditioned by recognitional capacities that are also engaged in ordinary
perception. By contrast, proponents of a full-blown conventionalist account
of depiction deny that there are perceptual and psychological constraints on
pictorial representation. Pictorial signs, like linguistic signs, are arbitrary and
they have no inherent connection to what they signify: pictures can be
understood only through reference to the rules through which signs are
coordinated with their referents. Even where these rules have sedimented
into habit or custom, the codes of recognition that enable viewers to recognize

what a picture represents are socially constructed rather than natural, and so must be learned or acquired.

The analysis of an artwork as a system of signs holds out the prospect of a unified theory that can accommodate both pictorial and linguistic representation. However, in its more extreme, conventionalist form it threatens to erase the salient differences between the two. A more promising strategy is adopted by the philosopher Nelson Goodman in his book *Languages of Art*. While Goodman – in common with other symbol theorists – seeks to identify cognitively significant affinities between verbal and non-verbal symbols, he also shows how non-verbal symbol systems such as pictures, diagrams, maps and models, differ from verbal systems.[19] Whereas most advocates of the semiotic approach refer somewhat vaguely to a plurality of 'systems of representation', without identifying the features that distinguish one system from another, Goodman provides a detailed analysis of the individuating characteristics of each of the different systems he discusses. John Hyman is surely right to observe: 'Without this precision, conventionalism can provide historians and critics with a range of convenient and attractive metaphors, but it cannot amount to a testable theory of art.'[20] Hyman, together with many others, assumes from the outset that Goodman defends a conventionalist theory of art, guided perhaps by some of Goodman's more provocative remarks. However, I shall argue that Goodman's analysis of the syntactic and semantic properties of non-linguistic symbol systems effectively undermines the claim that a picture can be interpreted in accordance with a set of rules or conventions that correlate signs with referents. Far from reducing painting to writing, he shows why perceptual discrimination is central to looking at pictures but does not play the same role in other symbol systems.

A Symbol Theory of Art

In the Introduction to *Languages of Art* Goodman warns that 'the reader must be prepared to find his convictions and his common sense – that repository of ancient error – often outraged by what he finds here'.[21] Perhaps the most deeply held of these convictions is that we know what a picture represents because it resembles its subject. Consider, for example, Goya's portrait, *The Duke of Wellington*, which hangs in London's National Gallery (Plate 10). Surely it is the visual similarity between the picture and the Duke that makes it a picture of the Duke rather than, say, a picture of the Duchess or the Duke's London residence, Apsley House. The reader of these pages, who has already encountered several challenges to the copy theory of representation, is unlikely to be outraged by Goodman's observation that resemblance is not *sufficient* for depiction. Indeed, his arguments against what he terms the naive view of representation have been widely accepted. What is at issue is whether these arguments suffice to support his claim that, once understood correctly, 'Resemblance disappears as a criterion of representation' – that is, it is neither sufficient nor necessary.[22]

Goodman considers two different versions of the resemblance theory: i) *A* represents *B* if and only if *A* appreciably resembles *B*, and ii) *A* represents *B* to the extent that *A* resembles *B*. Neither formulation can withstand critical scrutiny. As Goodman points out, resemblance is reflexive and symmetric: if *A* resembles *B*, then *B* resembles *A*. But representation is clearly asymmetric: Goya's painting represents the Duke of Wellington, but the Duke doesn't represent the painting. Moreover, although nothing resembles the Duke so much as the Duke, the Duke does not represent himself. There are many things that resemble each other without one being a representation of the other. An identical twin resembles but does not represent his brother, and a car off an assembly line is not a picture of any of the other cars off the line.[23]

The resemblance theory of depiction is evidently inadequate as it stands: that *A* resembles *B* does not suffice to make *A* a representation of *B*. However, rather than investigating whether it is possible to retain the central intuition of the resemblance theory – perhaps by modifying the way in which the theory is formulated or by incorporating it within a more sophisticated account that provides an alternative means of explaining the difference between resemblance and representation – Goodman summarily declares that resemblance plays no role in explaining depiction:

> The plain fact is that a picture, to represent an object, must be a symbol for it, stand for it, refer to it; and that no degree of resemblance is sufficient to establish the requisite relationship of reference. Nor is resemblance *necessary* for reference; almost anything may stand for almost anything else. A picture that represents – like a passage that describes – an object refers to, and more particularly, *denotes* it. Denotation is the core of representation and is independent of resemblance.[24]

It is this argument – rather than Goodman's criticisms of the naive version of the resemblance theory – that has awakened the fiercest opposition. Lopes writes of Goodman's 'extraordinary insouciance' in moving from rejection of the resemblance theory to the claim that 'what a picture symbolizes is a matter of what symbol system or language it belongs to, as if the resemblance theory of depiction were the only possible perceptual theory'.[25] And Budd has argued that although Goodman's argument is both valid and sound, 'it inflicts no harm on the idea that it is of the essence of a picture that it looks like what it depicts, since it only shows that *looking like* is not fully constitutive of *depiction*, not that it is not a necessary condition of it'.[26]

I shall return in the next section to the question whether Goodman's construal of depiction as denotation entails the claim that pictorial reference is independent of resemblance or whether this stronger claim is an inessential addition to his theory, and hence can be excised without doing damage. For the moment, I want to follow Goodman in assuming that we must first rid ourselves of the 'dogma' that depiction can be defined in terms of resemblance before we can provide a more adequate characterization. This leaves open the possibility, tentatively explored by Goodman himself in later writings, that resemblance may yet have a role to play in a full account of pictorial representation.[27]

Denotation is just one of a variety of ways in which symbols can refer. Goodman also discusses other species of reference such as exemplification, expression, literal and metaphorical reference, and mediate reference through a chain of links that include both denotation and exemplification.[28] Here I shall focus exclusively on his account of denotation. Goodman takes up the term 'denotation' from linguistic analysis, where it is used to describe the relation that holds between a word, such as a name or a predicate, and the object or property that it stands for. The name 'Duke of Wellington' denotes the Duke of Wellington and the predicate 'decorated' denotes the receipt of military honours. To claim that denotation is the core of representation is thus to claim that pictures, like names and predicates, refer to or stand for what they represent.[29] Since Goodman denies that resemblance is sufficient to secure reference, he needs to provide an alternative means of explaining how pictures refer to their subjects. The first part of his answer is that denotation is possible only within a symbol system. Just as words and sentences possess meaning in virtue of the language, or linguistic system, to which they belong, so the meaning of a visual symbol is governed by the pictorial system to which it belongs. Denotation is system-relative: the same symbol or set of symbols can denote an object in one system and a different object in another system. (We are familiar with this phenomenon in natural languages: the word 'Rock' denotes a skirt in German and a mass of stone or solid mineral matter in English.) Goodman's full answer to the problem of pictorial reference thus requires that he specify the features that distinguish one symbol system from another. Although his account of these differences is couched in highly technical language – and thus is initially rather forbidding – the results are genuinely illuminating and help to reveal some important characteristics of visual representation that are given insufficient attention by other approaches.

Goodman describes *Languages of Art* as 'an approach to a general theory of symbols', including maps, diagrams, models, sketches, sculptures and musical scores, as well as texts and pictures.[30] In a summary such as this it is not possible to do justice to the full range of topics that he addresses. My goal is to isolate one important strand that runs through the book, namely how pictorial denotation is be distinguished from verbal denotation. Nonetheless, to understand Goodman's solution to this problem, we need to broaden the frame of reference to include another type of symbol system, which he terms a 'notation'. A notation is, in respects yet to be defined, radically unlike a picture. Goodman's analysis of the properties that are required of a notational system results in the identification of five mutually independent conditions that may or may not be satisfied by other systems.[31] These conditions are: unambiguity, syntactic disjointness, syntactic differentiation, semantic disjointness and semantic differentiation. As we shall, whereas a linguistic system, such as a natural language, satisfies some but not all these conditions, a pictorial system, such as a painting, typically violates all five. By examining the properties of a notational system, Goodman arrives at a new and highly original means of distinguishing different types of symbol system from one another.

Let us start by considering the distinction between syntactic and semantic conditions. Once again, Goodman has taken these terms from linguistic analysis, where 'syntax' is used to describe the ordering and combination of words in phrases and sentences and 'semantics' refers to aspects of meaning, whether at the level of individual words or complete sentences. What Goodman terms a symbol *scheme* is a purely syntactical ordering and combination of characters. A symbol scheme can be analysed without reference to what, if anything, the characters stand for or represent. A symbol *system*, on the other hand, requires the coordination of a scheme with a realm of compliants – that is to say, it consists of a symbol scheme correlated with a field of reference.[32] Syntactic conditions, then, pertain solely to the internal ordering or structure of a symbol scheme; semantic conditions pertain to the relation between the characters of a scheme and what, if anything, those characters denote. The significance of this distinction will become clear once we consider the specific conditions that characterize a notational system.

The first requirement of a notational system is that the characters that make up the symbol scheme must be *disjoint*: no mark may belong to more than one character. Thus, for example, in musical notation, the same mark cannot be both a crotchet and a quaver. Similarly, in a natural language that uses the Roman alphabet, the same mark cannot be both an 'a' and a 'd'. This is a syntactic condition on a symbol scheme: without it, the scheme could not function as it does. We must be able to assume that a mark in one scheme is either a crotchet or a quaver, and that a mark in another is either an 'a' or a 'd', otherwise halfway through a piece of music or a text, the same mark might form a different character, making it impossible to read on with any certainty. In practice, of course, especially in the case of manuscripts, but also when reading old typefaces such as Gothic, it can be difficult to determine to which character a mark belongs. For this reason, the second requirement on a notational system is that the characters of its scheme be *effectively differentiated*. Goodman acknowledges that this may sometimes involve considerations of context: in musical notation a mark can be identified as a quaver rather than a crotchet by working out that otherwise there would be too many beats to the bar, and in a written text a mark can be identified as an 'a' rather than a 'd' by considering the other letters of the word to which it belongs.[33]

Whereas a natural language has a notational scheme, and thus can satisfy the requirements of disjointness and effective differentiation, a picture violates these requirements and so is non-notational. A natural language such as English, which uses the Roman alphabet, is disjoint and differentiated: there is no character between 'c' and 'd', and it is always possible, in principle, to determine to which character a mark belongs. By contrast, a picture belongs to what Goodman terms a *syntactically dense* scheme. This type of scheme allows for infinitely many characters such that between any two there can always be a third. In a picture, a line can always be a bit longer or shorter and a colour can always be a bit lighter or darker. But why is this distinction important? The payoff comes when we recognize that since the characters in a pictorial scheme are not disjoint, small differences in the inscription of the marks are syntactically significant. In a notational scheme, it only matters what character a mark belongs to – the significance of the mark is exhausted once we have determined whether it is an 'a' or a 'd'. Substituting one typeface for another, or writing one letter larger or smaller than another, has no syntactic effect: the marks rock, ROCK and ROCK all inscribe the same characters. But in a pictorial scheme differences such as a heavier line, a more rounded shape or a darker colour are syntactically relevant since they play a role in determining the character that has been inscribed.

The semantic conditions that must be fulfilled by a notational system closely parallel the syntactic conditions that must be fulfilled by a notational scheme. *Semantic disjointness* requires that no two characters have the same compliant in common. What this means can best be understood by considering a natural language such as English, which fails to meet this requirement. The terms 'doctor' and 'Englishman' semantically intersect since they can be used to denote one and the same individual.[34] Moreover, some words and phrases in English are ambiguous: for example, the word 'wood' denotes both the hard fibrous substance that forms the trunk and branches of a tree and an area of land densely covered with trees. For this reason, English is not a notational system. To meet the requirement of *semantic differentiation* every character in the scheme must have a corresponding class of compliants. The denotation of pitch in a musical score is notational since both the characters and their compliants are finitely differentiated (middle C, C sharp, D, and so forth) and there is a one-to-one correspondence between the notes marked on the staff and the pitches sounded by an instrument.[35] However, the verbal language for tempos (unlike metronome marks) is not notational: the marking *rallentando* (getting gradually slower) can be performed in a variety of different ways.[36] The system allows for an intermediate tempo between any two notated tempi.

Goodman terms a system that fails to meet the requirements of semantic disjointness and differentiation *semantically dense*. Pictures are semantically dense since for every two compliance classes the system provides for the possibility of a third. Just as there is an infinite number of characters that can be formed by minute differences in the inscription of the marks, such as the length of a line or the shade of a colour, so there is an infinite number of possible compliance classes to which these characters can be correlated. A slightly darker red pigment can denote a slightly darker red coat and a slightly shorter line can denote a slightly shorter ribbon. It is central to Goodman's theory that there need not be a one-to-one correlation between symbols and what they represent: 'Pictures may function as representations within systems very different from the one we happen to consider normal; colours may stand for their complementaries or for sizes, perspective may be reversed, or otherwise transformed, and so on.'[37] Consider, for example, how a red coat shows up green in the negative of a colour photograph. A pictorial system that provides for complementary colour relations would allow different shades of green to denote different shades of red. Goodman argues that, appropriately interpreted, a picture produced in accordance with this system would yield the same information as a picture painted in normal colours.[38]

The foregoing analysis of different types of symbol system initially appears to result in a wholly negative characterization of pictorial representation: whereas linguistic systems can meet the syntactic conditions but not the remaining semantic conditions on a notational system, pictorial systems typically fail to satisfy any of the five requirements. However, if we return to the question of how pictures differ from descriptions, we can see that Goodman has, in fact, provided the required positive characterization.

Whereas linguistic systems are syntactically and semantically differentiated, pictorial systems are *dense throughout*:

> Nonlinguistic systems differ from languages, depiction from description, the representational from the verbal, paintings from poems, primarily through lack of differentiation – indeed through density (and consequent total lack of articulation) – of the symbol system ... A system is representational only insofar as it is dense; and a symbol is a representation only if it belongs to a system dense throughout or to a dense part of a partially dense system.[39]

Although syntactic and semantic density is sufficient to distinguish pictorial representations from descriptions, further specification is needed if pictures are to be distinguished from other representational systems such as diagrams, maps and line-graphs. Even a simple symbol system such as an ungraduated thermometer meets the requirement of syntactic and semantic density: minute differences in the height of the mercury column denote minute differences in temperature.

How, then, is pictorial representation to be distinguished from other dense systems? Goodman's answer is that whereas diagrams and other non-pictorial systems are *attenuated*, pictorial systems are *relatively replete*. To take a reading from a thermometer we need only consider the height of the column; everything else, such as the colour of the mercury and the thickness of the column, is devoid of syntactic and semantic relevance. By contrast, every feature of a painting or a drawing is potentially meaningful. The difference between pictorial and diagrammatic systems lies in the number of features that can be ignored as contingent. Goodman brings this argument home by means of a thought experiment. Imagine that an electrocardiogram and a Hokusai drawing of Mount Fujiyama both have the same undulating black line against a white background. In the diagram only one aspect of the line has meaning: the relative position of any point that it traverses. But in the drawing the weight of the line, its texture, its relation to other lines and shapes, and its size relative to the picture are all potential bearers of meaning. Whereas, theoretically at least, there is a sharp distinction between dense and articulate, i.e. disjoint and differentiated, schemes, repletion is a matter of degree since a greater or lesser number of features can be relevant in different symbol systems.[40] Compared to an electrocardiogram, a drawing is relatively replete – that is to say, a comparatively greater number of features are relevant to the determination of meaning. Even the qualities of the paper on which it is drawn are potentially significant: nothing can be ruled out, nothing can be ignored.[41]

Rules and Conventions

Despite his professed wariness of the terms 'convention' and 'conventional', which he describes as 'dangerously ambiguous', Goodman does not explicitly distinguish his position in *Languages of Art* from a conventionalist theory of depiction.[42] Indeed, a number of his more notorious statements actively invite this interpretation. The difficulties begin with his insistence: 'Denotation is the core of representation and is independent of resemblance.'[43] Most readers have rightly taken his claim that denotation is 'free' to entail that there need be no intrinsic relation between a symbol and what that symbol stands for or represents.[44] What this means can be explained through an anecdote told by one of Kant's biographers. The story goes that Kant was discussing a military battle with some officers one evening when a young lieutenant accidentally knocked over a glass of wine. To save the young man's embarrassment, Kant is supposed to have used the spilled wine to represent the enemy troops and to have made further marks on the table to show how the battle unfolded.[45] It is possible, of course, that the wine just happened to form a shape that resembled a military battalion and that it was this that gave Kant his genial idea. But any such resemblance would have been purely contingent. For a spillage to denote enemy troops there does not need to be an intrinsic relation between the mark and what it is used to signify: Kant could have used the stain to represent his home town of Königsberg or the Duke of Wellington, just as he could have placed his hat on the table or used a button off his coat instead of the spilled wine.

If all that Goodman had to say about representation were contained in his claim that denotation is the core of representation, he would undoubtedly be committed to conventionalism. In the absence of any other connection between a sign and what it signifies, there must be what Peirce terms a 'rule that will determine its Interpretant'.[46] Otherwise, we have no way of knowing what the sign refers to or denotes. However, we need to distinguish between Goodman's formal reminder that, from a logical point of view, anything may stand for anything else, and the full account of pictorial representation that he gives in the rest of the book. The difference between the two can be explained by considering one of Goodman's own examples, which ties in nicely with the anecdote about Kant. We are asked to imagine a situation in which troops have commandeered a museum, and a briefing officer, for want of anything better, uses the pictures from the walls to represent enemy emplacements.[47] Just as with Kant's spilled wine, there need not be any visual resemblance between a picture and what it is used to denote: given the appropriate principles of coordination, Goya's *Duke of Wellington* could stand for Napoleon. Goodman is therefore right to argue: 'Almost any picture may represent almost anything; that is, given picture and object there is usually a system of representation, a plan of correlation, under which the picture represents the object.'[48] If someone designates that henceforth X should be taken to represent Y, then X can be used to represent whatever is Y. However, this argument is valid only if 'representation' is used in the restrictive sense of denotation. As Arthur Danto has pointed out, it is puzzling why Goodman adds the qualification 'almost', for surely there are no limits to denotational reference.[49]

The confusion arises from Goodman's failure clearly to distinguish between two different meanings of the term 'representation'. The example of the military briefing is intended to show that the use of a picture to denote something does not by itself constitute *pictorial representation*. It is this second sense of the term that is being used when Goodman claims that 'taken as mere markers in a tactical briefing or used as symbols in some other articulate scheme [pictures] do not function as representations'.[50] At the heart of Goodman's symbol theory of art is the claim that the relation between a symbol and what it denotes is determined by the symbol system to which it belongs: it is only within a specific symbol system that something is a symbol of a given kind. For a picture to function as a pictorial symbol it must belong to a system that is syntactically and semantically dense and relatively replete. The briefing officer who uses Goya's *Duke of Wellington* to denote Napoleon employs the picture within a system that is disjoint and differentiated: each picture on the wall is correlated with a determinate compliant. This clearly violates Goodman's specifications for a pictorial symbol system. He is therefore entitled to conclude that:

> denotation by a picture does not always constitute depiction ... To represent, a picture must function as a pictorial symbol; that is, function in a system such that what is denoted depends solely on the pictorial properties of the symbol.[51]

I take this to be Goodman's considered view, for it reveals how his detailed examination of the differences between a notation and other symbol systems can be connected to the rest of his theory. Pictures represent through denotation within a symbol system. But it is only when a picture is employed within a system that satisfies the requirements of density and repleteness that it can be characterized as a depiction. Anything can be used to represent anything else, given the appropriate 'plan of correlation', but not every representation qualifies as a pictorial representation.

The full consequences of this argument become apparent when we recall the specific requirements that a pictorial symbol system must satisfy. The standard way of accounting for the difference between pictures and descriptions is to observe that, unlike a verbal description, a picture resembles what it represents. Since Goodman rejects this account, he needs to provide an alternative means of distinguishing painting from writing. His strategy, as we have seen, is to identify symbol systems through their formal properties rather than the nature of the individual symbols they employ. Since nothing depends on the internal structure of the symbol, resemblance drops out of his account as a criterion for distinguishing pictures from descriptions: pictorial symbol systems differ from notational systems in virtue of being syntactically and semantically dense and they differ from other representational systems in virtue of being relatively replete. Goodman contends that all three identifying features of a pictorial symbol system 'call for maximum sensitivity of discrimination'.[52] Syntactic and semantic density 'demand endless attention to determining character and referent', while density 'demands such attention along . . . more dimensions'.[53] Whereas reading a text requires that we sort the marks on the page into a determinate set of characters, to each of which there is a corresponding denotatum, looking at pictures for their informational content requires that we attend to subtle differences in the shape, colour and ordering of the marks since every difference potentially makes a difference in what is denoted. Goodman's theory of art explains why perceptual discrimination plays a role in understanding pictures that it does not play in other, articulate symbol systems. Unlike perceptualism, however, which takes the experience of the viewer as primary, his theory is grounded in an analysis of the structural features of different symbol systems rather than the study of psychological effects.

With these observations in place, we are now able to address the question left hanging at the start of the previous section: does Goodman's symbol theory of art issue in a convention theory of depiction, as most commentators assume, or does it allow for the possibility that – suitably qualified and shorn of its definitional function – the concept of resemblance still has a role to play in explaining how pictures represent? Those such as Hyman, who claim that Goodman is a thoroughgoing conventionalist, draw a hard and fast distinction between a naturalized account of depiction, which holds that 'a viewer's ability to perceive the content of a picture depends on her knowledge of the appearances of the objects it depicts,' and a conventionalist account, which holds that 'a picture, like a text or graph, is composed and interpreted in accordance with a set of rules or conventions that correlate symbols with denotata'.[54] Hyman then has easy play in showing that whereas, for example, there are iconographic conventions that fix the symbolic attributes of saints, there are no rules of this kind that govern ordinary pictorial reference. This objection misses its target, however, since Goodman explicitly rejects the view that Hyman attributes to him. Contrary to what many of his critics believe, Goodman states unequivocally: 'Understanding a picture … is not a matter of bringing to bear universal rules that determine the identification and manipulation of its component symbols.'[55] Once again, the key to his position is to be found in his analysis of the specific syntactic and semantic conditions that a pictorial symbol system must satisfy.

Rules or conventions are generalizations that require the identification – and reidentification – of basic elements whose behaviour can be regulated. Lexicons and grammars can be provided for a natural language because a linguistic system is made up of distinct units – letters, phonemes, words, phrases, sentences – that are determinate and discriminable. Unlike a natural language, or the notation of music using graphic symbols, a dense scheme does not have a disjoint and differentiated set of characters that are tokens of recognizable types. Instead, as we have seen, a pictorial scheme potentially has an infinite number of characters, since any small difference in the inscription of the marks will result in a different character. Recall once again Clark's attempt to 'stalk' Velásquez's *Las Meniñas* (Plates 6 and 7) and the way in which, as he got closer to the painting, the image broke up into 'a salad of beautiful brushstrokes'. There is no limit to the diversity of colours, shapes and patterns out of which a painting can be made; individual brushstrokes, just like chalk or pencil marks, can be placed on top of each other or blended, and they can vary in weight, density and texture, as well as in direction and rhythm. Even a mosaic, which is made up of individual tesserae, does not have a disjoint set of characters, since no two tesserae are ever exactly the same and they can be put together in any combination. Clark's hope that he could uncover the process by which the artist had transformed 'appearances into paint' was defeated by the recognition that the marks that make up a hand, a ribbon or a piece of velvet do not match up on a one-to-one basis with constituent elements of the objects they represent. It is only in a semantically articulate system that individual characters can be directly correlated with discrete compliance classes: in a dense system 'concrete symbol-occurrences do not sort into discriminably different characters but merge into one other, and so also for what is denoted'.[56] The sensitivity of discrimination required to interpret character and referent, and the impossibility of telling whether any two symbols belong to the same type, renders the goal of providing determinate rules that correlate symbols with denotata unrealizable for pictorial representation.

It is clear, then, that Goodman's position differs in important respects from the conventionalism proposed by other advocates of the semiotic approach, such as Kahnweiler and Bryson, who claim that pictorial signs can be understood on the model of linguistic signs.[57] But we have yet to see how

– or, indeed, whether – his theory can make good the evident shortcomings of this approach without becoming entrapped, once again, in the naive account of resemblance that he rejects at the start of *Languages of Art*. The analysis of the concept of resemblance in *Languages of Art* is restricted to showing that it is neither necessary nor sufficient for depiction. As Lopes points out, 'Goodman is not interested in the *roots* of reference – how referential relations are established. His remarks about what determines what a picture represents are entirely negative.'[58] Goodman's characterization of depiction as a species of denotation is intended to serve as a corrective to the ingrained assumption that we know what a picture represents because it looks like its subject: only once representation is 'disengaged from perverted ideas of it as an idiosyncratic process like mirroring, and is recognised as a symbolic relation that is relative and variable' can a more satisfactory account be provided.[59] However, even if we accept Goodman's core insight that nothing is intrinsically a representation and that representation is always relative to a symbol system, we are still faced with the task of explaining how pictorial reference is secured. Lopes has argued that this omission in Goodman's theory is best filled by a hybrid account that combines the insights of the symbol theory of art with a naturalized account of depiction that draws on the psychology of perception.[60] The recognition that a picture must belong to a symbol system that determines which features are taken to be salient or relevant suffices to undermine the naive resemblance theory of representation. But the symbol theory of art does not exclude the possibility that perceptual mechanisms of recognition play a central role in understanding what a picture represents.

In publications written after the appearance of *Languages of Art* Goodman offers several concessions to his critics without abandoning his core claim that the 'apprehension [of resemblance] does not assure, nor its absence preclude, understanding what a picture represents.'[61] He willingly accepts that 'many pictures resemble their subjects', but he insists that this does not provide a secure basis for explaining depiction:

> Resemblance may be as difficult a notion as meaning, but for a different reason. Whereas meanings are elusive, resemblances are ubiquitous. Any two objects resemble each other in some respect. The problem is to specify the sort of resemblance that is required for pictorial representation.[62]

Narrowing down the concept of resemblance to visual resemblance does not solve the problem, since pictures can resemble their subjects in any number of ways. It is far from clear what role the identification of similarities plays in understanding pictures that represent fictional objects, such as unicorns, or cases where we have no independent access to what is depicted. Most of us are willing to assume that Goya's *Duke of Wellington* resembles the Duke of Wellington without any knowledge of what the Duke of Wellington actually looked like. Goodman does not need to deny the existence of visual similarities between a picture and its subject to point out that the specification of which similarities are relevant is relative to a symbol system and thus context-dependent. Even in supposedly clear-cut cases, we still have to determine which properties to look for. There are a wide range of variables at play both at the level of perception and at the level of depiction. Just as there is no single way that something looks, but rather many ways of seeing, so there is no firm, invariant relation between picturing and what is depicted.

Much of Goodman's theory of art is counter-intuitive, but here he is on firm ground. To walk through a collection of paintings that spans different periods and cultures is to be made aware of the sheer diversity of pictorial styles and the seemingly limitless variety of means through which artists have depicted the same, relatively stable repertoire of subjects. An Impressionist painting that captures subtle effects of light and atmosphere has no less claim to objectivity than an architect's drawing or a meticulously observed Dutch still life. The same arrangement of fruit and flowers, or the same subject for a portrait, will be painted in different ways by different artists. To Goodman's question, 'Which is the more faithful portrait of a man – the one by Holbein or the one by Manet or the one by Sharaku or the one by Dürer or the one by Cézanne or the one by Picasso?', there is clearly no right answer.[63] Every artist selects, orders and emphasizes different properties of the subject in accordance with her own sense of what is significant or effective. This recognition opens the way for an account of pictorial diversity that not only accommodates the variety of ways in which pictures can represent their subjects but also acknowledges the disclosive potential of different modes of pictorial representation.

Seeing and Reading

In Chapter 1, I observed that both perceptualism and the symbol-based approach to art derive inspiration from Gombrich's groundbreaking book *Art and Illusion*. Although Goodman does not share Gombrich's interest in the psychology of pictorial perception, focusing, as we have seen, on the formal and structural properties of artworks as symbolic systems, rather than on the production of effects in the mind of the viewer, he fully endorses Gombrich's claims concerning the selectivity of vision and the limits of likeness. In *Languages of Art* he contends that '[t]he case for the relativity of vision and of representation has been so conclusively stated elsewhere that I am relieved of the need to argue it at any length here', noting that 'Gombrich, in particular, has amassed overwhelming evidence to show that the way we see and depict depends upon and varies with experience, practice, interests and attitudes'.[64] Recent advances in cognitive science have supported Gombrich's conclusions, and there is now a broad consensus that vision is an attention-directed system that selects and processes information from the visual field, filling in gaps and integrating saccades – rapid eye movements that last between 20 and 200 microseconds – into short- and long-term visual memories.[65] It follows that if what we see is dependent upon what we look for – that is to say, on which aspects of the visual field are identified as relevant or important – a picture must also be highly selective. As Gombrich observes, 'so complex is the information that reaches us from the visible world ... no picture will ever embody it all. That is not due to the subjectivity of vision but to its richness'.[66] Much of *Art and Illusion* is taken up with showing that the artist cannot simply copy what she sees, but must first employ a schema or design through which she can organize and give form to her experiences: once we acknowledge that representation is never duplication and that even the most realistic painting can only produce its effects through the resources of the medium, we are obliged to concede that concepts also play a role in pictorial perception.

It is unsurprising, then, that Gombrich has been interpreted, by some readers at least, as endorsing a convention theory of depiction.[67] However, in *Art and Illusion* and in his later writings, he trenchantly rejects the claim that learning to understand a picture requires mastery of an arbitrary code that links signs with their referents, insisting that recognition of the conventional elements of depiction need not issue in full-blown conventionalism.[68] I take Gombrich and Goodman to be in basic agreement on this issue despite their differing assessments of its consequences. What separates them is Gombrich's continued adherence to the idea that there is a standard of truth by which different systems of representation can be measured. In particular, he has argued that the method of geometrical perspective described by Alberti in the fifteenth century, and developed and refined by subsequent generations of artists, is true to experience in a way that is unmatched by other representational systems.[69] A static multicoloured surface cannot duplicate the moving, three-dimensional world. However, Gombrich contends that through a process of trial and error artists have discovered how to provide visual cues that can trigger the same responses in the mind of the viewer: a landscape artist need not use green pigment to represent green grass as long as the disposition of the colours on the canvas succeeds in conveying the appearance of a sunlit lawn.[70] Gombrich's standard of truth is therefore based not on a relation of correspondence or identity between the painting and its subject – that is to say, on a comparison of the motif with the image – but 'on the potential capacity of the image to evoke the motif'.[71]

Viewed under the appropriate conditions, it is undoubtedly the case that pictures produced in accordance with the laws of geometrical perspective are able to provide us with 'object-presenting experiences', even if this does not constitute a fully-fledged illusion in the sense in which Gombrich uses this term.[72] There are good grounds for assuming that pictorial perception relies on the same perceptual and cognitive capacities that enable us to discriminate objects in our environment and to reidentify them under changed conditions of light, distance, viewing angle, and so forth. And it seems plausible to suggest that our brains have evolved to interpret visual cues with a rapidity and plasticity that artists can exploit for their own purposes. If this is right, then realism cannot simply be a matter of the viewer's familiarity with an entrenched system of representation as Goodman argues.[73] Whether or not a system is standard for a given culture is only one factor determining its effectiveness: there are also perceptual and psychological factors that determine our ability to discern what a picture represents. No matter how familiar we might be with the works that Braque and Picasso produced during their Cubist period, a painting such as *The Portuguese* (Plate 9) does not allow the same 'instant and effortless recognition' that Gombrich extols in Renaissance art.[74] But nor, as we shall see, is it intended to.

Goodman's claim in *Languages of Art* that 'vestiges' of the resemblance theory 'persist in most writings on representation' suggests that he wishes to extirpate it entirely.[75] As we have seen, however, he is more plausibly interpreted as challenging our naive or pre-theoretical assumptions. His demonstration that resemblance is not sufficient for depiction, and that apprehending what a picture represents is always relative to the symbol system to which it belongs, reveals the limits of a strictly naturalistic account of pictorial representation. The distinction between having to read a picture and simply seeing what it represents serves to remind us that a process of interpretation is involved even when it seems as if we merely register its content. Goodman's aim is not, as Hyman and others have suggested, to establish that depiction is entirely dependent on conventions. Instead, he seeks to undermine the strict dichotomy between the natural and the conventional. By showing that no firm line can be drawn between the two, he seeks to undermine the entrenched dualism that opposes two different sources of knowledge, one grounded in the realm of nature and the other in the realm of human cultural practice. The system of geometrical perspective provides a highly effective means of pictorial representation. However, since pictures are necessarily selective both about which properties they show their subjects having and how these properties are represented, it cannot be said to reveal the world 'as it is' independent of interpretation. In place of Gombrich's claim that there is a single standard of truth, Goodman reminds us that there are many equally valid ways of seeing and representing the world.

Goodman's anti-realism is closely linked to his cognitivism. In his book *Ways of Worldmaking* he puts forward the thesis that 'the arts must be taken no less seriously than the sciences as modes of discovery, creation and enlargement of knowledge in the broad sense of advancement of understanding'.[76] He rejects what he terms 'the usual contrasting of the scientific-objective-cognitive with the artistic-subjective-emotive', arguing that 'art, like science, provides a grasp of new affinities and contrasts, cuts across worn categories to yield new organisations, new visions of the world we live in'.[77] If a work of art simply mirrored or reflected reality, it could not advance our understanding in the way that Goodman suggests. Only once we give up the idea that there is a single right way of depicting the world can we explain why art has genuine cognitive potential. A new style of painting, or a new system of representation, does not necessarily improve on or correct what went before except insofar as an established style or technique may have become formulaic or overly restrictive.[78] Moreover, not all art aims at the production of an 'object-presenting experience'. This is as true of earlier periods in which the symbolic content or ritual function of art was given priority over mimetic accuracy as it is of the avant-garde movements of the twentieth century, whose rejection of the very project of fidelity to nature and the production of a convincing representation of reality was based on a profound distrust of pictorial immediacy and a demand for critical self-awareness about the means and methods of representation.

I want to conclude this chapter by examining these issues in relation to the interpretation of Cubism with which I began. As early as 1912, the poet and critic Apollinaire declared: 'Cubism differs from the old schools of painting in that it is not an art of imitation, but an art of conception which tends towards creation.'[79] That same year, Jacques Rivière observed: 'The true purpose of painting is to represent objects as they really are; that is to say, differently from the way we see them.'[80] The transition from an art of perception to an art of conception was understood in a variety of different ways, ranging from the claim that the Cubists depicted an object from a plurality of viewpoints, thereby capturing the durational character of experience, through to more speculative claims concerning the higher truth that is apprehended by the mind rather than the senses.[81] The origins of the semiotic interpretation of Cubism can be traced back to these ideas, but it also has its roots in the work of the linguist Ferdinand de Saussure, whose theory of the arbitrary character of the linguistic sign was presented in a series of lectures given in Switzerland between 1907 and 1911 – that is to say, at roughly the same time as the development of Cubism. In the absence of any evidence showing that Braque and Picasso were aware of Saussure's ideas, advocates of the semiotic approach have argued that there was a simultaneous breakthrough in the fields of art and language. The first person to describe Cubism in semiotic terms seems to have been Kahnweiler, who argued:

> These painters turned away from imitation because they had discovered that the true character of painting and sculpture is that of a *script*. The products of these arts are signs, emblems, for the external world, not mirrors reflecting the external world in a more or less distorting manner. Once this was recognised, the plastic arts were freed from the slavery inherent in illusionistic styles.[82]

Kahnweiler was also the first to propose that Picasso's discovery of the mutability of the pictorial sign was prompted by his acquisition in 1912 of a Grebo mask in which the eyes are represented by projecting cylinders and the mouth by two parallel bars. Although Picasso had been collecting African and Iberian artefacts since 1908, Kahnweiler suggests that his transformative encounter with a work of non-Western art enabled him to recognize that the 'human face "seen" or rather "read", does not coincide at all with the details of the sign, which ... would have no significance if isolated'.[83] The same shape can be used to represent an eye, a mouth, the neck, or any other part of human anatomy, as long as it is placed within a context that fixes its meaning. In the case of a mask, the meaning of the sign is dependent upon our knowledge of the shape of the human face and the characteristic ordering of its parts. It is only because a face is something with which we are so familiar that we can read the cylinder as an eye; seen in isolation it no more represents an eye or a mouth than it does anything else.

Kahnweiler's ideas were subsequently developed by art historians such as Yves-Alain Bois and Rosalind Krauss, who argued that there are close analogies between the insights of structural linguistics and the second, 'synthetic' period of Cubism when Braque and Picasso began to explore the possibilities of collage.[84] This new technique, sometimes termed *papiers collés*, involved pasting pieces of newspaper, printed oilcloth, wallpaper and other commercially manufactured products directly onto the surface of the canvas. With great economy of means, Braque and Picasso assembled their pictures out of discrete elements that were allowed both to retain their independence and to enter new relations. The visual simplicity of the collages, which are often made up of just a few marks and pieces of paper, belies a sophisticated investigation into the nature of the pictorial sign. By recombining found materials, such as fragments of written text, sheet music, bottle labels and even slips of *faux bois* paper, the two artists juxtaposed multiple systems of reference that the viewer must piece together or synthesize. The letters 'j-o-u' cut from a newspaper might be read as the first part of the word *journal* or as a shortened form of the word *jouer* (to play). But the piece of paper with its printed text could also be given a separate, pictorial function as part of a still life where it might serve as a representation of a tabletop or some other familiar object.[85] With seemingly inexhaustible inventiveness, Picasso and Braque showed that the same shape or mark could be made to carry different meanings depending on its relation to other elements in the picture. However, the claim that the Cubists discovered 'the principle of semiological arbitrariness and, in consequence, the nonsubstantial character of the sign' can easily lead to misunderstanding if it is not qualified, as Bois reminds us, by the recognition that a sign can only function 'within a system that regulates its use'.[86]

In a justly celebrated analysis of Picasso's *Violin* of autumn 1912 (Plate 11), Krauss places great emphasis on the fact that the two pieces of newsprint that are pasted onto the support have been cut from the same sheet of paper: both match along one edge, but one has been turned over to reveal its reverse side. The lower piece is integrated into a schematic charcoal drawing of a violin so that its shape assumes the profile of part of the violin's body and the lines of print are allowed to stand for the grain of the wood. Unmistakeably pasted onto the surface, the newsprint sits flat on top of the support, 'resolutely frontal, facing the viewer'.[87] But the addition of two differently sized sound holes encourages us to read the violin as placed at an angle, with the smaller *f* hole indicating perspective diminution. The second piece of newsprint is placed higher up, its left edge cupping the pegs and scroll of the instrument. Here the piece of newspaper serves as a background so that 'the lines of type now assume the look of stippled flecks of graphite, the painter's visual shorthand for atmospheric surround'.[88] If Krauss's reading is correct, then Picasso has used one and the same sheet of paper to represent both opacity and depth and figure and ground. Whereas the different sizes of the *f* holes still conform to the traditional method of representing foreshortening, the two pieces of newsprint secure their reference through the binary opposition between 'front and back' and 'light and shade'.

With reference to Peirce's categorization of different types of sign, Krauss uses her interpretation of *Violin* to show that 'with the new medium of collage, [Picasso] entered a space in which the sign has slipped away from the fixity of what the semiologist would call an iconic condition – that of resemblance – to assume the ceaseless play of meaning open to the symbol, which is to say, language's unmotivated, conventional sign'.[89] By 'unmotivated' she means that the sign has no fixed relation to its referent, whether causally (an index) or through resemblance (an icon). An unmotivated sign is what Peirce terms a 'symbol'. The invention of collage thus marks a 'momentous' change – 'a change not within the system of illusion from one type to another, but a conversion from one whole representational system, roughly called iconic, to another, roughly called symbolic'.[90] Notwithstanding the brilliance of Krauss's analysis, I believe that we should reject this conclusion. Just as a cylinder can only be interpreted as an eye or a mouth within the 'system of values' established by the anatomy of the human face, so the different meanings accorded to the pieces of newsprint depend upon their relation to the iconographic representation of the violin, which exploits our awareness of the look of a familiar object. Krauss's proposal that the medium of collage allows Picasso to demonstrate the arbitrary character of the pictorial sign fails to acknowledge the extent to which even a work as compressed and elusive as *Violin* remains firmly anchored in perceptual experience.

Rather than marking the transition from one system of signs to another, as Krauss contends, the invention of collage is best seen as a deepening and further extension of the ongoing investigation into the structures and processes of depiction that had characterized Cubism from the outset. During the first, 'analytic' period of Cubism, Braque and Picasso explored the minimum requirements for recognition, sometimes representing an object through a single attribute, such as an *f* hole for a violin or an ellipse for the top of a glass. The departure from the Renaissance system of representation is made clear by the mocking addition in one of Braque's paintings of a 'realistic' depiction of a nail, which casts an illusionistic shadow on the painting's surface.[91] In the words of the critic Clement Greenberg, by the end of 1911 both artists 'had pretty well turned traditional illusionist paintings inside out'.[92] In the final, 'hermetic' phase of Analytic Cubism, the breakdown of coherent pictorial space and the dissolution of the integrity of form approaches the brink of full abstraction. However, both artists seem to have realized that the removal of identifiable subject matter would have broken the complex interplay between the depiction of recognizable objects and the independent reality of the marks on the surface of the painting.

The technique of collage provided a means of overcoming this impasse by securing, once again, determinate reference to the external world. Illusionistic effects, achieved through drawing directly onto canvas or by pasting in pictures, *faux bois* and other *trompe l'oeil* devices, could be isolated so that they no longer deceived the eye. However, the experimental, improvisatory nature of Cubism militates against the idea that Braque and Picasso sought to establish an alternative system based on the arbitrary character of the sign.

Without the expectations generated by the context of use, the meaning of a sign remains indeterminate. This is as true of a pencil mark or a brushstroke as of one of Picasso's pieces of newsprint. A curved line can represent the profile of someone's nose or the prow of a ship: everything depends on its relation to other signs. What Bois terms the 'relative motivation' of the sign requires that any mark or unit, whether it belongs to a dense system such as painting or an attenuated system such as writing or musical notation, be given a positive value.[93] For the visual art of painting, this is determined not only by our familiarity with the symbol system to which the work belongs, but also by our knowledge of how things look.

5

The Specifically Visual

Relational Differences

In Chapter 2, I drew a distinction between two different conceptions of painting, both of which can already be found in Alberti's treatise *On Painting*. The first conception, which is rooted in classical theories of mimesis, holds that the artist should strive to represent as accurately as possible the way in which objects reveal themselves to sight. For Alberti, this is to be achieved by obeying the laws of mathematical perspective, which permit the artist to represent on a flat surface a cross section through the visual cone formed by the rays of light that travel from the surfaces of objects to the eye. A painting should be like a 'window onto the world', opening transparently onto the scene it represents. By contrast, the second conception identifies a painting as a composition, a purposively structured unity that is organized in accordance with its own internal rules and principles. If the artist is to seize the attention of the viewer and to present his *historia* in an effective way, he needs to select and order its constituent elements appropriately. These two conceptions of painting, which remain in constant tension throughout Alberti's treatise, are brought together, somewhat disarmingly, in the final pedagogical section, where he reminds the prospective artist that he 'should be attentive not only to the likeness of things but also and especially to beauty, for in painting beauty is as pleasing as it is necessary'.[1] Whereas the demand for 'likeness' (*similitudo*) requires that the painter adhere as closely as possible to the way in which objects present themselves to normal vision, the demand for 'beauty' (*pulchritudo*) requires that he consider the symmetry, proportion, cohesion and lucidity with which the various parts of the painting are combined into an effective and pleasing whole. If one axis connects the painting to the world, a second equally important axis connects the different parts of the painting to each other.

Up to this point I have primarily been concerned with explaining how pictures represent and with providing an account of the complex relation between the marks out of which a picture is made and recognition of its subject matter or content. I now want to turn to the broad set of issues that are traditionally grouped under the heading of composition, but which extend to include a wide range of other features, including facture and the handling of the medium, the relative intensity and saturation of colour, the contrast between gradations of light and dark, and the organization of the contents of the painting in relation to the twin boundaries of the framing edge and the picture plane. It is important to recognize that these 'design features' are properties of the painting rather than of what it represents.[2] It is Bellini's painting *Virgin and Child Enthroned with Saints* (Plate 4) that has a patterned surface on which the brushstrokes are blended into each other, not the scene depicted. Less obviously, the location of the two nearest figures just behind the picture plane and the low angle of vision that ensures we gaze upwards at the Virgin and Child are features of the way in which the depiction has been constructed rather than of the scene itself. The orientation of the figures, the disposition of light and shade, and even the texture of the marked surface, can enter and inform our awareness of the painting's content. To see the painting as a painting rather than as a window onto the world is to recognize that these features are the result of choices made by the artist and that they can vary independently of what is represented.

I have identified two different axes or lines of enquiry, one of which runs between the painting and its model in nature, and the other of which is internal to the painting itself. It is a weakness of Alberti's theory of depiction – and, indeed, of any theory that identifies painting with the accurate representation of the world as it reveals itself to sight – that it does not consider how these two axes intersect. A similar problem confronts Gombrich's illusion theory of pictorial perception insofar as he detaches the viewer's awareness of the marked surface of a painting from her awareness of what that surface represents: although the viewer can alternate between attending to the marks on the surface and entering the illusion that they sustain, she cannot attend to both at the same time. One of the advantages of Wollheim's theory of 'seeing-in' is that it shows how this account can be corrected. The distinctive phenomenology of representational seeing permits simultaneous attention to both surface and subject: attention to a painting's design features (its configurational aspect) and attention to its subject matter or content (its recognitional aspect) stand in a relation of reciprocity and mutual enhancement.[3] In the experience of looking at a painting it is not always clear whether we are responding to the way in which the artist has presented the subject or to features of the scene depicted; the two interact with one another, mutually enriching and complicating our awareness of the materiality of the surface and what the marked surface represents.[4]

On the interpretation that I defended in Chapter 4, this account is extended rather than contradicted by Goodman's analysis of the density and relative repleteness of pictorial symbol systems: since every difference in the order, texture, brightness, colour and disposition of the marks on the surface of the canvas is potentially significant, viewing a painting requires 'maximum sensitivity of discrimination'.[5] In their sophisticated versions at least, both perceptualism and the symbol-based approach to art give equal weight to a picture's design features and thus provide for an integrative theory of depiction. But we have yet to investigate whether it is possible to provide a broader theory of design features that possesses the same degree of rigour that Goodman brings to the analysis of verbal and non-verbal symbol systems. *Languages of Art* is tightly focused on the problem of reference, analysing the syntactic and semantic structures through which symbols are correlated with referents. Goodman maintains that what a picture refers to is always relative to the symbol system to which it belongs; not only are the ways of seeing and picturing 'many and various', but none can lay claim to be 'the way of seeing or picturing the world as it is'.[6] This raises the question – unanswered in *Languages of Art* – whether it is possible to provide a systematic analysis of the relational differences that distinguish one pictorial representation from another.[7] If no two artists ever depict the same motif in exactly the same way, how are these differences to be characterized? Are we confronted with an irreducible plurality of ways of seeing and picturing, as Goodman suggests, or is it possible to identify underlying structural features that would allow us to make meaningful comparisons between the design features of different paintings even in cases where the depicted content or subject matter is not the same?

The Problem of Style

The term that is standardly used to characterize differences in form rather than content is 'style'. Etymologically, it derives from the Latin word *stilus*, which was used to denote a pointed instrument for writing on wax tablets; by extension, it came to be employed figuratively to characterize an author's own, individual way of formulating and presenting his ideas.[8] Recognition that a painter, like a writer, has his own style, and that this can be used to distinguish the work of one artist from another, is already to be found in Quintilian. This usage continued throughout the Renaissance, where the term was virtually interchangeable with the Italian *maniera*, the expression of an artist's personality through his individual 'manner' of painting.[9] When Gombrich addresses the 'riddle of style' at the start of *Art and Illusion* he takes this to mean 'Why is it that different ages and different nations have represented the visible world in such different ways?'[10] However, it was not until the eighteenth century that the concept of style began to acquire its modern historical bias. The fusion of the ancient rhetorical understanding of style with the concept of historicism – the belief that works of art can only be understood in relation to the practices, institutions and ideals of the culture in which they were produced – is generally accredited to the German art historian Johann Joachim Winckelmann, whose groundbreaking *History of the Art of Antiquity* was published in 1764.[11] Winckelmann was the first to employ stylistic analysis as a means of reconstructing the evolution of art through various phases, each of which is characterized by a distinctive set of traits or features. He also sought to link changes in artistic style to specific cultural and political developments, arguing for instance that there is a connection between the democratic freedoms instantiated in the Athenian city-state and the aesthetic freedoms that characterize the high period of Greek art.

The idea that works of art are an expression of the collective spirit of a nation or an age is most fully articulated in Hegel's *Lectures on Aesthetics*, delivered between 1818 and 1831. Hegel's conviction that 'every work of art belongs to its own time, its own people, its own environment' and that 'scholarship in the field of art demands a vast wealth of historical, and indeed very detailed facts' was enormously influential in shaping the fledgling discipline of art history.[12] Even those who rejected other elements of Hegel's philosophy accepted that the task of the art historian was not merely to situate artworks in their appropriate context, but to organize the history of art into a unified narrative. If every work of art is the product of an historically specific constellation of interests and values, then historical knowledge is essential to understanding the art of the past. The assumption that artworks produced under the same social and cultural conditions are likely to share certain features in common also allowed art historians to proceed in the other direction: stylistic analysis could be used as a means of dating and classifying an artwork for which there was a lack of other evidence linking it to a particular artist or school. The concept of style thus provided both a structure for the history of art – a means of organizing the diversity of artworks into broader categories and sequences of development – and a set of procedures for identifying when, where, and sometimes by whom, an artwork was made.

In his essay 'In Search of Cultural History', first delivered as a lecture in 1967, Gombrich sought to show that '*Kulturgeschichte* has been built, knowingly and unknowingly, on Hegelian foundations that have crumbled'.[13] Gombrich argued that the great project of categorizing artworks into stylistic categories that express the 'spirit of the age' – Classical, Romanesque, Gothic, Renaissance, Baroque, Rococo, Neoclassical, Romantic – arose from a collectivist and deterministic conception of history that had long since ceased to be viable. Even the supposedly neutral and descriptive use of style labels as a tool for the attribution and dating of artworks is open to challenge, since 'description can never be completely divorced from criticism'.[14] In the course of the late nineteenth and early twentieth centuries the march of styles was consumed in a blaze of 'isms', each of which took the place of its predecessor with ever greater rapidity. The sheer profusion of media and practices that characterized so-called 'advanced art' threatened to render the term redundant, and few critics today would seek to characterize an artist's work solely on stylistic grounds. Already at the close of the nineteenth century, the art historian Heinrich Wölfflin spoke of the 'uprooting' of style, observing that in his own time 'styles change like fancy dresses being tried on for a masquerade'.[15] His search for a 'weightier' conception of style led him to focus on the art of the High Renaissance and the Baroque, two periods in which stylistic differences were strongly marked. However, even when employed in relation to the art of the past, the concept of style remains difficult to define with any precision.

The problem arises, at least in part, from the sheer multiplicity of style terms. An artist can be said to have his or her own individual style, which, in turn, can be subdivided into early, middle and late style. Style labels are also used to identify recurrent features or constancies that link the work of different artists. Thus, for example, a period style such as Gothic is used to identify characteristic attributes of medieval art from the mid-twelfth century onwards, while a school style – such as the school of Giotto or the school of David – is based on the identification of features that are common to the work of artists who studied under or were strongly influenced by the same master. Other collective labels include regional styles that group together artists from the same geographical area – such as the school of Leiden or the Swabian school – and the names of artistic movements such as Impressionism and Futurism, where membership is seen to involve sharing at least some of the same goals and techniques. This suprapersonal conception of style is also extended to identify so-called universal styles such as classicism or naturalism that are not restricted to the work of a particular artist, period or school, but reappear in varying forms at different times and places.

Many of these stylistic categories seem to be little more than convenient placeholders that start to break down when subject to closer scrutiny. Not only are the boundaries between historical periods subject to constant revision, but the classification of individual, regional and period styles frequently results in overlapping and contradictory designations.[16] The imposition of unity that lies behind the identification of a collective or group style can obscure important differences: although Gérard, Girodet, Gros and Ingres all studied under David, they developed their own individual interests and techniques. Similarly, artists who belong to a specific movement, such as Impressionism or Futurism, do not all paint in the same style. Degas is categorized as an Impressionist based on his participation in the group's exhibitions and his interest in the representation of modern life rather than a commitment to *plein-air* painting and the use of small touches of pure colour. Most problematic of all are universal style terms such as classicism and naturalism: the employment of single label to characterize tendencies that are supposedly found in the art of ancient Greece, the Renaissance and nineteenth-century France invites considerable misunderstanding, not least because it suggests that there is a common set of commitments underpinning markedly disparate practices.

It is unsurprising, then, that there has been extensive debate not only about how style terms are to be understood, but whether the concept of style can be freed from its historicist underpinnings. Some art historians, such as Svetlana Alpers, have sought to avoid using the concept of style altogether, arguing that it is wrong to assume that 'a frankly external system of style classification' can tell us something about the properties of individual works.[17] A less radical solution has been proposed by James S. Ackermann, who contends that stylistic change can be characterized without recourse to a deterministic model of historical development. Once we acknowledge that the history of art is motivated by 'a constant incidence of probings into the unknown, not a sequence of steps towards the perfect solution', it is possible to develop a more nuanced, context-sensitive approach that avoids the pitfalls of historical collectivism and aesthetic transcendentalism.[18] Ackermann argues that the concept of style remains an 'indispensable historical tool' since 'by defining *relationships* it makes various kinds of order out of what otherwise would be a vast continuum of self-sufficient products'.[19] The alternative would be an atomistic conception of art, in which individual artworks are treated as discrete entities that can be studied only in isolation. Even art historians such as Alpers who remain wary of the concept of style acknowledge that 'the historical nature of the stylistic problematic ... has been the basis for the most serious thinking about style and art'.[20] The relation between the concept of style and larger processes of historical change remains central to art-historical enquiry. Yet it is far from clear how these two dimensions are to be brought together in the study of individual artworks.

Strong Revisionism

These debates form the context for Wollheim's strongly revisionist theory of pictorial style. His position is grounded in a deep-rooted scepticism about the historical explanation of works of art. In particular, he rejects the claim that there is a 'special feature of the visual arts ... which has, allegedly, the consequence that if we are to understand painting, sculpture or graphic art, we must reach an historical understanding of them'.[21] In a series of lectures and articles, and in his book *Painting as an Art*, he drew a set of distinctions that are intended to dispel confusion and to reorder the way that style concepts are employed.[22] Criticizing what he describes as 'the extreme theoretical poverty of the existing discussion', he argued that these distinctions should provide the basis for future empirical work on the subject.[23] His paper, 'Pictorial Style: Two Views', first published in 1979, concludes with a list of maxims designed to guide a research project of the appropriate kind.[24] In his final article on the topic, published in 1995, he expressed his disappointment that this project had yet to be carried out, but he reiterated his belief in the '*a priori* or intuitive appeal' of his position, claiming that it 'furnishes the most natural way of ordering the material of style'.[25] His proposals are thus intended to be of practical as well as theoretical significance; if accepted, they should transform the way in which both critics and art historians analyse the stylistic properties of works of visual art.

Wollheim's first, ground-clearing move is to distinguish between, on the one hand, individual style, or the style of a particular artist, and on the other, all the various other style labels, including period style, school style and universal style, which he brings under the category of general style. The key to his position lies in the claim that only individual style has psychological reality: it forms part of the artist's 'mental store', and it directly influences the way in which he paints.[26] The concept of individual style is *generative*: it explains how an artist comes to paint in a certain way by characterizing the actual processes and decisions that guide the artist's work. By contrast, general style terms are merely *taxonomic*: they are developed by critics and art historians as a means of organizing the diversity of works and approaches with which they are confronted when they turn to the art of the past. General style terms provide a means of grouping different sets of characteristics for our convenience. They offer a shorthand for identifying what is considered particularly interesting, significant or distinctive from a particular standpoint at a particular moment in time. They are thus relative to a certain point of view and can and do vary with changes in the discipline of art history.

As we might expect, the positive or constructive part of Wollheim's theory resides in his account of the psychological reality of individual style. He has devoted considerable attention to explaining how an artist's conscious thoughts and beliefs – as well as other desires, attitudes and emotions of which he may be unaware – shape his activity as a painter. One of his most suggestive lines of enquiry concerns the way in which an artist's style is formed not only by his ideas about painting but also by characteristic modifications of his bodily movements: an artist's disposition to paint in a certain way reaches deep into the limbs and muscles, and is thus more properly characterized as possessing 'psycho-motor reality'.[27] By contrast, Wollheim's account of general style is largely negative: he argues that insofar as art historians fail to identify a 'productive system' that can account for a period, school or universal style, such designations serve merely to cluster or colligate certain features together.[28] Since it is hard to see what could qualify as a productive system other than the psychological and physiological traits of an individual artist, the productivity requirement effectively rules out the possibility of providing a non-intentionalist account of pictorial style. Wollheim concedes that the view he advocates:

> cannot be expected to find favour, or even to possess intelligibility, outside a broader framework within which the art of painting may be set. This framework ... presupposes that, in trying to understand a painting, in trying to grasp its meaning, we should always see it as (what after all it is) the product of a human mind: the mind of its painter.[29]

The question raised by Wollheim's strong revisionism is whether this framework suffices to provide a full understanding of pictorial style. I shall argue that it does not and that his proposals serve to exorcize rather than to explain what Alpers terms the 'historical basis of the stylistic problematic'.[30] The radical consequences of Wollheim's theory derive not from the distinction between individual style and general style, which is widely accepted, but from two further theses that he builds on to this distinction. These are, first, *the description thesis*: the claim that general style terms are merely taxonomic; and second, *the relativization thesis*: the claim that general style terms are relative to the changing point of view of those who seek to understand the art of the past. Let us consider each of these theses in turn, starting with the relativization thesis.

It follows from the relativization thesis that 'style-descriptions can be written and rewritten unconstrained by anything except prevailing art-historical interests'.[31] Unlike individual style, which is '*in* the artist who has it', both psychologically and physically, general style 'lacks reality': not only may art historians define general styles in any way that seems useful, there is no 'fact of the matter' for them to get right or wrong.[32] The relativization thesis thus issues in a radically constructivist conception of what constitutes art-historical enquiry. This conception is not only at variance with current practice, it also seems unnecessarily restrictive. The identification of shared stylistic features continues to play an important role in the attribution of paintings, supplemented in many cases by archival research and the empirical evidence provided by microscopy, chemical analysis, mass spectrometry and radiocarbon dating. While classification on stylistic grounds alone must always remain uncertain, the provision of independently verifiable evidence through modern conservation techniques allows for an ongoing process of correction and corroboration, which provides an appropriate measure of objectivity. Wollheim's account fails to accommodate the possibility that there can be a hermeneutically sensitive search for an increasingly correct employment of general style terms, in which any proposed revision in the scope or reference of the term must respond to and demonstrably improve on previous categorizations, while itself remaining open to revision in the light of new evidence and interpretations.[33]

This argument would do little damage to Wollheim's theory, however, if the first of his two theses turns out to be correct. The description thesis holds that general style terms are merely tools of classification and that 'the attribution of a style to a painter [has] no explanatory force in respect of his work'.[34] Wollheim's claim that only an account of the actual processes through which an artist comes to produce a work of art in a certain style has explanatory value is simply another way of stating his view that in order to understand a work of art we need to consider the activity from which it issues. I have already expressed reservations concerning Wollheim's attempt to impose on seeing-in a standard of correctness based on the fulfilled intentions of the artist. In Chapter 3 I argued that awareness of the artist's intentions – however broadly construed – is only one component in understanding the meaning of a painting. If this is correct, then other factors can also play a role, including knowledge of a work's place in the history of art and its classification according to period, school and region. The distinction between a generative conception of style and a merely taxonomic conception is invidious because it fails to acknowledge that locating an artwork in the appropriate stylistic category can change the way in which it is understood and interpreted. In Goodman's typically succinct formulation, the assumption that concepts of style are merely 'curatorial devices for sorting works according to origin' is misleading since it assumes that 'attribution is alien to aesthetics'.[35]

The dating of a painting – and the consequent ability to establish a meaningful context for comparison – not only directs our attention to salient properties of the work, it also helps us to identify its distinguishing features. To recognize Leonardo's painting of thirteen figures seated at a dinner table as a representation of the Last Supper requires familiarity with a specific pictorial tradition; similarly, appreciation of the artist's innovation solution to the arrangement of the figures – all of whom are arrayed along one side of the table – requires understanding how this differs from earlier representations of the same subject, such as Giotto's well-known fresco in the Scrovegni Chapel in Padua, which shows some of the apostles seated with their backs to the viewer.[36] Erwin Panofsky has argued that we cannot even identify the primary or literal subject matter of a painting unless we know what style it is in. In his well-known essay 'Iconography and Iconology', he discusses the right-hand panel of Roger van der Weyden's *Middelburger Altarpiece* (c. 1445, Gemäldegalerie, Berlin), which depicts the apparition of the infant Christ before the kneeling figures of the three Magi.[37] The ability to identify the child as Christ and the three figures as the Magi depends, of course, on knowledge of the biblical narrative and the relevant iconographic conventions. However, Panofsky goes on to argue that even the 'pre-iconographical' interpretation of the painting as depicting an apparition of a child – irrespective of who the child is taken to be – depends on knowing that it is in the style of Renaissance naturalism. We deduce that the child hovers in mid-air from the fact he is 'depicted in space with no visible means of support'. Yet there are many earlier pictures in which objects 'seem to hang loose in space in violation of the law of gravity, without thereby pretending to be apparitions'.[38] It is only because we identify the painting as being in one style rather than another that we are able to discount the possibility that the artist has simply placed the child against an abstract ground for decorative or dramatic effect.

The limits of Wollheim's approach should now be clear. If knowledge about shared stylistic features plays an indispensable role in arriving at a correct interpretation of the meaning of an artwork, then the adoption of an explanatory framework that is exclusively focused on the intentions of the artist proves to be too narrow. Stylistic analysis is essentially comparative, identifying similarities and drawing distinctions between artworks within a dynamic structure that undergoes continual change and transformation. Rather than isolating the concept of style from wider questions of historical development, we need to find an effective and non-prejudicial way of bringing the two together.

A Logic of Depiction

I now want to examine whether it is possible to establish a framework for the comparative analysis of works of visual art that can meet the twin requirements of objectivity and explanatory value. It should enable us to characterize differences in the formal organization of artworks irrespective of their subject matter and without direct reference to the intentions of the artist, since these are frequently inaccessible. I have already observed that neither perceptual nor symbol-based theories of pictorial representation provide an adequate set of resources for carrying out this project. For this reason, I want to look instead at the proposals put forward by the art historian Heinrich Wölfflin in his book *Principles of Art History*, which was first published in 1915. This remains the most ambitious attempt to draw up a set of 'criteria' (*Maßstäbe*) through which the 'historical transformations' of style can be defined.[39] As in his earlier writings, Wölfflin centres his discussion on the High Renaissance and the Baroque. However, as the original German title – *Kunstgeschichtliche Grundbegriffe* [Fundamental Concepts of Art History] – clearly signals, his goal is not simply to describe historical developments specific to the sixteenth and seventeenth centuries, but to identify the most basic concepts of art-historical analysis. I begin with a discussion of Wölfflin's own views as these are articulated in *Principles of Art History*, before going on to consider more recent attempts to provide a philosophically rigorous reconstruction of his position. I show that if Wölfflin's theory of style is to form the basis for a philosophically defensible account of the relational properties that govern the formal organization of works of visual art, it needs to be extricated from the cyclical conception of history within which it was originally articulated. Nonetheless, the reconstruction of the fundamental concepts as purely formal or relational categories runs the risk of severing stylistic analysis from the explanation of historical change. I therefore conclude by returning to Wölfflin's account of the transformations of style, showing that his explanation of the 'decorative' significance of the five pairs of concepts provides an important corrective to the formal-logical reconstruction of his views.

To grasp the distinctive character of Wölfflin's project it is helpful to compare his approach with that of the Swiss historian Jacob Burckhardt, under whom he studied at the University of Basel.[40] Burckhardt was sceptical of Hegel's philosophy of history, insisting that his own work was guided by detailed historical knowledge rather than philosophical system-building. However, he, too, sought to explain the development of art as part of a larger process of cultural history. His best-known book, *The Civilization of the Renaissance in Italy* (1860), is as much concerned with the legal, political and financial structures of the Italian city-states as it is with art and literature.[41] Wölfflin accepts Burckhardt's claim that since artworks are shaped not only by the ideas of the artist, but also by the social and intellectual environment in which they are produced, the history of art cannot be reduced to the study of individual artists, no matter how significant their contribution might be. However, he points out that the analysis of cultural phenomena as reflections or manifestations of the 'world-outlook' of different historical periods runs the risk of losing what is specific to the visual arts. Art needs to be studied not only in relation to external social factors, but also in relation to internal patterns of influence. It is not enough to place artworks in their original social and historical context: we must also seek to uncover the 'inner development of form' as this changes over time.[42]

Wölfflin begins *Principles of Art History* by identifying two different 'roots' of style. The first root, which he terms social or cultural, branches into the familiar categories of individual style, national style and period style. The study of each of these offers 'grateful tasks' to the descriptive art historian.[43] For Wölfflin, what links them together is the assumption that art can be analysed in terms of 'expression' (*Ausdruck*), whether this be the expression of the temperament of the individual artist or of the spirit of a nation or an age. He acknowledges that this is a legitimate and valuable area of enquiry, as is the analysis of art in terms of its quality. However, he insists that these two possibilities do not exhaust the field. Alongside the social or cultural root of style, there is also a specifically 'visual root' that can be studied independently of other factors:

> This book is occupied with the most universal forms of representation. It does not analyse the beauty of Leonardo or Dürer but the element in which that beauty became manifest. It does not analyse the representation of nature according to its imitative content . . . but the mode of perception which lies at the root of the representational arts in the various centuries.[44]

Wölfflin maintains that 'there can be discovered in the history of style a substratum of concepts referring to representation as such'.[45] These concepts operate at a level that is logically prior to expression since they do not impose constraints on the expressive possibilities available to the artist. Rather, they provide the means through which different expressive contents are first realized. The important point for us to note here is that Wölfflin's analysis of the fundamental concepts of art history is intended to take place at a level that *subtends* the distinction between individual and general style. He envisages 'a history of the development of occidental seeing, for which the variations in individual and national characteristics would cease to have any importance'.[46] Indeed, in the original foreword to *Principles of Art History*, he entertained the possibility of an 'art history without names', which was to be exclusively concerned with transformations in the mode of representation without reference to individual artists or to the wider social context in which art was produced.[47]

As I have already indicated, Wölfflin presents his account of the fundamental concepts of art history through a close analysis of Western art of the sixteenth and seventeenth centuries, including not only painting, but also sculpture and architecture. They consist of five pairs of contrasting concepts: (i) linear and painterly, (ii) planimetric and recessional, (iii) closed form and open form, (iv) composite unity and fused unity, and (v) absolute clarity and relative clarity. In each case, the first member of the pair is derived from a characteristic property of the classic art of the High Renaissance, while the second derives from the freer art of the Baroque. Nonetheless, Wölfflin believes that by focusing on the underlying visual schemata rather than the expressive content of the art of his chosen period he has succeeded in identifying a set of formal possibilities that – with appropriate modification and extension – can also be used to characterize the art of other times and places. Wölfflin's argument for the universal relevance of his theory is based on a periodic model of historical change in which the same basic process repeats itself in every varying form throughout the course of history. He maintains that the transition from the first to the second member of each pair of concepts 'follows a natural logic, and cannot be reversed', likening the process to a stone rolling down a hillside that may vary its course but not its direction.[48] Once the movement from one set of properties to the other has worked itself out, a new cycle begins that obeys the same 'internal necessity'. An equally sweeping conception of history is to be found in the work of Wölfflin's contemporary, Alois Riegl, who describes the history of art as a single overarching movement from a 'haptic' or tactile mode of apprehension to an increasingly 'optic' and subjective mode of vision.[49]

If Wölfflin's fundamental concepts are to be deployed outside of this deterministic model of history, we need to find an alternative means of establishing their validity. This requires that we reject not only his cyclical conception of historical change, but also his claim that there is a necessary pattern of development governing the transition from one form of representation to another. The most radical way of approaching this problem is to recast the concepts as relational categories that can appear in any order or configuration, without geographical or temporal restriction on their scope of application. On this view, it is only once the fundamental concepts are freed of their historical content that they can serve as tools for the analysis of pictorial style. This strategy has been adopted by Andreas Eckl and Lambert Wiesing, both of whom undertake a 'formal-logical' reconstruction of the five pairs of concepts.[50] Eckl takes his starting point from Wölfflin's own, admittedly rather loose analogy between the fundamental concepts and Kant's deduction of the categories in the *Critique of Pure Reason*.[51] Eckl acknowledges that Wölfflin's five pairs of concepts are abstracted directly from experience, and thus cannot stand comparison with Kant's analysis of the pure concepts of the understanding. However, contrary to Wölfflin's own views, he contends that it is possible to provide a 'transcendental-philosophical grounding' of the fundamental concepts by demonstrating that they identify necessary conditions of the possibility of pictorial representation.[52]

Wiesing also argues that Wölfflin's five pairs of concepts can be reconstructed as transcendental rather than empirical conditions that any pictorial representation whatsoever must satisfy. However, he suggests that the appropriate context for understanding Wölfflin's ideas is to be found in a predominantly German tradition of formalist aesthetics. The key insight of this tradition is that 'the relation between forms is what is decisive about forms'.[53] By analysing a picture as a complex of relations, its adherents seek to identify properties that belong to the picture rather than to what the picture represents. As Wiesing observes, formalist aesthetics 'is concerned with the question: what are the structural features of a representation that make the representation possible but do not themselves represent anything?'[54] Insofar as art historians such as Riegl and Wölfflin succeed in elucidating the 'logical' rather than the 'factual' conditions of visual representation, they can be said to have contributed to a '*transcendental* theory of the possibilities of making visible'.[55] Wiesing shows that the analysis of immanent pictorial relations – what he terms the 'logic of depiction' – differs in important respects from the standard theory of logical relations that was worked out by Peirce and others in the nineteenth century. The categories of relational logic – transitivity, symmetry and reflexivity – provide a means of characterizing the *extension* of concepts – that is to say, the relations between the objects to which concepts refer, rather than *intensional* differences in the way in which objects are represented. According to Wiesing, the formal logic of relations 'bypasses what is specifically aesthetic'.[56] Since pictorial representation allows the same objects to be depicted in a potentially infinite variety of ways, a further set of categories is needed to characterize the intensional properties that distinguish one representation from another. Wölfflin's fundamental concepts of art history can be used to make good this deficit once it is recognized that they describe the formal possibilities that stand at the artist's disposal.

Fundamental Concepts of Art History

With these considerations in mind, we can now look closely at each of Wölfflin's five pairs of concepts. Let us start by considering the contrast between the 'linear' and the 'painterly'. The basic distinction is between a clear presentation of forms through the use of line and the merging of forms into each other and into their environment through use of broader marks and patches. This is how Wölfflin describes the difference between the two styles:

> Linear style is the style of distinctness, plastically felt. The evenly firm and clear boundaries of solid objects gives the spectator a feeling of security, as if he could move along them with his fingers . . . The painterly style, on the other hand, has more or less emancipated itself from things as they are. For it, there is no longer a continuous outline and the plastic surfaces are dissolved. Drawing and modelling no longer coincide with the underlying plastic form, but only give the visual semblance of the thing.[57]

In the first case, objects are presented as discrete and isolatable from one another, with their boundaries sharply defined; in the second, they are fused together so that it is no longer clear where one thing stops and something else begins. The characterization of the linear style as 'tactile' and the painterly style as 'visual' is metaphorical since both are modes of visual representation. Similarly, Wölfflin's identification of the painterly style as an art of 'semblance' and the linear style as a representation of things 'as they are' can only be understood in an extended sense. Nonetheless, the aptness of these descriptions quickly becomes apparent when we relate them to specific examples. As a representative of the linear style, I have chosen Dürer's *Self-Portrait with a Thistle*, 1493 (Plate 12), and as a representative of the painterly style Rembrandt's *Self-Portrait with Two Circles*, of 1661–2 (Plate 13).

Dürer's painting reveals that the use of line to define forms is not restricted to the outline of objects but also provides a means of modelling the folds of cloth and the features of the face. We can see at once why Wölfflin likens the linear style to the movement of the hand as it feels along the body, for both give a sense of solidity and physical presence. The clarity of presentation allows even the smallest details to be apprehended without difficulty. The spiky, angular leaves of the thistle – variously interpreted as a pledge of fidelity to the artist's fiancé and as an allusion to Christ's crown of thorns – accentuate the precision of the representation and draw our attention downwards to the artist's hands, where each finger is separately articulated. The emphasis on what is solid and tangible is sustained through a strong, pliable line that both connects and distinguishes individual forms.

If we turn from Dürer's self-portrait, painted at the age of 22, to Rembrandt's *Self-Portrait with Two Circles*, painted in the final years of his life, we can see that line no longer plays a central role and that even the contours of objects are left broken and indeterminate. The dominant ordering device is the deployment of light and shade, or what Wölfflin terms a grouping into 'patches' (*Fleckenerscheinungen*).[58] It is not merely that Rembrandt's handling of paint is broader and more vigorous, with a pronounced facture that allows the brushstrokes to remain visible even at a distance. Rather, the delineation of individual objects is subordinated to the realization of an overall visual impression in which the forms are allowed to fuse and merge into one another. What matters is less the definition of the individual elements, whose precise shape remains elusive, than the totality of their relations. Rembrandt does not depict every detail of his clothing or the exact pattern of the material: instead, he seeks to capture the appearance of the whole as it is revealed by the play of light, which both illuminates and obscures. Instead of the permanent and enduring, we are offered the transitory and indeterminate – a 'semblance' that is disclosed to subjective vision for a passing moment.[59]

The second pair of concepts, 'planimetric' and 'recessional', characterizes differences in the way in which the contents of a painting are ordered in relation to the picture plane. All representational painting involves some degree of recession, but as the term suggests a strictly planimetric composition is organized in strata that line up parallel to the surface of the picture, while a strongly recessional composition depreciates the plane, emphasizing the relation between the foreground and the background. The significance of this distinction can be seen by comparing Bellini's *Virgin and Child Enthroned with Saints* (Plate 4) with Tintoretto's *The Presentation of the Virgin* (Plate 14). Bellini opens a fictive space behind the architectural frame that is sufficiently deep to hold the image of the seated Virgin and the saints, but he uses this to arrange the figures in three separate bands or strata. By aligning the contents of the painting with the picture plane, he creates a sense of order and repose: it is as if we were gazing into a world more regular and harmonious than our own that is nonetheless arranged for our contemplation. Tintoretto decisively rejects this mode of organization in *The Presentation of the Virgin*. The viewer is invited to follow the pointing arm of the massive foreground figure up a precipitously diminishing staircase to the figure of the kneeling Virgin, who is dwarfed by her surroundings. This dramatically recessional composition, with its resulting juxtapositions of scale, creates a powerful feeling of energy and movement. The near station point of the viewer, the proximity of the figures in the foreground and the use of violent foreshortening all contribute to the sense of vertiginous recession into depth.

Wölfflin contends that all successful art displays 'necessity', the sense that nothing can be changed without loss, but is at it must be.[60] The purpose of his third pair of concepts, 'closed form' and 'open form', is to show that this can be achieved in different ways. Closed form is characterized by a stable equilibrium between the parts, realized through the pronounced use of verticals and horizontals, and a balance around the middle axis. Once again, Bellini's *Virgin and Child Enthroned with Saints* provide us with a good example. The emphatically symmetrical composition, with the Virgin and Child at the centre, is supported by an underlying geometry that establishes exact relations between each of the figures and the surrounding architectural structure. Open form, by contrast, avoids the sense of regularity and order that is produced by such visible 'scaffolding' in favour of a more dynamic and seemingly contingent mode of presentation. Whereas closed form 'makes of the picture a self-contained entity, pointing everywhere back to itself', open form 'everywhere points beyond itself and purposely looks limitless, although, of course, secret limits continue to exist'.[61] Wölfflin borrows from mechanics the idea of an oscillating or labile balance to describe the achievement of a freer sense of order. Tintoretto's *The Presentation of the Virgin* is no less structured than Bellini's *Virgin and Child Enthroned with Saints*. However, rather than placing the figures in a clear relation to the edge of the picture, Tintoretto allows the framing edge to cut through the depicted scene, as if we were looking at 'a piece cut haphazard out of the visible world'.[62]

The last two pairs of concepts are more resistant to summary, at least in part because they elaborate on, and further extend, the distinctions we have already discussed. Wölfflin uses the term 'composite unity' to describe an articulated compositional structure in which each element retains its independent function while also remaining a necessary part of the whole: it seems as if the parts could be isolated from one another and continue to be recognizable. With the transition to 'fused unity' this independence is abandoned in favour of the dominating total motif. A painting in a strongly linear style such as Dürer's *Self-Portrait with a Thistle* allows us to identify individual objects and individual parts of objects with ease. But if we try to focus on the objects depicted in Rembrandt's *Self-Portrait with Two Circles*, such as the painter's hat or his palette and brushes, they seem to recede from our grasp. The same is true of the painter's features; we can no longer trace the structure of the jaw or the angle of the nose as we can with Dürer, though there is no loss of vividness or power of expression.

In explicating the final pair of concepts, 'absolute clarity' and 'relative clarity', Wölfflin observes that whereas the classic style of the High Renaissance aims at 'an exhaustive revelation of form', the Baroque style, wherever possible, will leave something to be guessed at, emphasizing the indeterminate and changing character of appearances.[63] The parallelism of the table and the picture plane in Leonardo's *Last Supper* obeys the requirements of a planimetric composition; but the seating of the figures along one side of the table is also a pictorial device that allows the spectator to view the facial expressions and gestures of each of the disciples without them blocking one another from view. Wölfflin points out that 'of the twenty-six hands – Christ's and the twelve disciples' – not one has "dropped under the table".[64] Tintoretto, by contrast, deliberately obscures the faces and limbs of some of his protagonists, delighting in the use of strong light and shadow. The 'relative clarity' of the Baroque must still be comprehensible, but the ordering of the scene should appear an 'accidental by-product' rather than something that has been purposefully arranged in the interests of the viewer.[65]

If Wölfflin's claim to have identified the 'most general forms of representation' is to be defended without recourse to his periodic theory of history, we need to show that he has succeeded in identifying relational properties that can be used to characterize other forms of pictorial representation rather than just specific features of the art of the High Renaissance and the Baroque. Here I shall focus on Wiesing's interpretation, which recommends itself on the grounds of elegance and simplicity. However, I shall follow Eckl in reducing Wölfflin's five pairs of concepts to three: since the last two pairs do not represent independent relational properties they fall to Ockham's razor.[66] The key to Wiesing's reconstruction of the fundamental concepts as a formal logic of depiction is the recognition that each of the pairs demarcates a basic polarity within which any picture whatsoever can be located. On this interpretation, the fundamental concepts are 'limit values' (*Grenzwerte*): they identify notional final points on a scale of possibilities.[67] Reduced to its essentials, the distinction between 'painterly' and 'linear' modes of representation is a distinction between different types of transition from one mark to another on the picture surface. Whereas painterly transitions are merging and fluid, linear transitions are differentiated and distinct. Since all pictorial representation is created by means of marks of some kind, the relation between the marks must be locatable somewhere on a scale between the pole of the purely linear and the pole of the purely painterly. These are notional or ideal types, for a purely linear picture would be devoid of any continuity between individual marks and a purely painterly picture would be fully amorphous.[68] However, there are innumerable intermediate possibilities: every picture achieves its own, individual 'balance' (*Ausgleich*) between these two extremes.[69]

The second pair of concepts, 'planimetric' and 'recessional', provides a means of characterizing two different ways in which the contents of a painting can be ordered in relation to the picture plane. On Wiesing's reconstruction, the opposition planimetric–recessional demarcates a further relational property of pictures: the relation between surface and depth. Once again two extremes are possible: depicted objects can be placed alongside one another so that they are arrayed across the picture plane or they can be placed behind one another so that they recede into depth. All pictorial representation must occupy a position somewhere between these two poles. Wiesing notes that in this respect images differ fundamentally from language: unlike linguistic description, visual representation is necessarily spatial. We can say 'Stan and Ollie are standing there' without specifying the spatial relationship of Stan to Ollie. But it is not possible to depict two figures without situating them somewhere on the spectrum of pure alongside one another (plane) and pure behind one another (depth).[70] The third pair of concepts, 'closed form' and 'open form', describes the relation between the contents of a picture and its boundary or framing edge. A fully closed ordering would issue in a symmetrical and strictly regular arrangement, while a fully open ordering would be accidental or arbitrary, without any acknowledgement of the shape of the support or the need to establish pictorial unity. All visual representation must be locatable somewhere on the scale between a maximally ordered and a maximally free relation between the parts.

Taken together, the three pairs of concepts identify 'transcendental limits' or what Wiesing terms the '*a priori* formal properties of a representation'.[71] It is possible that further pairs of concepts can be discovered: the claim is not that these three pairs of concepts are exhaustive, but that all visual representation involves *at least* the configurational features that they describe: they provide the minimum constituents of a formal logic of depiction. The reconstruction of the fundamental concepts of art history as relational categories frees them of any residual dependency on Wölfflin's cyclical theory of history. In principle at least, this allows them to be employed in any order whatsoever without prior constraints as to which of each pair should take precedence over the other: their application is without restriction in time or place.

I now want to return to the question whether stylistic analysis carried out on this basis can avoid the relativism and descriptivism that Wollheim believes to be the inevitable consequence of any attempt to characterize the specifically visual properties of artworks rather than the underlying psychological and physical processes through which an artist comes to paint as he does. The distinction between a generative and a taxonomic conception of style rests on the claim that there is an 'ineliminable gap' between the two: whereas a 'style description' reconstructs something that is real and causally effective, the provision of a 'stylistic description' is merely a project of classification, subject to the changing interests of each new generation of critics and art historians.[72]

The formal logic of depiction seeks to identify necessary structural features that any pictorial representation must possess. Rather than sorting artworks into a set of categories – labelled linear, painterly, planimetric, and so forth – the fundamental concepts of art history demarcate a scale of possibilities that allow the relational properties of artworks to be analysed. The characterization of an artwork as more or less linear, or more or less painterly, depends on the term of comparison. As Wölfflin points out, 'It is throughout a question of relative judgement. Compared with one style, the next can be called painterly.'[73] However, the judgments are relative to the artworks that have been selected, not to the subjective standpoint of the viewer: the fundamental concepts of art history provide a means of analysing properties that are *intrinsic* to works of visual art. Wollheim's restriction of explanatory force to an intentionalist account of pictorial meaning is more difficult to counter. However, the comparative analysis of artworks is not reductively 'taxonomic' in the sense in which he uses this term. Insofar as the fundamental concepts of art history enable us to understand the design features of an artwork as the result of a choice between a range of alternatives, they also fulfil an explanatory function: they disclose the abstract or formal possibilities that visual representation makes available to the artist.

In practice, of course, an abstract or formal possibility is not yet a concrete possibility. It would be anachronistic to suggest that an artist working in the fifteenth century could have employed compositional structures that were first developed in the sixteenth century. Wölfflin repeatedly stresses that the linear style was an historical achievement and that the 'solution' to the problem of pictorial order that characterizes the art of the High Renaissance – the identification of plastic limits through a firm and even line, the consistent acknowledgement of the plane, a balanced mode of distribution, the construction of the picture as a self-contained entity, and the clear and harmonious arrangement of the parts in relation to the central axis and the framing edge – was only arrived at through a lengthy process of discovery and experimentation. Similarly, Wölfflin argues that it was only after the consolidation of this style that artists could seek to find a way to overcome its restrictions. Many of the innovative features of Baroque art – the use of a dynamic recessional composition, the release of spatial energy through foreshortening and unusual vantage points, the integration of the parts into a single, dominating motif, and the emphasis on the momentary rather than the static and enduring – arose from the conscious rejection of a mode of pictorial organization that had come to be seen as too strongly willed, and hence as artificial and lacking in vitality.

The 'transcendental' reconstruction of the fundamental concepts put forward by Eckl and Wiesing is thus potentially misleading since it fails to acknowledge that there are historical constraints on the range of possibilities that are available to artists in different times and places. Artists cannot learn from or reject modes of pictorial composition they have never encountered.[74] Just as Leonardo could respond to Giotto's fresco of the Last Supper when painting his own version of the subject, but not the other way round, so the process of assimilation and rejection that characterizes the relation between the High Renaissance and the Baroque can only be traced in a single direction. I therefore want to conclude this chapter by considering whether there are aspects of Wölfflin's account that are excluded by the formal-logical reconstruction of the fundamental concepts that nonetheless turn out to have a crucial role to play in explaining stylistic change. In particular, I want to examine more closely the nature of the constraints that supposedly restrict the 'visual possibilities' available to artists at different historical periods. Once understood aright, the identification of such constraints does not carry any particularly demanding philosophical commitments, even though Wölfflin couches his argument in terms that are indebted to Neo-Kantianism and thus potentially misleading for the contemporary reader.[75]

The History of Vision

It might be thought that the task of identifying 'the most general representational forms' (*die allgemeinsten Darstellungsformen*), or what Wölfflin also terms 'the mode of representation as such' (*die Darstellungsart als solche*), is a sufficiently ambitious undertaking for a book that is primarily concerned with the history of art.[76] However, it is a striking feature of *Principles of Art History* that Wölfflin also conceives his project as a contribution to the history of vision. Throughout the text, he maintains that the five pairs of concepts not only serve to characterize 'forms of representation' but also 'forms of beholding': 'in these forms nature is seen, and in these forms art manifests its contents'.[77]

Wölfflin's claim that 'vision has its own history' can be interpreted in both a strong and a weak sense.[78] Taken in its strong sense, he is committed to the belief that human beings see the world in different ways and that it is possible to discern historical patterns of change or development in the 'forms' in which nature is seen. He even speaks of a 'development of the eye', referring not to physiological changes in the ocular system but to transformations in the way in which visual phenomena are apprehended.[79] In its weaker sense, the claim is simply that different historical periods have produced different forms of visual representation. The former is a claim about human beings and their perception of the world; the latter is a claim about the relational properties of artworks. Wölfflin does not keep these two claims distinct, and it is frequently unclear whether he is describing forms of beholding or forms of depiction. Throughout the text, he moves interchangeably between 'forms of seeing' (*Sehformen*), 'forms of apprehension' (*Vorstellungsformen*) and 'forms of representation' (*Darstellungsformen*) without ever fully clarifying the relation between them.[80] Is this simply an equivocation, a failure properly to distinguish two discrete areas of enquiry, one concerned with the nature of perception and the other with the nature of depiction? Or is there another, more productive way of understanding his project that allows us to see why the connection is important for the analysis of pictorial style?

There is nothing particularly problematic, of course, about the attempt to establish a close link between perception and depiction. The central thought behind perceptualist accounts of pictorial representation is that in recognizing the contents of pictures we draw on the same resources that are used in ordinary perception. According to John Hyman, for example, 'a viewer's ability to perceive the content of a picture depends on her knowledge of the appearances of the objects it depicts'.[81] More recently, Dominic Gregory has sought to demarcate a class of 'distinctively sensory representations' that includes both mental images and pictures.[82] Wölfflin's position differs from this intuitively plausible – but not, of course, unchallenged – approach to understanding pictorial representation insofar as he maintains that vision itself has a historical dimension and that the changes it undergoes over time run parallel to, and perhaps even help to determine, changes in the formal organization of artworks. It is this contention that lies behind his much-cited and, as I hope to show, much-misunderstood, declaration:

> Every artist finds certain visual possibilities before him, to which he is bound. Not everything is possible at all times. Vision itself has its history (*Das Sehen an sich hat seine Geschichte*), and the revelation of these visual strata must be regarded as the primary task of art history.[83]

In the foreword to the first edition of the book, published in Munich in 1915, Wölfflin observed that research into the basic organizing categories of art-historical enquiry had not kept pace with recent advances in empirical research, and he called for a history of art that would 'trace the emergence of modern seeing step by step'.[84] This would encompass not only changes in the formal organization of artworks (*Bildgestaltung*) but also changes in the way in which form is perceived or apprehended (*Bildvorstellung*).[85]

One way of making sense of Wölfflin's refusal to observe a firm distinction between the way in which things are seen and the way in which things are depicted – his willingness to treat the five pairs of fundamental concepts virtually interchangeably as 'forms of beholding' and as 'forms of representation' – is to recognize that his account is informed by a broadly Neo-Kantian conception of the mind according to which objects of experience are not simply *given* to us but taken up and transformed through the 'spontaneous' contribution of the cognitive faculties. The origins of this conception are to be found in Kant's first *Critique* and his attempt to show that 'although all our cognition commences *with* experience, yet it does not on that account all arise *from* experience'.[86] In the more radical version developed by the nineteenth-century philosopher Konrad Fiedler, with whose work Wölfflin was undoubtedly familiar, it is not only the faculty of understanding but also the faculty of sensibility that is capable of fulfilling a generative function. Once the faculty of sensibility is identified as spontaneous rather than merely receptive, it is possible to argue that there are different ways of apprehending the world through the senses and – with a characteristically Neo-Kantian twist – that this is something that can change or develop over time. For Fiedler, the creative activity of the artist is to be understood as a further development of the 'process of seeing': works of visual art give material, and hence enduring, form to an ordering of sensible experience that takes place primarily at the level of intuition rather than through the imposition of concepts.[87] In place of the conventional model of art as imitation, Fielder proposes a productive model in which artists can succeed in disclosing innovative ways of seeing the world.

Wölfflin's Neo-Kantian commitments are given their most explicit formulation in the Conclusion to *Principles of Art History*. With reference to the familiar metaphor of art as a 'mirror of life', he argues that even at the level of everyday experience 'beholding (*Anschauung*) is not just a mirror which always remains the same but a living power of apprehension (*eine lebendige Auffassungskraft*) which has its own inward history and has passed through many stages'.[88] He goes on to explain that what he has sought to describe through the contrast between the High Renaissance and the Baroque is precisely a 'change in the form of beholding' (*Wechsel der Anschauungsform*).[89] Wölfflin places considerable emphasis on the term *Anschauung*, rendered by Hottinger as 'beholding', but which in a Kantian context is standardly translated as 'intuition', guided by Kant's use of the term *Anschauung* for the Latin *intuitus*.[90] In the original German, Wölfflin's reference to *Anschauungsformen* or 'forms of intuition' is of unmistakably Kantian provenance and the informed reader is surely intended to recognize the allusion to the Transcendental Aesthetic of the *Critique of Pure Reason*. It is worth pausing to consider Wölfflin's terminology more closely. Consider, for example, the following passage from the foreword that was added to the sixth edition in 1922:

> It is greatly to the interest of the historian of style first and foremost to recognise what mode of imaginative process he has before him in each individual case. (It is preferable to speak of modes of *imagination*

(*Vorstellungsformen*) rather than modes of *vision* (*Sehformen*).) It goes without saying that the mode of imaginative beholding is no outward thing, but is also of decisive importance for the content of the imagination, and so far the history of these concepts also belongs to the history of mind. / The mode of vision, or let us say, of imaginative beholding, is not from the outset and everywhere the same, but, like every manifestation of life, has its development. The historian has to reckon with stages of the imagination.[91]

The key term here is *Vorstellung*, or rather *Vorstellungsformen*, which Wölfflin distinguishes from *Sehformen* through italics. The standard Kantian translation of *Vorstellung* is 'representation', again following Kant's use of the term *Vorstellung* for the Latin *repraesentatio*.[92] The underlying Kantian framework – if indeed this is the scaffolding on which Wölfflin is constructing his argument – is obscured by the decision to translate *Vorstellung* as 'imagination' and *anschauchliche Vorstellung* as 'form of imaginative process'. Kant, of course, reserves a separate term for the faculty of imagination (*Einbildung*), which in the first *Critique* fulfils a mediating function between sensibility and understanding.

On the Neo-Kantian reading, Wölfflin uses the term *Vorstellungformen* to draw attention to the productive or generative contribution of sensibility to objective experience, and thus to emphasize the continuity between the formative contribution of our powers of apprehension and the creative activity of the artist. Where Wölfflin overtly departs from Kant is in the historicization of the constituent elements of this account: the conditions of the possibility of experience are not viewed as static and a priori but as dynamic, and thus as subject to change both culturally and historically. Here Wölfflin is on common ground with other Neo-Kantian philosophers, of whom Ernst Cassirer is probably best known in the English-speaking world.[93] The 'stages' to which Wölfflin refers in the final sentence are not simply different imaginative possibilities that can be entertained at will but rather different ways of organizing and giving form to experience itself.

Further support for this Neo-Kantian interpretation is provided by the direct comparison that Wölfflin draws between his analysis of the five pairs of fundamental concepts and Kant's deduction of the categories (the pure concepts of the understanding) in the *Critique of Pure Reason*:

We can call them categories of beholding (*Kategorien der Anschauung*) without danger of confusion with Kant's categories (*Kategorien*). Although they clearly run in one direction, they are still not derived from one principle. (To a Kantian mentality they would look merely adventitious.)[94]

Wölfflin's main concern here is to emphasize that he has arrived at the fundamental concepts empirically through the close analysis of a selection of different artworks rather than through a process of philosophical deduction. This is the reason why, from a Kantian standpoint, they will appear to be adventitious or merely 'thrown together' (*als bloß 'aufgerafft' erscheinen*). However, in the context of the first *Critique*, Wölfflin's reference to '*Kategorien der Anschauung*', with its strange slippage between the 'categories of the understanding' and the 'forms of intuition', is puzzling, to say the least. Is Wölfflin suggesting that he has identified other categories – distinct from causality, unity, plurality, etc. – that are operative at the level of sensibility? Or has he failed to mark an important distinction between the different levels of Kant's account? It is at this point, I believe, that we should recognize the limits of the Neo-Kantian interpretation of *Principle of Art History*. Rather than attempting to give further precision to distinctions that seem to have been quite loosely formulated, it is more fruitful to acknowledge that although Wölfflin appears to be indebted to a broadly Kantian conception of the mind's productive and transformative powers, which was taken up and developed by philosophers such as Fiedler and Cassirer, he takes this conception for granted rather than providing independent arguments in its support.

Although there are resources available that might be used to develop this account, especially in recent Kant scholarship that has reassessed the role of sensibility in the first *Critique*, I want to propose another, less demanding way of making sense of Wölfflin's position.[95] This requires that we examine the role that Wölfflin attributes to the concept of visual pleasure, or what he also terms the 'idea of beauty', in establishing the connection between vision and artistic representation.[96] An additional benefit of this approach is that it helps us to understand why he believed that the fundamental concepts can be used to explain the development of non-representational art forms such as architecture and design rather than being restricted to painting and sculpture. Finally, and most importantly, it provides grounds for resisting the temptation to recast the five pairs of concepts *exclusively* in attentional or aspectual terms. Although each of the concepts can be characterized as identifying a specific modality of 'visual attention', this risks severing the connection between 'forms of beholding' and 'forms of representation' that we are trying to explain.

Let us return, once again, to the distinction between the 'linear' and the 'painterly'. Whatever we make of Wölfflin's contention that this pair of concepts can be used to capture a far-reaching transformation that took place in European art over the course of the sixteenth and seventeenth centuries, there doesn't seem to be anything in the distinction itself that could warrant his claim that this transformation required 'a decisive readjustment of eye' (*eine einschneidende Umgewöhnung des Auges*).[97] I take Wölfflin's use of the contrast linear–painterly to characterize differences in the design features of artworks to be uncontroversial. As we have seen, in relation to two-dimensional works of representational art, the distinction can be used to identify different kinds of transition between the marks out of which the picture is made. In the linear style the marks tend towards being distinct and individually identifiable, whereas in the painterly style they tend to be fluid and merging. However, in keeping with his claim that the fundamental concepts are both 'forms of representation' and 'forms of beholding', Wölfflin also presents the distinction as means of distinguishing two different ways in which one and the same object or groups of objects can be *seen*: 'linear vision sharply distinguishes form from form, while the painterly eye on the other hand aims at that movement which passes over the sum of things.'[98]

Wölfflin elucidates both claims with reference to two paintings of elaborately costumed figures by Bronzino and Velásquez. Whereas Bronzino's *Portrait of Eleanor of Toledo* (c. 1544, Uffizi, Florence) is characteristic of the linear style in the 'metallic distinctness of lines and surfaces', Velásquez's *Portrait of the Infanta Margarita* (1656, Kunsthistorisches Museum, Vienna) does not render the exact shape of the embroidered patterns on the Infanta's dress but rather the 'shimmering image of the whole'.[99] In a telling aside, Wölfflin observes of Bronzino's painting:

> No human eye can see things in this way – I mean with this even firmness of line. Not for a moment does the artist depart from the absolute distinctness of the object. It is as if, in the representation of a bookcase, an artist were to attempt to paint book by book, each equally clearly outlined, while an eye attuned to appearance only grasps the shimmer playing over the whole in which, in varying degrees, the separate form is submerged.[100]

Wölfflin acknowledges that a strongly linear depiction, in which everything is represented with the same degree of clarity, does not correspond to how anyone actually sees the world, for it is not possible to view a plurality of spatially distributed objects with the same level of attention all at once. Nonetheless, the way in which he formulates this argument suggests that what lies at the basis of the distinction between the linear and the painterly is a distinction between two different kinds of visual attention.[101]

Artists working in Europe in the sixteenth and seventeenth centuries may have elected to organize the design features of their work in identifiably different ways, but it seems implausible to suggest that artists throughout this extended period were not able to shift their attention at will from a focus on the details of the individual constituents of, say, a bookcase to an encompassing apprehension of the bookcase as a whole. The attention-directed character of the human visual system allows us to move with relative facility between the isolation of individual objects and a more unified view in which the parts 'fuse' into a whole, but there is no reason to believe that this capacity was unavailable or impeded at an earlier historical period. How, then, are we to make sense of Wölfflin's insistence that the linear and the painterly style represent two 'radically different modes of vision' (*von Grund aus verschiedenen Arten des Sehens*) and that this distinction can be used to identify constitutive differences between the arts of the sixteenth and seventeenth centuries?[102] Unless other factors are operative, the recasting of the fundamental concepts as forms of visual attention renders baseless the claim: 'Every artist finds certain visual possibilities before him, to which he is bound', for there doesn't seem to be any impediment, historical or otherwise, that might prevent artists from alternating between a unified and a non-unified mode of seeing. As Arthur Danto and Noël Carroll have pointed out, the human visual processing system evolved over time, but it does not have a 'history' in the sense that would be required here.[103] It may well be the case, as Bence Nanay has argued, that this claim needs to be modified in light of recent research into the 'neural plasticity' of the brain.[104] However, the ability to switch visual attention from the isolated apprehension of individual objects to the larger whole of which they form a part is more plausibly identified as a basic human capacity rather than as a historical achievement whose origins can be identified in a specific period of recent European history

To find a way out of this impasse, we need to give proper weight to Wölfflin's variant formulation: 'The great contrast between linear and painterly style corresponds to radically different interests in the world.'[105] The appeal to the concept of 'interest' (*Interesse*) initially appears to provide a rather weak basis for developing an alternative account, but its importance becomes clear when Wölfflin goes on to note: 'From differently orientated interests in the world, each time a new beauty comes forth.'[106] Elsewhere, he writes of the specific 'attraction' or 'appeal' (*Reiz*) of the painterly, observing that the transition away from the firm, clear outlines of the linear style 'is determined by a new sense of beauty, by the feeling for the beauty of that all-pervading mysterious movement which, for the new generation, at the same time meant life'.[107] The opposition between what is felt to be 'living' and the ebbing away of vitality that accompanies the loss of conviction in established forms of visual organization runs like a golden thread throughout his discussion of all five pairs of concepts.

The word that Wölfflin uses most frequently to capture this dimension of the fundamental concepts is 'decorative', a term that he deploys in opposition to the concept of 'imitation'. Although he acknowledges that each of the five pairs of concepts can be used to identify both decorative and imitative features, the decorative is given primacy in accounting for the historical development from one style to another. Indeed, Wölfflin contends that 'the history of art is not secondarily but absolutely primarily a history of decoration'.[108] While it is sometimes used in a narrower sense to refer to pattern or ornament, the more expansive meaning is still to be found, for example, in Matisse's use of the term in his 'Notes of a Painter'.[109] It can also be carried over without difficulty to analyse non-representational art forms, or, more accurately, it has its original application in this domain, from which it was taken up and employed to analyse the representational arts. It is noteworthy that the distinction between the linear and the painterly was first formulated by Wölfflin to characterize differences between Renaissance and Baroque architecture.[110] It was at a later stage that he came to realize that the distinction could also be used to characterize representational art forms such as painting and sculpture.

The crucial point for our discussion here lies in Wölfflin's contention: 'Only where decorative feeling has changed can we expect a transformation of the mode of representation.'[111] This is best approached by considering another of the five pairs of concepts: the opposition between closed (tectonic) form and open (atectonic) form. The basic distinction here is between a kind of ordering that makes itself readily apparent to the viewer – for example, through an emphasis on vertical and horizontal structures or a regular distribution of accents – and a kind of ordering that deliberately weakens the sense of lawfulness through a freer composition and the avoidance of symmetry. It is important to recognize that for Wölfflin closed form is itself an historical achievement. In comparison to the work of Leonardo or Raphael, when we look at the work of a fifteenth-century artist such as Martin Schongauer, 'We have the feeling that nothing is properly secured. Vertical and horizontal do not grip each other.'[112] Nonetheless, he describes the transition to open form in the seventeenth century as an intentional destabilization of the emphasis on visible order and structure that had come to predominate in the High Renaissance: closed form begins to seem artificial or, at least, too deliberate, too calculated in its relation to the viewer, leading artists to look for ways in which their work could be organized without giving the impression that it had purposely been made for contemplation.

Wölfflin acknowledges that the placing of the primary motif in the centre of the picture to establish a strongly symmetrical composition, as for example in Leonardo's *Last Supper* or Raphael's *The School of Athens*, represents a 'specially severe tectonic type'.[113] However, he emphasizes that the 'only important point for us is that the arrangement was once possible at all, while later it was no longer possible'.[114] Even when Rembrandt seeks to exploit the 'monumental effect' of closed form in his *Supper at Emmaus* (1648, Louvre, Paris) by placing the figure of Christ centrally in front of a niche, the effect is destabilized by allowing the figure to be 'swamped in the exaggerated space'.[115]

What, then, is the nature of the 'impossibility' of tectonic pictorial organization that Wölfflin seeks to characterize here? It is not a legal or practical impossibility, since Wölfflin makes no reference to the circumstances of the painting's commission or to constraints imposed by the Church or other official bodies. Nor, as we have seen, are there any grounds for assuming that artists in the seventeenth century lacked the basic human capacity to direct their visual attention, or that Rembrandt was somehow unable to attend to the appearance of regular pattern or order, whether in the natural or the man-made world. Once the question is formulated in this way, the only plausible answer is that the 'impossibility' lies in the perceived limitations of strict tectonic ordering as a satisfactory or desirable way of composing the picture. By the mid-seventeenth century, the use of closed form would have appeared overly rigid and artificial, or, to use Wölfflin's favoured term, lacking in vitality. Certain options ceased to be available, not as an abstract possibility, but as an effective means of giving expression to the interest in drama, spatial energy and movement that characterizes Baroque art. Once this process was underway, a reversion to the geometrical regularity of the older style would have looked archaic and thus carried a different affective power, and perhaps even a different range of meanings, from its original deployment in the High Renaissance.

We are now able to appreciate the significance of the rider that Wölfflin attaches to the claim that 'vision has its own history'. Having observed that the fundamental concepts 'can be treated as forms of representation or as forms of beholding', he adds that 'it is dangerous to speak only of certain "states of the eye" (*Zustände des Auges*) by which conception is determined: every artistic conception is, of its very nature, organised according to certain notions of pleasure (*Gefallen*)'.[116] Understood correctly, Wölfflin's claim that 'Every artist finds certain visual possibilities before him, to which he is bound' need not carry any controversial commitments concerning historical changes in the human visual processing system. Rather, it rests on the well-attested connections through which the work of one artist can be seen as responding to and developing the work of another. The identification of the decorative as a key factor in the explanation of stylistic change allows us to see that there are developments internal to the history of art that cannot fully be accounted for through reference to other factors, even if these factors cannot be isolated from broader social and cultural developments in the way that Wölfflin sometimes seems to suggest.

A defence of Wölfflin's position cannot be complete without considering Gombrich's objection that the five pairs of fundamental concepts do not provide a neutral descriptive framework for analysing structural differences between artworks since they contain a hidden norm. He points out that unlike the categories used by natural scientists, most stylistic labels were coined as terms of criticism or opprobrium. If we forget the origin of these terms, and succumb to the mistaken belief that they identify 'natural classes', we run the risk of overlooking their evaluative character. Gombrich contends that the 'morphological' approach to art history reached its apogee in *Principles of Art History*, which purports to equip the reader with a set of purely descriptive categories but is guided all along by a 'normative idea'. This idea, which Gombrich identifies with 'Vasari's idea of perfection', is already familiar to us from our discussion of *Art and Illusion* in Chapter 3: 'It rests on a firm conviction about the purpose of art and the means of achieving this end. The purpose . . . is the plausible evocation of a sacred or at least significant story in all its naturalistic and psychological detail, the means the mastery of representation.'[117] Gombrich endorses Vasari's claim that the classic style of the High Renaissance represents an 'optimum solution beyond which one cannot go with impunity'. Whether covertly – as in the case of Wölfflin – or explicitly, all other styles are measured against this ideal: the various style labels are 'only a series of masks for two categories, the classical and the non-classical'.[118] What this shows, according to Gombrich, is that:

> there are limits to historical relativism. Such a morphology of styles as we have we owe to the stability and identifiability of a classical solution. There is something like an 'essence' of the classic that permits us to plot other works of art at a variable distance from this central point.[119]

Wölfflin explicitly rejects this view. It is not a 'magic trick' or a careless omission that leads him to give equal weight to the two poles of his schema. Rather than giving priority to either the Classical or the Baroque, he claims that there is no overarching normative standard against which they can be measured: they are 'two conceptions of the world, differently orientated in taste and in their interest in the world, and yet each capable of giving a perfect picture of visible things'.[120] Although the painterly style is the later of the two, 'it is not a higher stage in the solution of one problem of the imitation of nature, but a totally different solution'.[121] Contrary to the tradition of thought that extends from Vasari to Gombrich, he contends that the historical transformations of art cannot be understood primarily in terms of progress in the imitation of nature. The differences between Dürer and Rembrandt, or between Bronzino and Velásquez, do not derive from a greater technical facility in the 'mastery of representation' but from a different feeling for beauty. Wölfflin's central insight is that differences in the design features of works of art cannot be captured in terms of greater or lesser mimetic accuracy, since 'even the most perfect imitation of natural appearances is still infinitely different from reality'.[122]

For Wölfflin, as for Goodman, there is a close connection between the diversity of 'ways of seeing' and the diversity of 'ways of picturing'.[123] Both emphasize the degree of ordering and selectivity that is involved even in so-called ordinary perception; and both hold that there is no single 'standard of correctness' against which depiction can be measured, since pictures can emphasize or disclose different aspects of visual experience. Nonetheless, although Wölfflin appears to be committed to a radically pluralistic conception of art as a form of 'worldmaking' – which, as Goodman acknowledges, can be traced back to nineteenth-century Neo-Kantianism – his account is rooted in a historical conception of stylistic change that imposes constraints on what is 'possible' at any given time.[124] That these constraints are grounded in a specific 'feeling for beauty' rather than a more demanding account of the plasticity of vision makes them no less effective as determinants of artistic style. The fundamental concepts of art history provide at least a minimal objective basis for the comparative analysis of the specifically visual features of artworks, while at the same time, providing a framework for understanding their historical transformation.

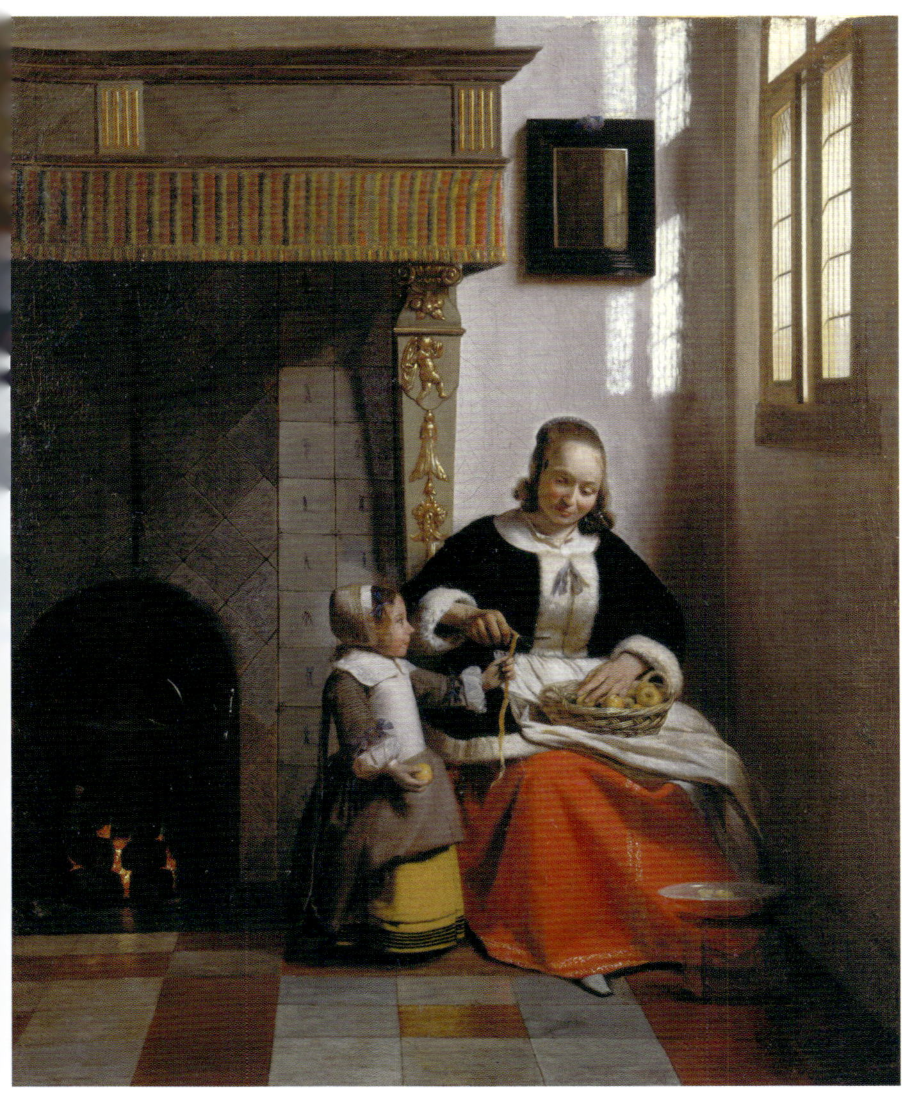

Plate 1 Pieter de Hooch, *A Woman Peeling Apples*, c. 1663, oil on canvas, 71 × 54 cm. (Wallace Collection, London / Bridgeman Images.)

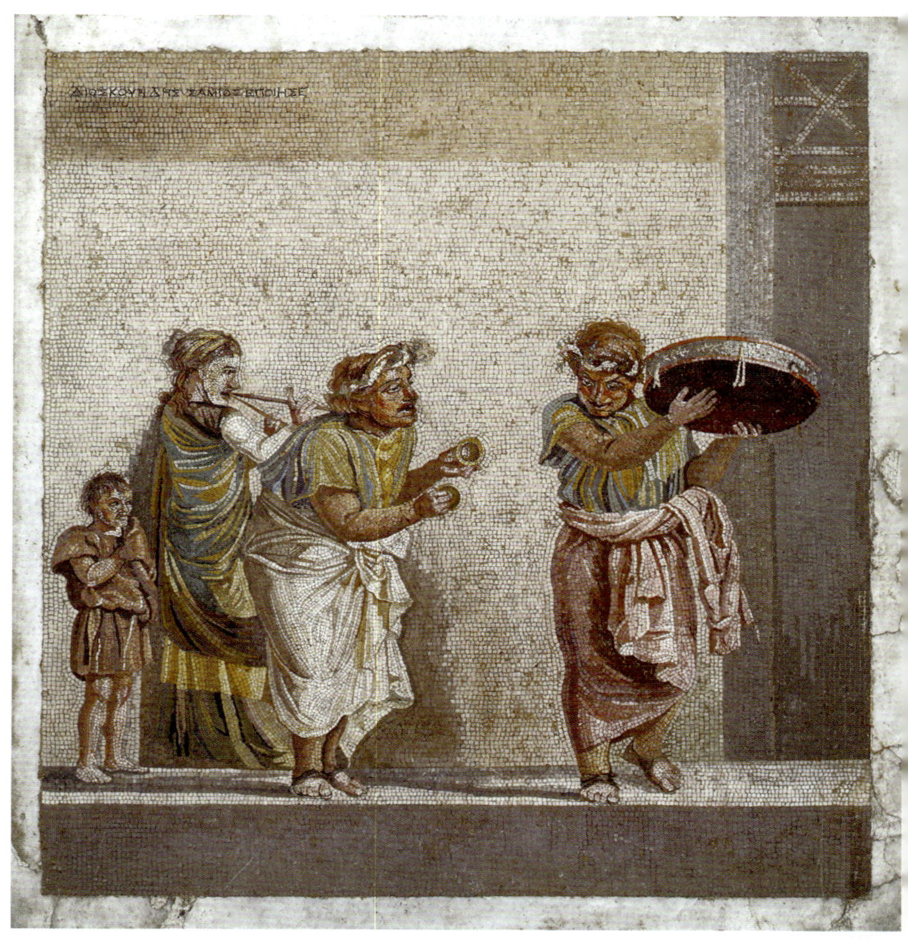

Plate 2 Dioskourides of Samos, *Strolling Masked Musicians*, 2nd century BC, limestone and marble tesserae, 41.5 × 43.5 cm. Found in Villa of Cicero, Pompeii. (Museo Archeologico Nazionale, Naples. Photo © Luisa Ricciarini / Bridgeman Images.)

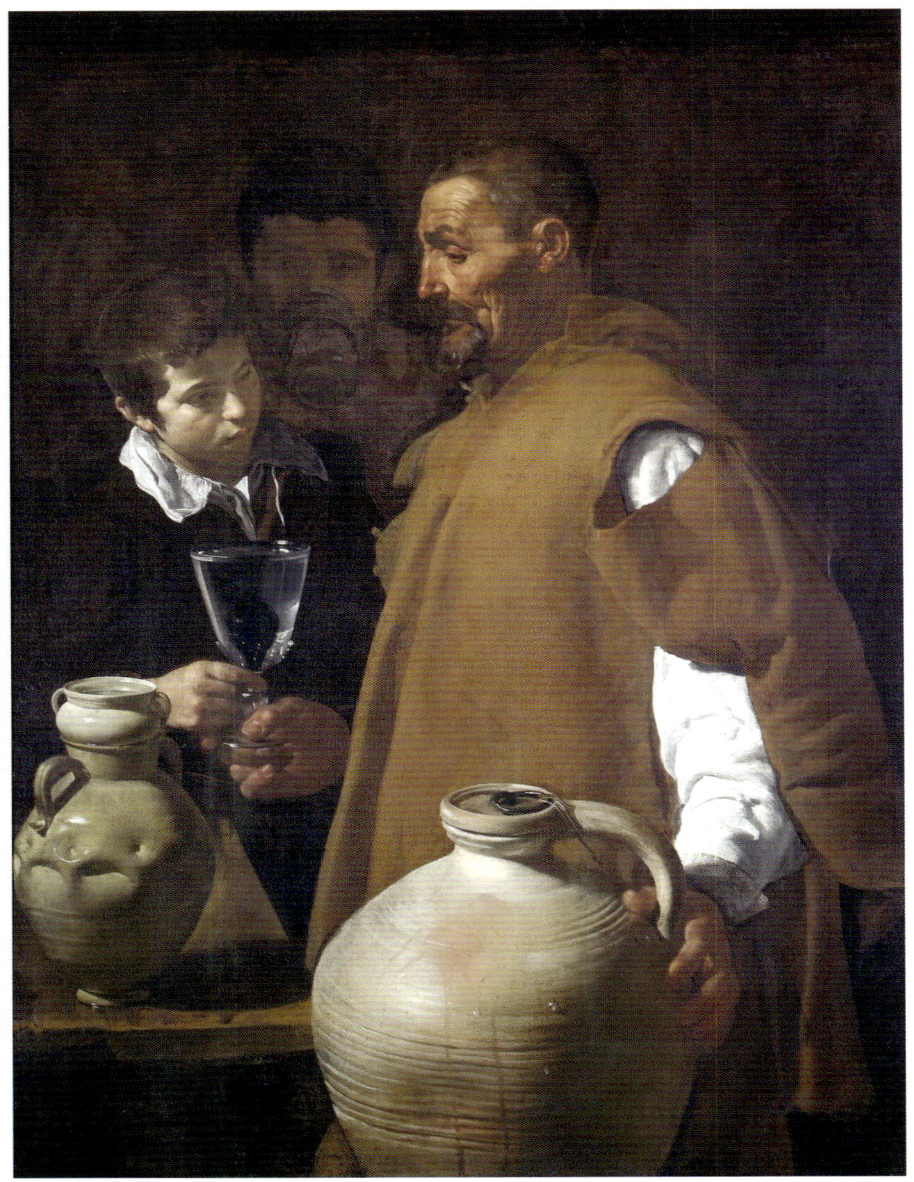

Plate 3 Diego Velásquez, *The Waterseller of Seville*, c. 1620, oil on canvas, 106.7 × 81 cm. (Apsley House, The Wellington Museum, London © Historic England / Bridgeman Images.)

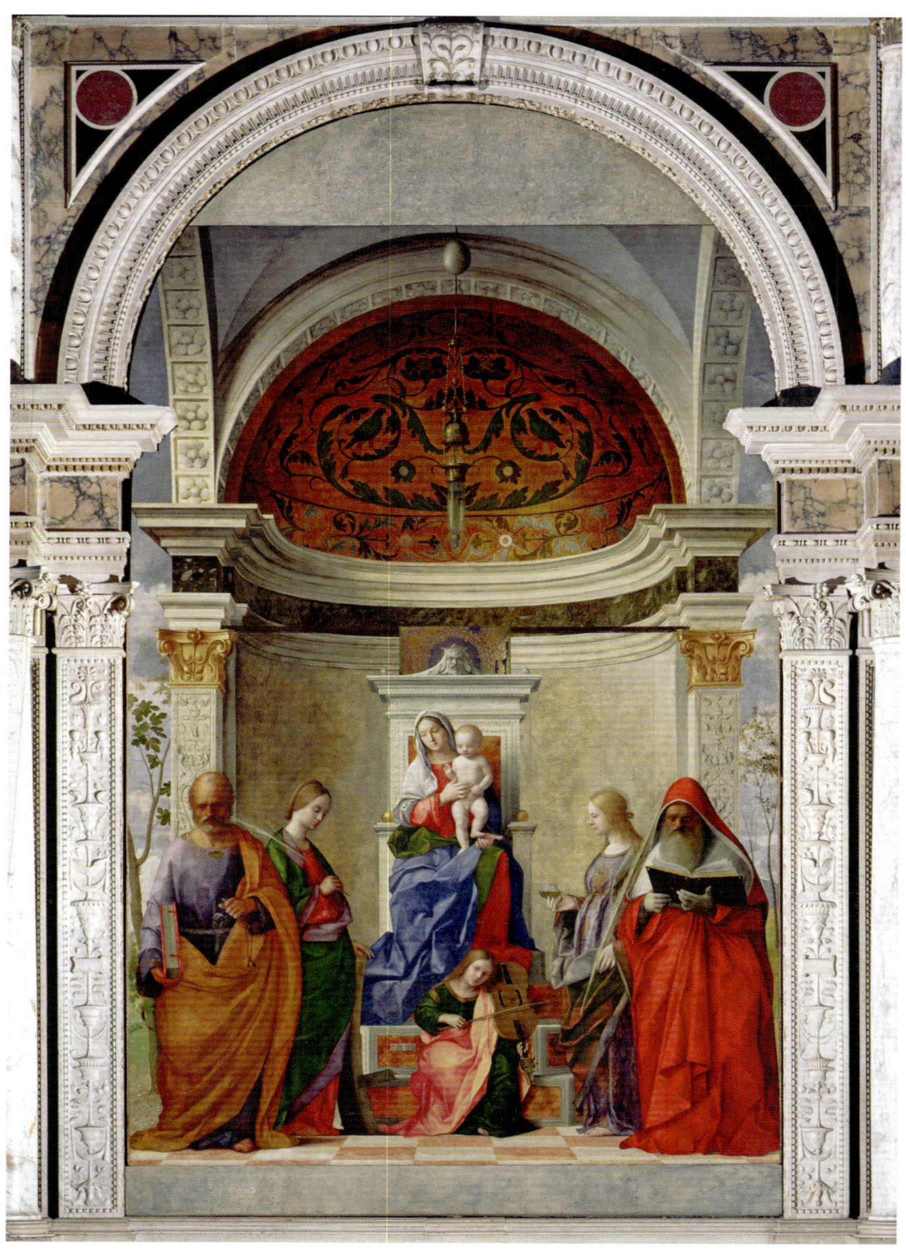

Plate 4 Giovanni Bellini, *Virgin and Child Enthroned with Saints (S. Zaccaria altarpiece)*, 1505, oil on canvas, transferred from wood, 402 × 273 cm. (Church of San Zaccaria, Venice, Cameraphoto Arte Venezia / Bridgeman Images.)

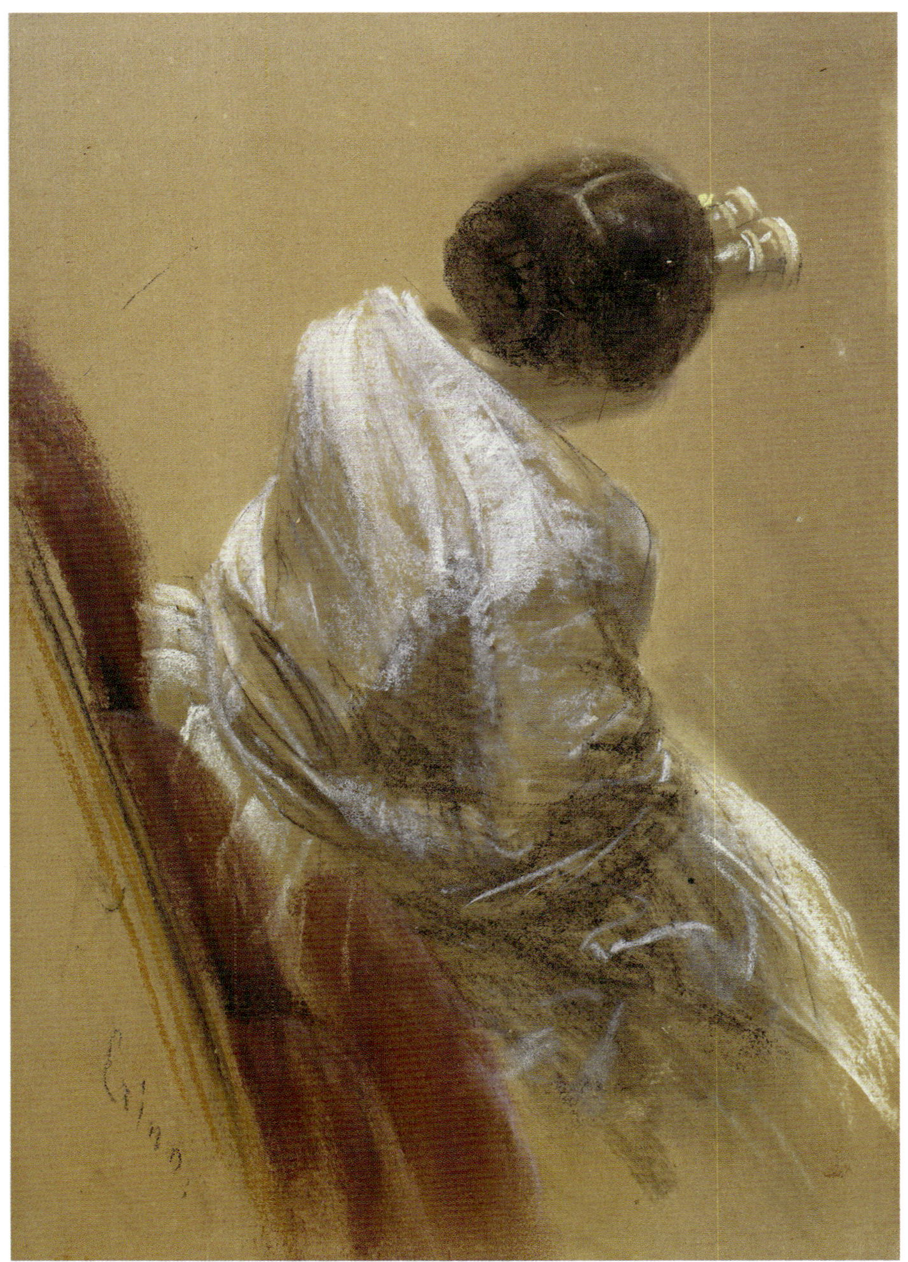

Plate 5   Adolph Menzel, *Lady with Opera Glasses*, c. 1850, coloured chalks on paper, 28.2 × 19.4 cm. (Bpk / Kupferstichkabinett, Staatliche Museen zu Berlin, Germany. Photo: Jörg P. Anders.)

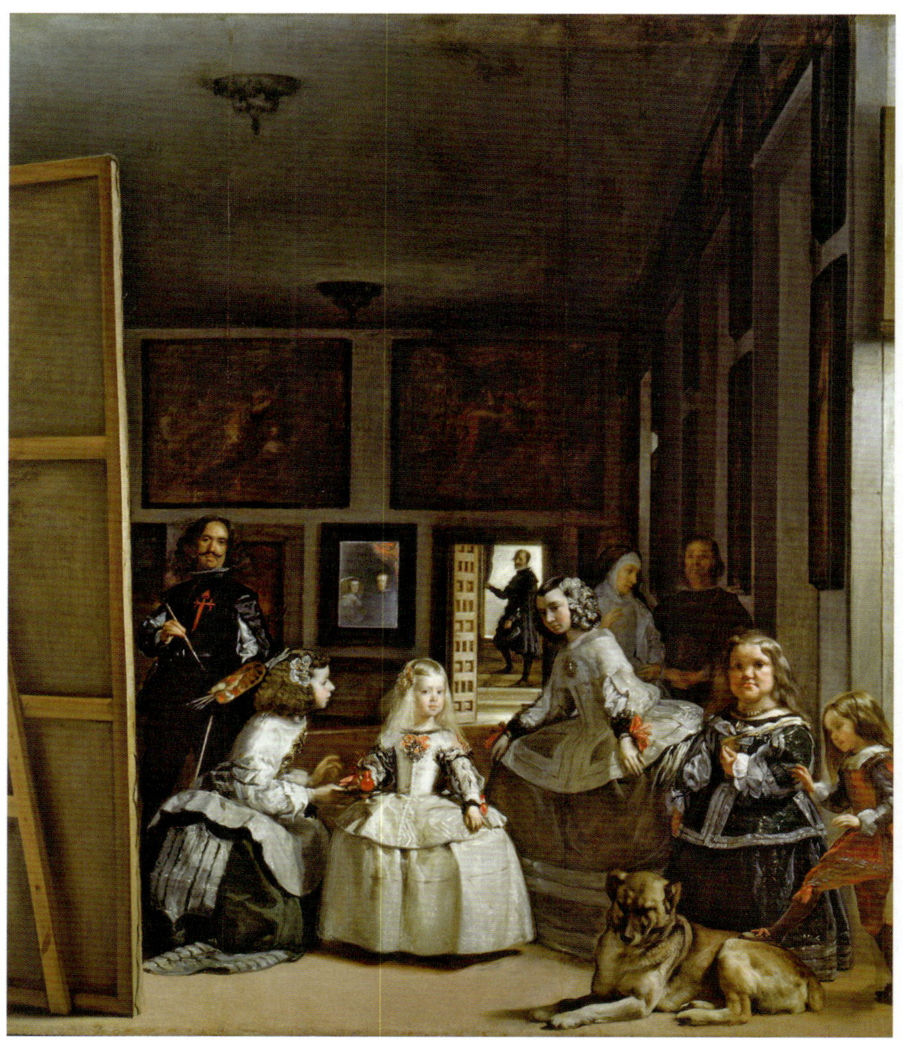

Plate 6 Diego Velásquez, *Las Meniñas*, c. 1656, oil on canvas, 318 × 276 cm. (Museo del Prado, Madrid / Bridgeman Images.)

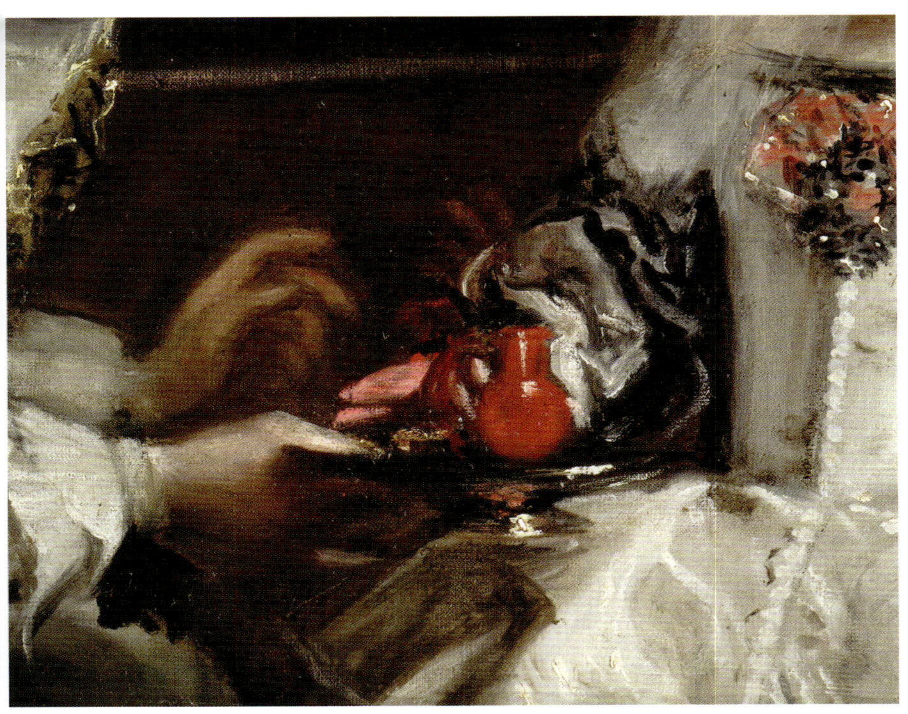

Plate 7 Diego Velásquez, *The hands of Maria Augustina Sarmiento and the brooch of the Infanta Margarita Maria*, detail of *Las Meniñas*, c. 1656 (Museo del Prado, Madrid / Bridgeman Images.)

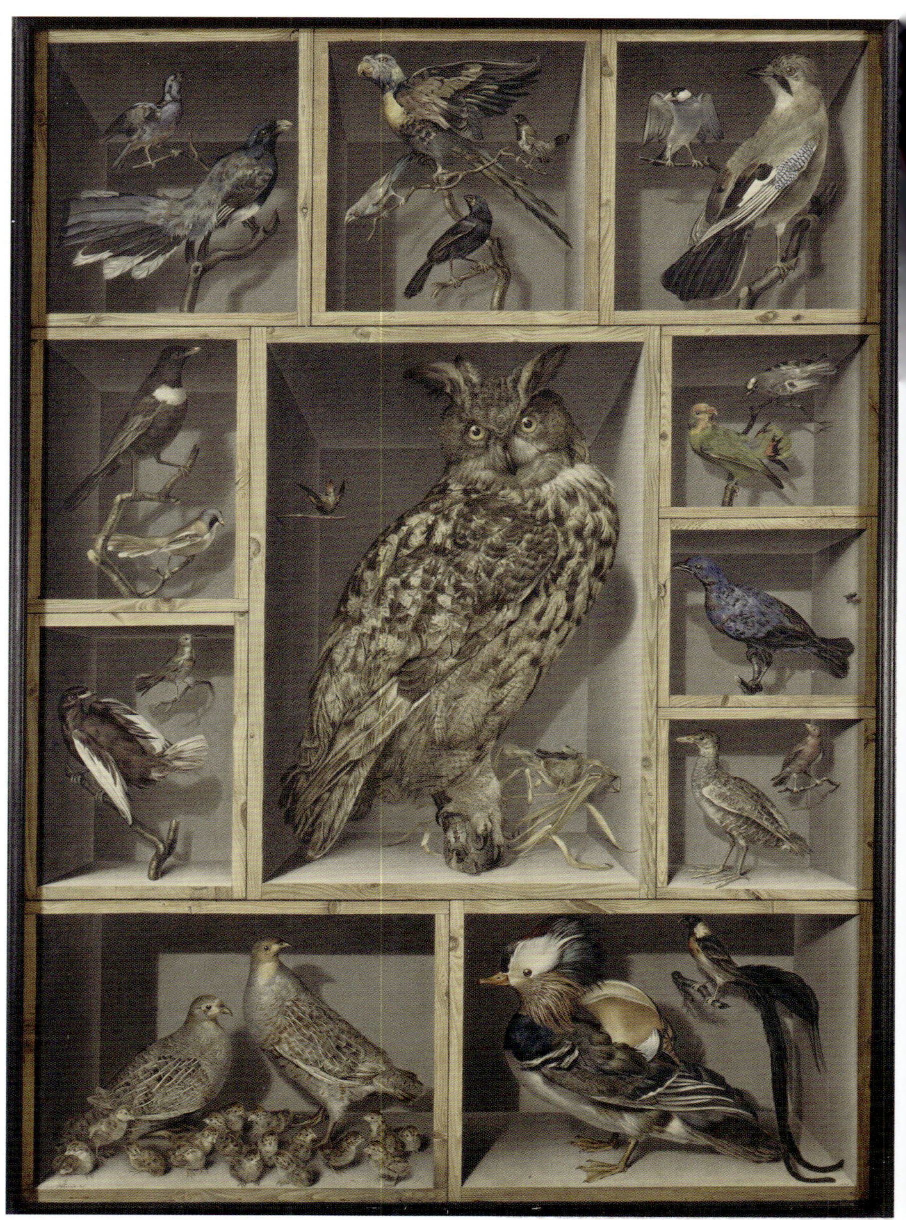

Plate 8 Alexandre-Isidore Leroy de Barde, *Still-Life with Exotic Birds*, c.1810, watercolour on paper, 124.6 × 88.5 cm. (Musée du Louvre, Paris, D.A.G. Photo © RMN-Grand Palais / Gérard Blot.)

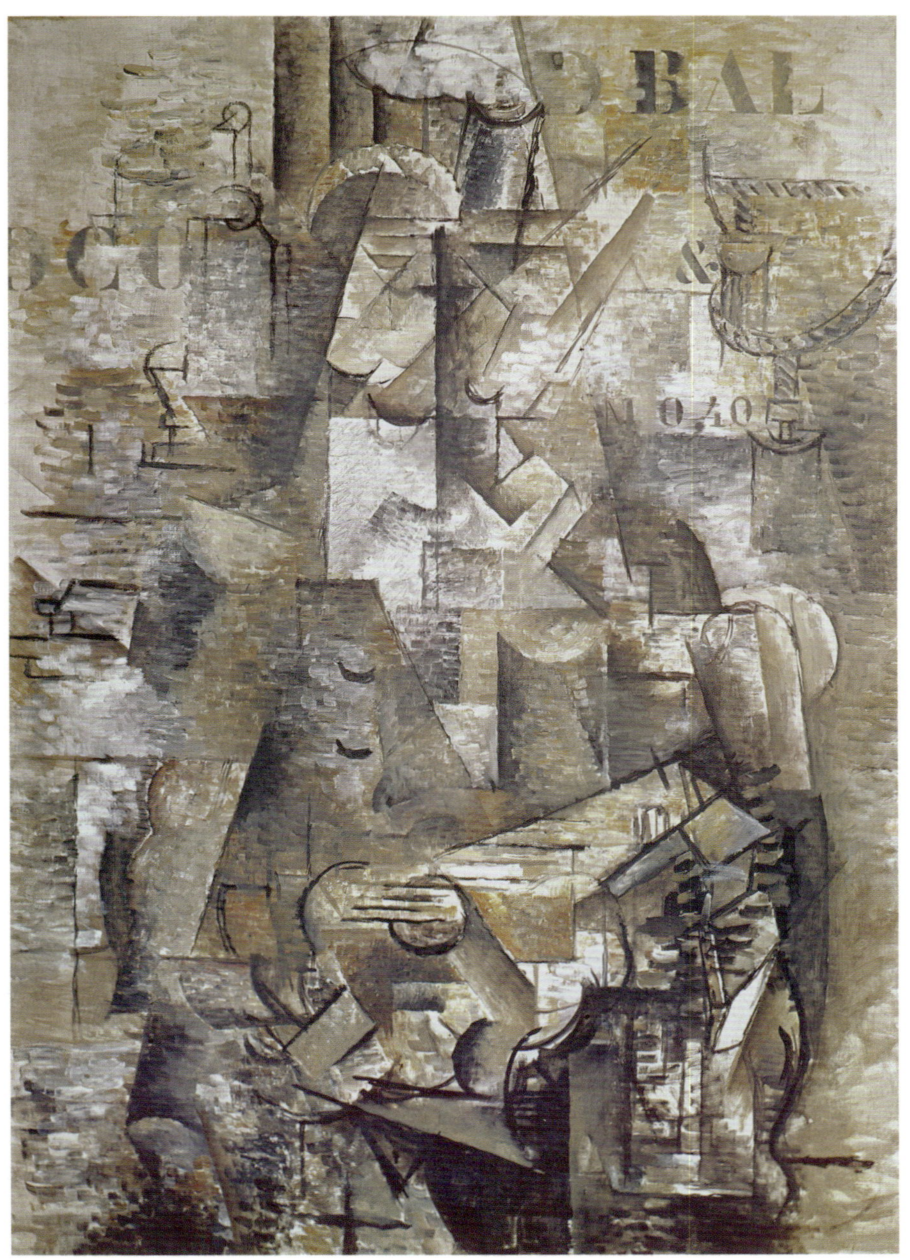

Plate 9 Georges Braque, *The Portuguese (The Emigrant)*, 1911–1912, oil on canvas, 117 × 81.5 cm. (Öffentliche Kunstsammlung, Basel / Bridgeman Images. © DACS.)

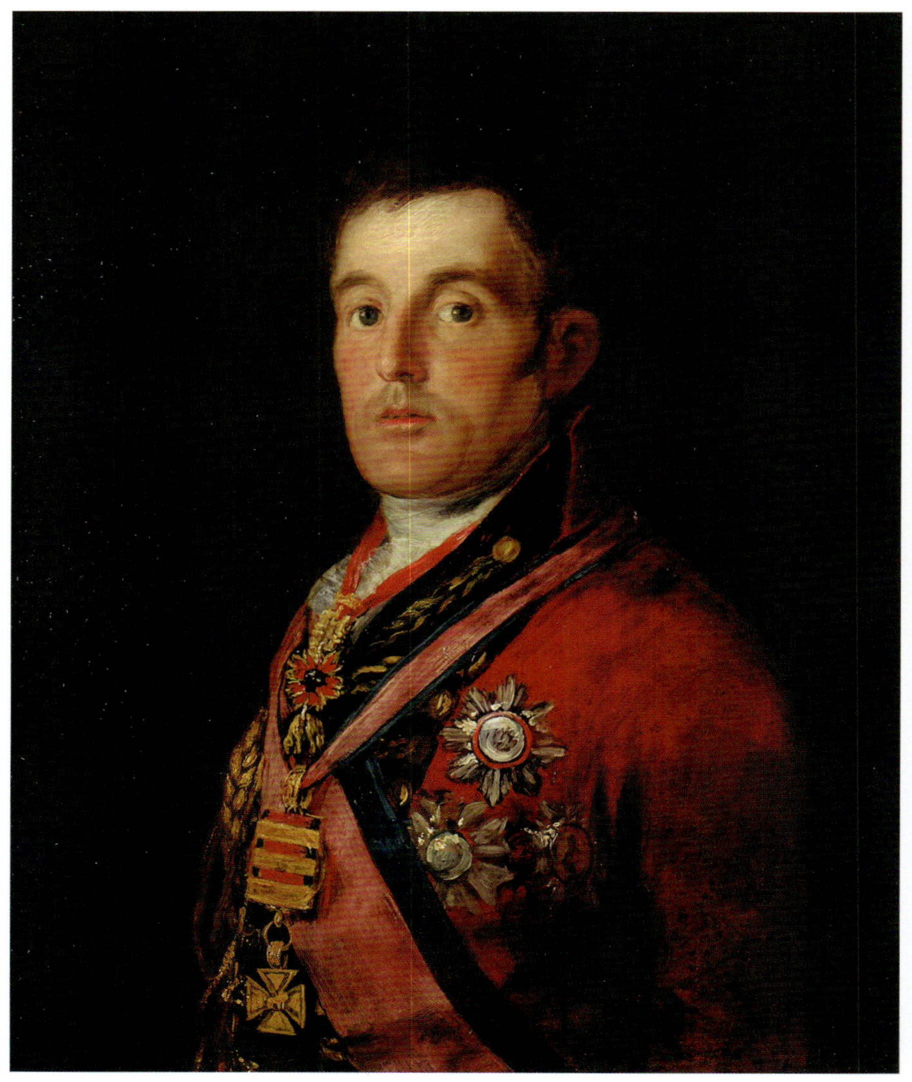

Plate 10 Francisco de Goya, *The Duke of Wellington*, 1812–14, oil on mahogany, 64.3 × 52.4 cm (National Gallery, London / Bridgeman Images.)

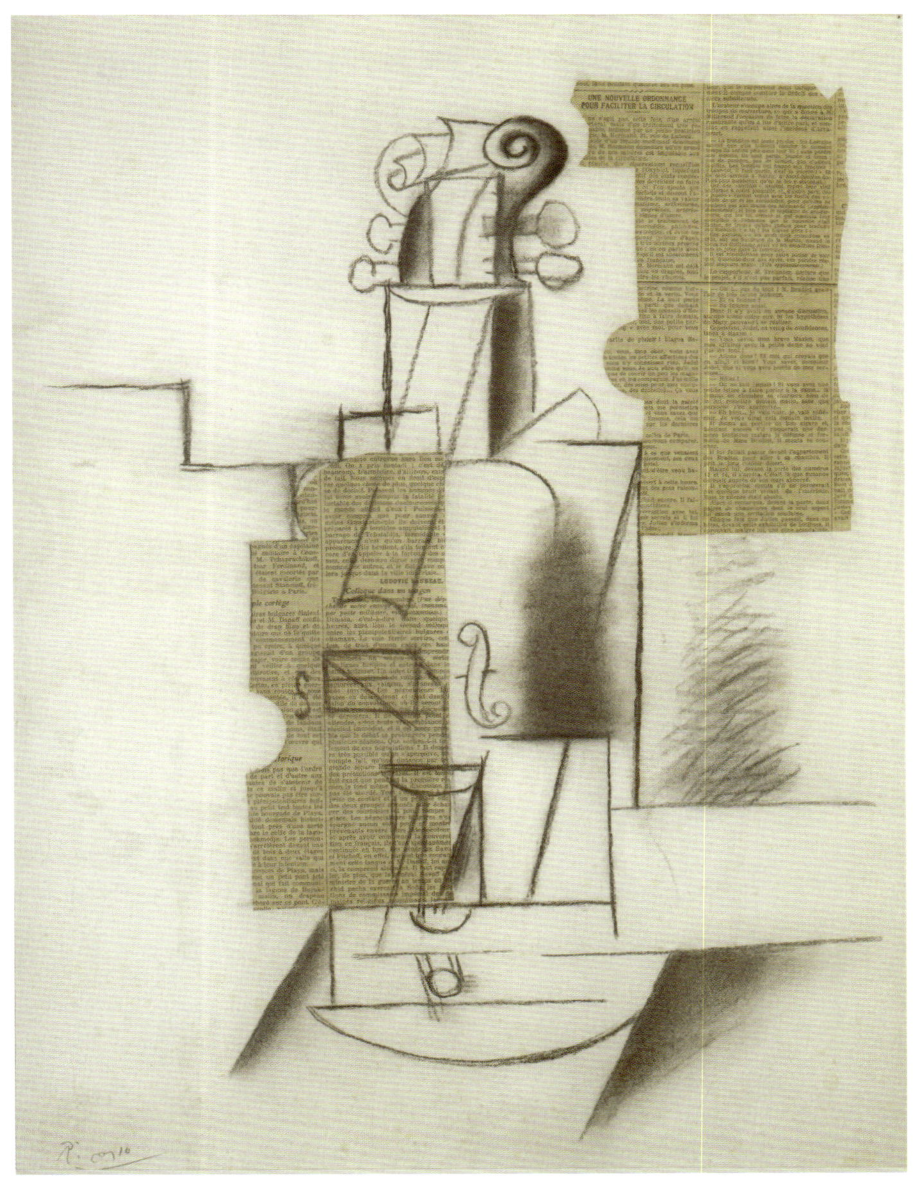

Plate 11 Pablo Picasso, *Violin*, 1912, pasted paper and charcoal, 62 × 47 cm. (Musée National d'Art Moderne – Centre Georges Pompidou, Paris. © Succession Picasso / DACS. Photo © Centre Pompidou, MNAM-CCI, Dist RMN-Grand Palais.)

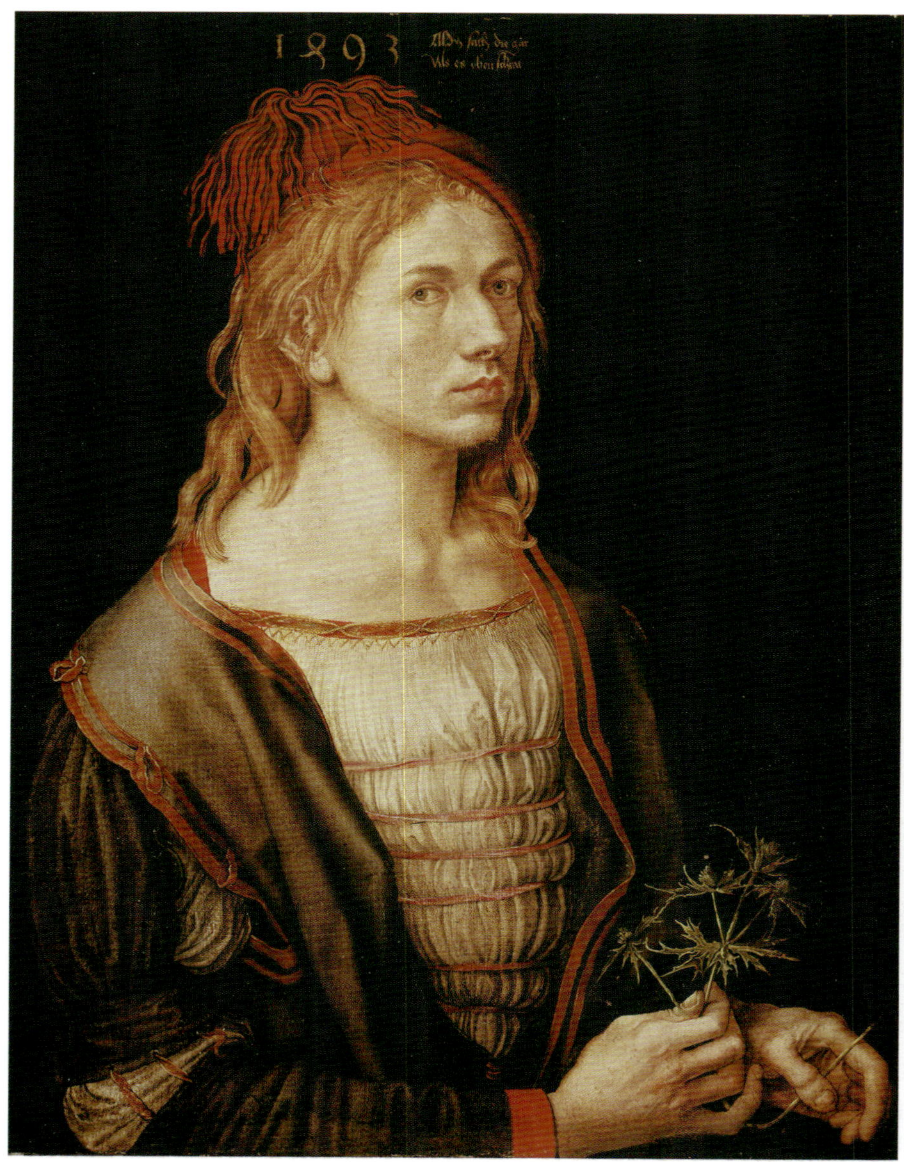

Plate 12 Albrecht Dürer, *Self-Portrait with a Thistle*, 1493, oil on velum, 56.5 × 44.5 cm. (Musée du Louvre, Paris. Photo © Luisa Ricciarini /Bridgeman Images.)

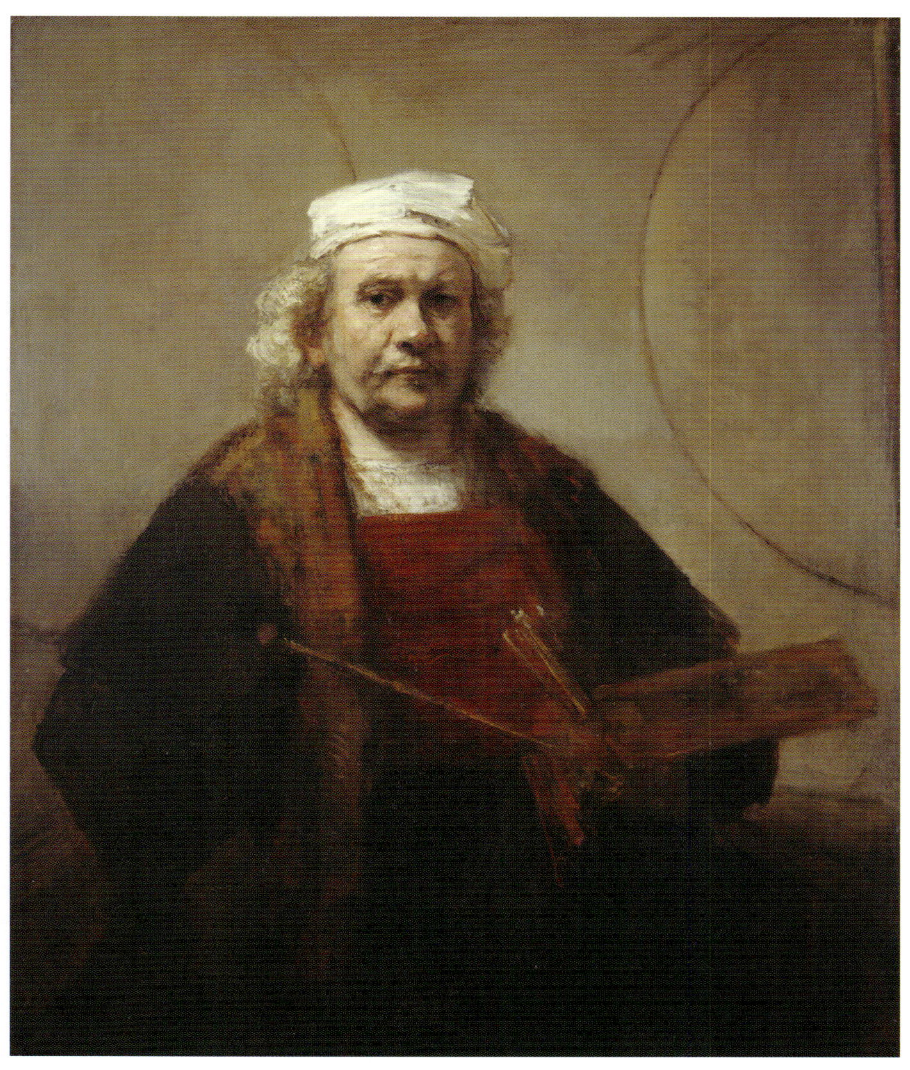

Plate 13 Rembrandt van Rijn, *Self-Portrait with Two Circles*, 1661–62, oil on canvas, 114.3 × 94 cm. (The Iveagh Bequest, Kenwood House, London, © Historic England / Bridgeman Images.)

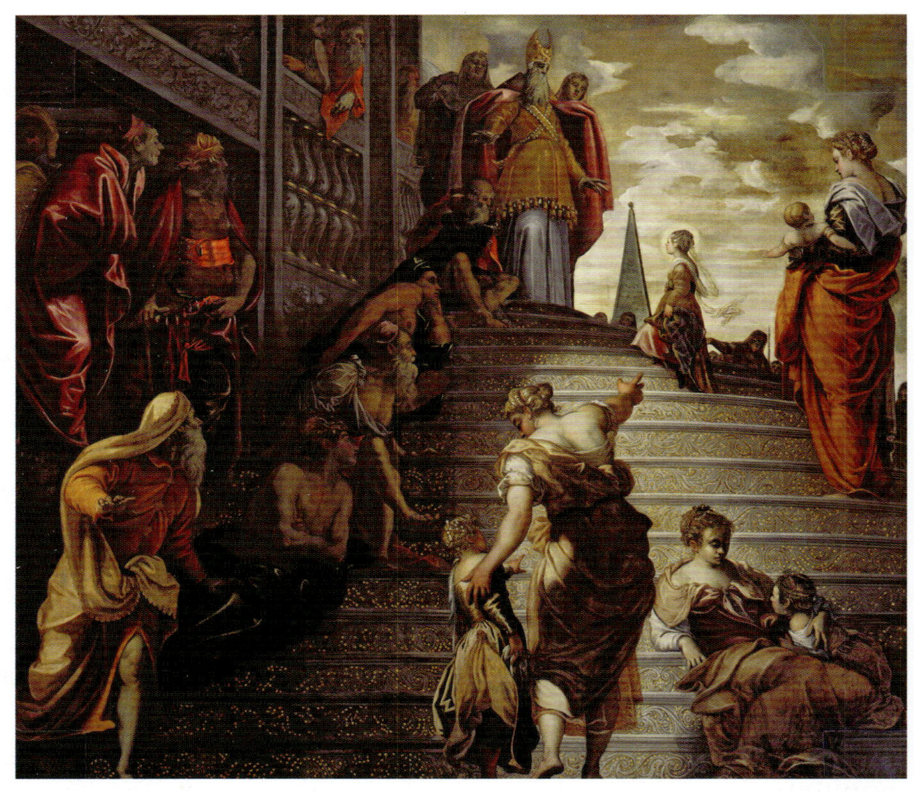

Plate 14 Jacopo Tintoretto, *The Presentation of the Virgin*, 1552, oil on canvas, 400 × 480 cm. (Madonna dell'Orto, Venice, Cameraphoto Arte Venezia / Bridgeman Images.)

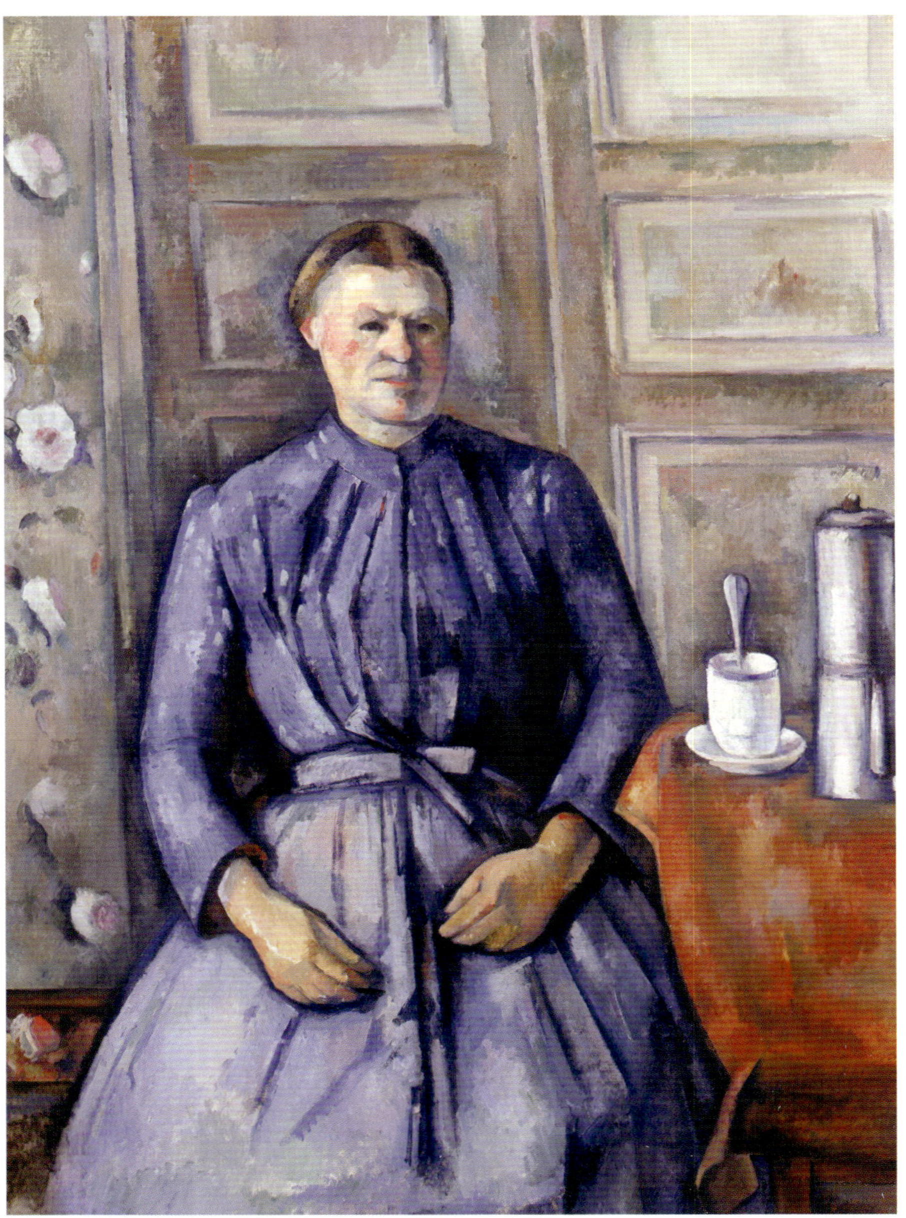

Plate 15 Paul Cézanne, *Woman with a Coffee Pot*, c. 1890–95, oil on canvas, 130.5 × 96.5 cm. (Musée d'Orsay, Paris / Bridgeman Images.)

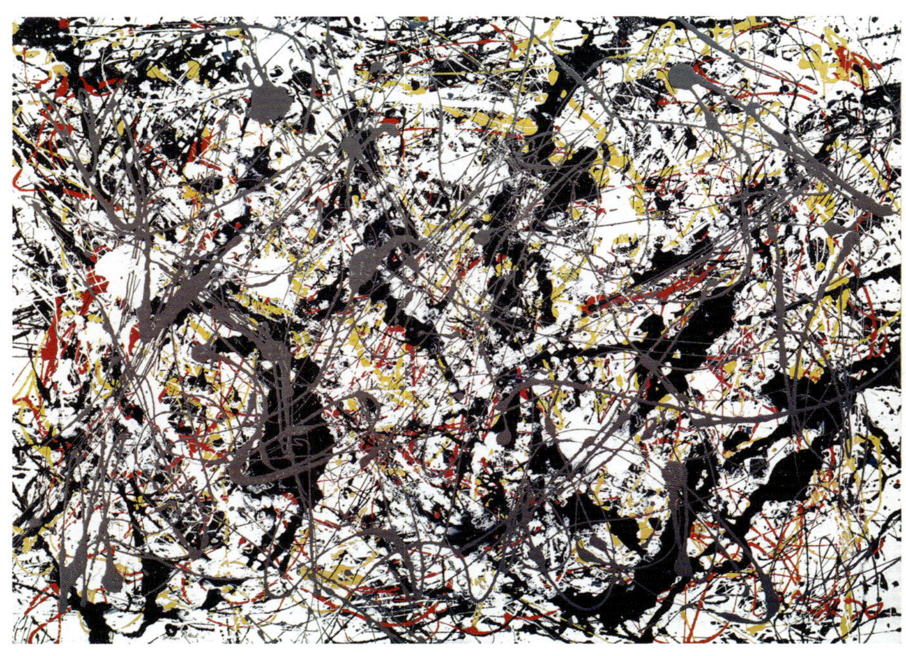

Plate 16 Jackson Pollock, *Silver over Black, White, Yellow and Red*, 1948, oil and enamel on paper laid over canvas, 61 × 80 cm. (Musée National d'Art Moderne, Centre Pompidou, Paris / Bridgeman Images. © DACS.)

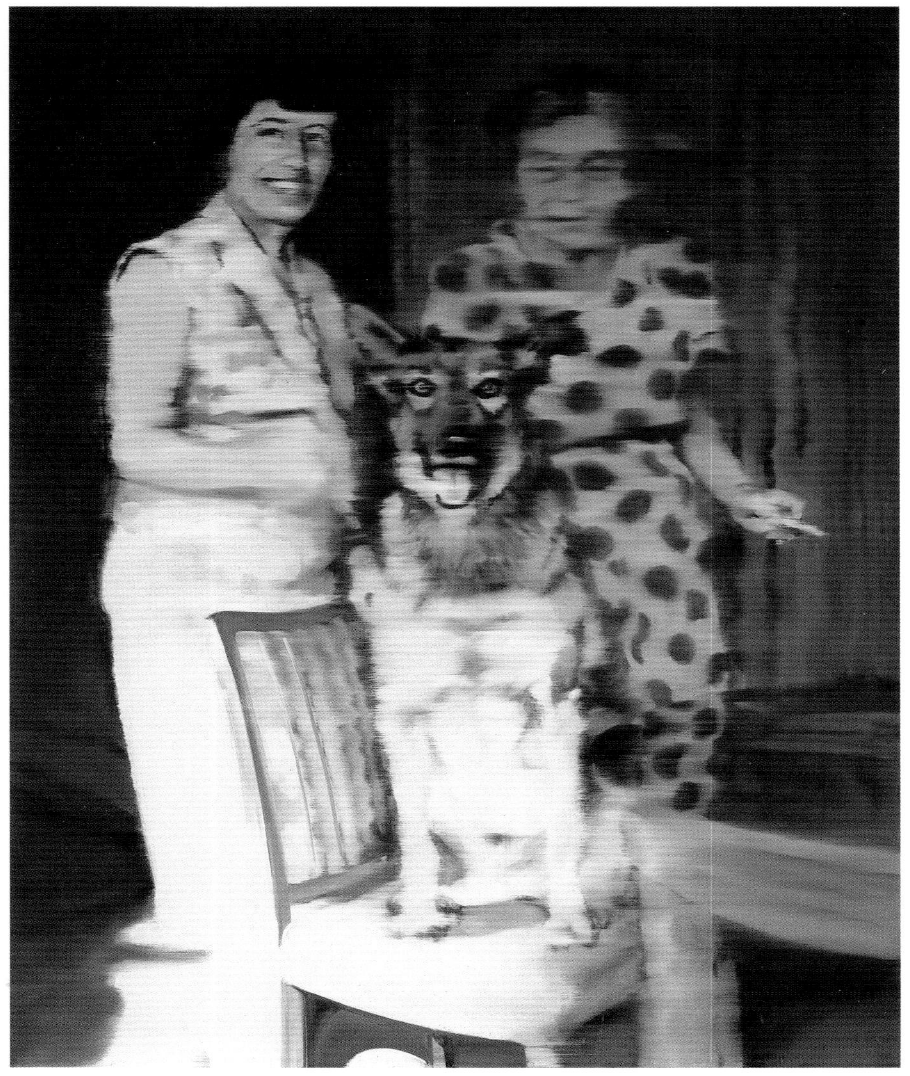

Plate 17 Gerhard Richter, *Christa and Wolfi*, 1964, oil on canvas, 150 × 130 cm. (Joseph Winterbotham Collection, 1987.276, The Art Institute of Chicago. © Joseph Richter.)

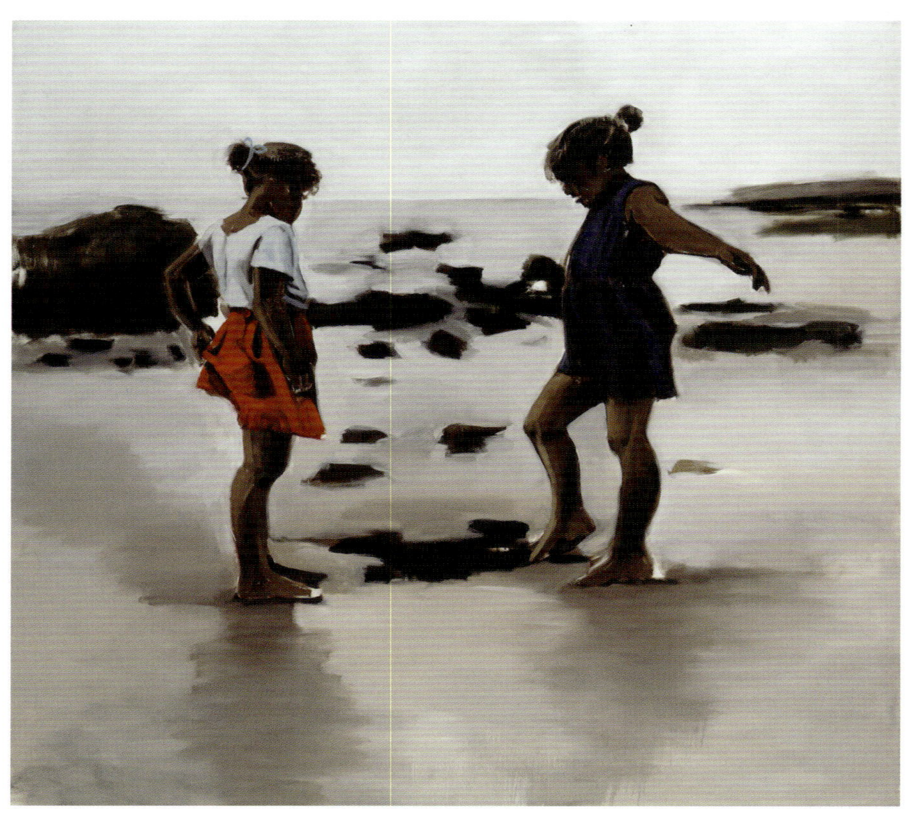

Plate 18 Lynette Yiadom-Boakye, *Condor and the Mole*, 2011, oil on canvas, 230 × 250 cm. (Arts Council Collection. Courtesy of the Artist, Corvi-Mora, London, and Jack Shainman, New York. Photography: Marcus Leith.)

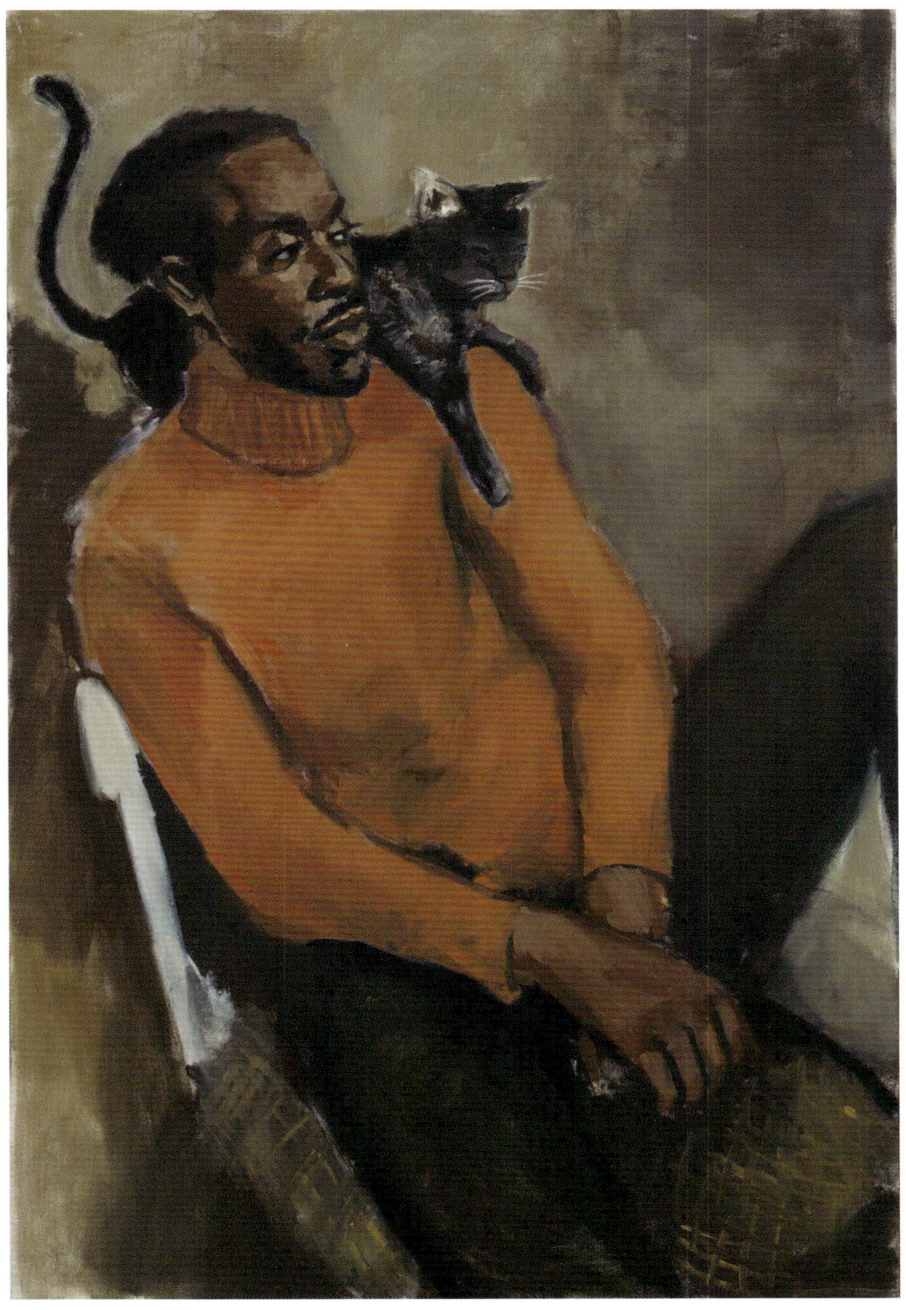

Plate 19 Lynette Yiadom-Boakye, *In Lieu of Keen Virtue*, 2017, oil on canvas, 200 × 130 cm. (Private Collection. Courtesy of the Artist, Corvi-Mora, London, and Jack Shainman, New York. Photography: Marcus Leith.)

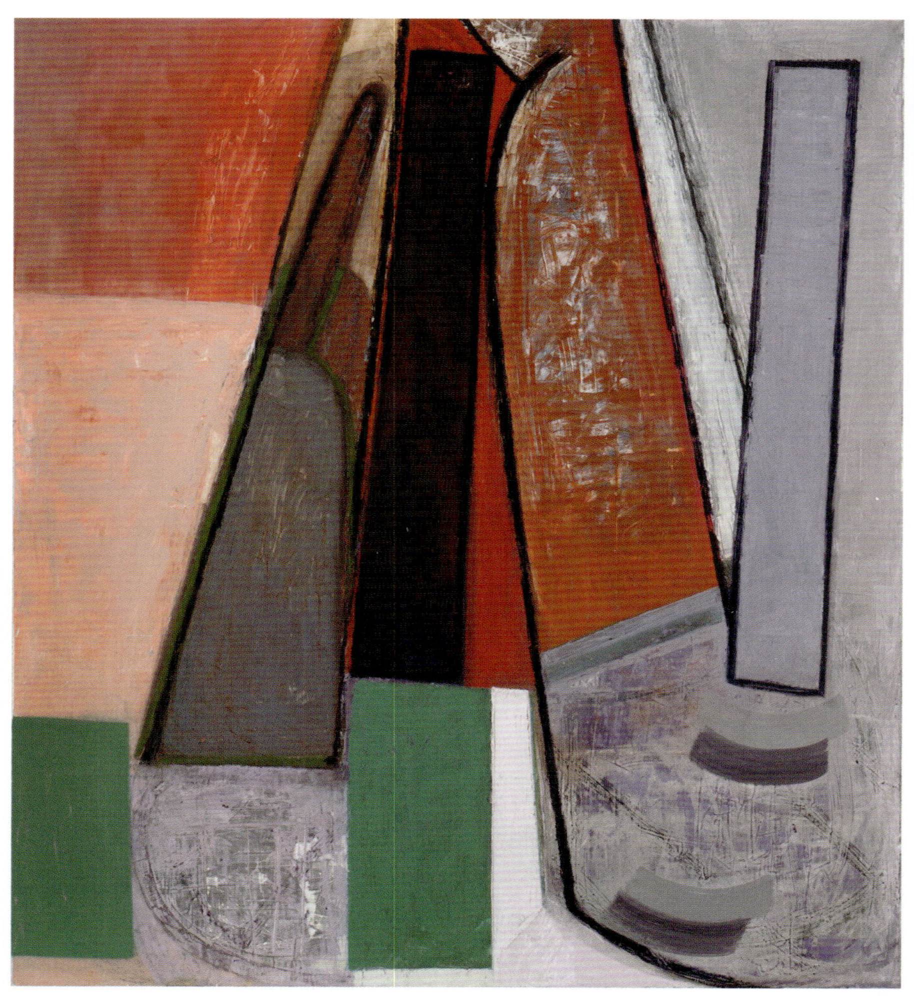

Plate 20 Amy Sillman, *Finger x 2*, 2015, oil on canvas, 190.5 × 167.6 cm. (Collection of the Metropolitan Museum of Art. Courtesy of the Artist.)

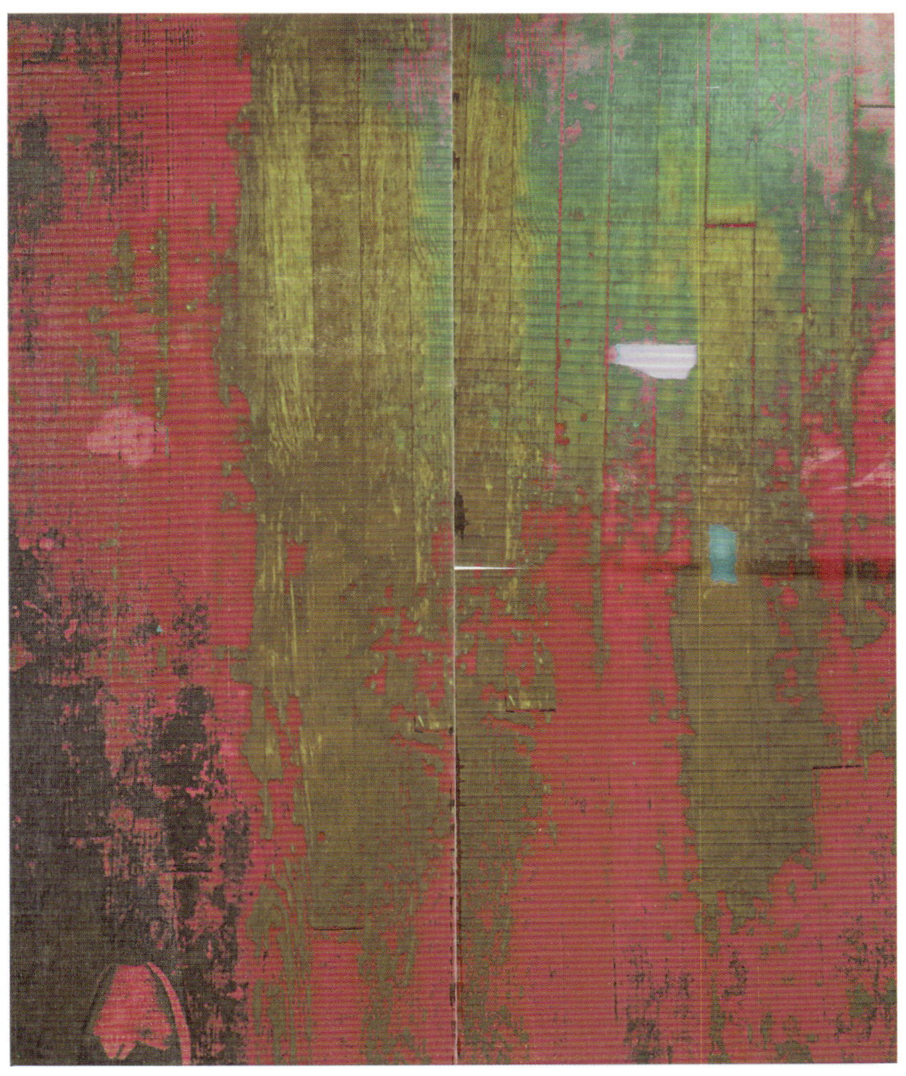

Plate 21 Wade Guyton, *Untitled*, 2016, Epson UltraChrome HDR inkjet on linen, 213.4 × 175.3 cm. WG3982. (Udo and Anette Brandhorst Collection, Munich. © Wade Guyton. Courtesy of the Artist.)

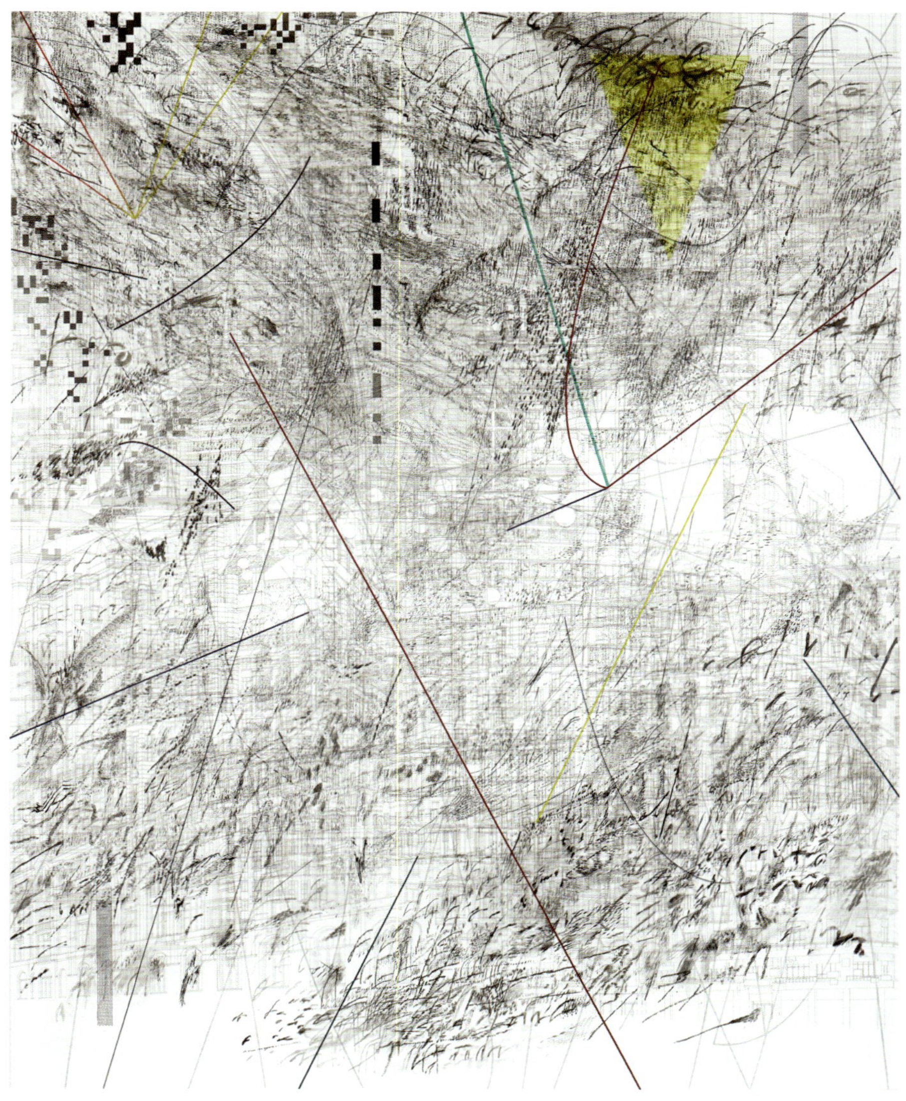

Plate 22 Julie Mehretu, *Mogamma, A Painting in Four Parts: Part 3*, 2012, ink and acrylic paint on canvas, 457.2 × 365.8 cm. (Tate Modern, London. © Julie Mehretu. Courtesy of the artist and Marian Goodman Gallery).

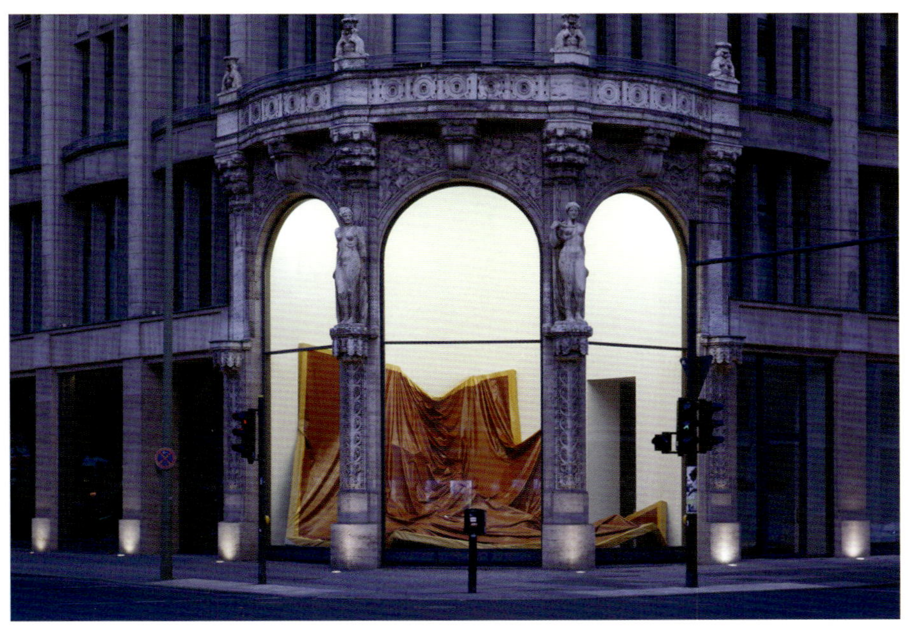

Plate 23 Angela de la Cruz, *Larger Than Life (Knackered)*, 2004, oil and acrylic on canvas, 260 × 400 × 1050 cm. Installation view, Corner Space of Galerie Thomas Schulte, Berlin, 2015. (Photo by Sergio Belínchon. Courtesy the artist and Galerie Thomas Schulte).

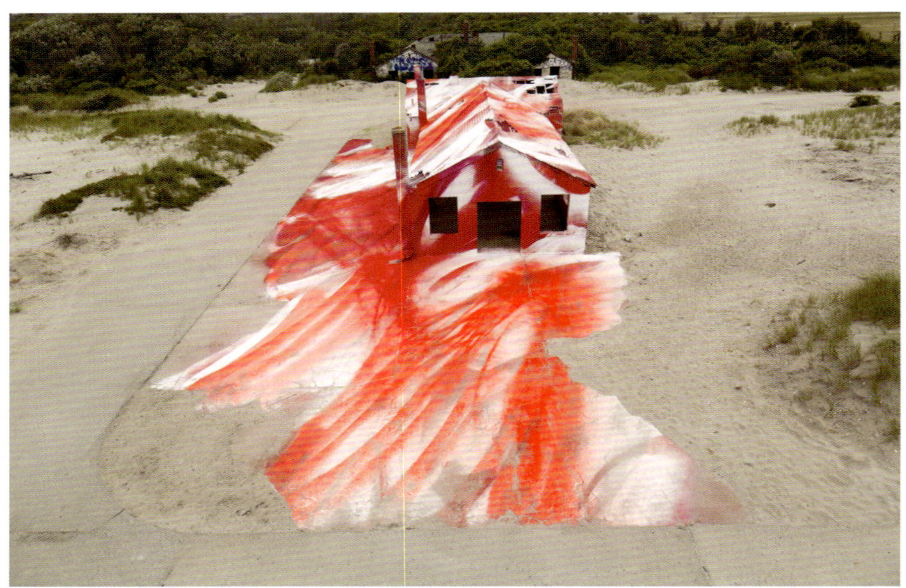

Plate 24 Katharina Grosse, *Rockaway*, 2016, MoMA PS1's *Rockaway!* series, New York, USA, acrylic on wall, ground and various objects, 600 × 1,500 × 3,500 cm. (Photo: Pablo Enriquez; Courtesy of MoMA PS1. © 2022 Katharina Grosse and VG Bild-Kunst, Bonn.)

6

Modernism and the Avant-Garde

The Limits of Formalism

Philosophy of art normally takes place at a safe distance from the artistic fray, occupying an elevated standpoint from which it can oversee rival positions without risk of being drawn into the conflict. However, the emergence of a full-blown formalist theory of painting is closely tied to developments in avant-garde art practice in the late nineteenth and early twentieth centuries.[1] The articulation of formalism as a theoretical doctrine by Roger Fry and Clive Bell was part of a campaign to persuade an insular and sceptical British public of the significance of recent French art, spearheaded by the organization of two large-scale exhibitions of modernist painting and sculpture at the Grafton Galleries in London in November 1910 and December 1912. The first exhibition, entitled 'Manet and the Post-Impressionists', featured among others the work of Cézanne, Van Gogh and Gauguin. The author of the catalogue introduction claimed that these artists had rejected the residual naturalism that still characterizes Impressionism in favour of a new emphasis on pictorial structure and design; rather than adopting a 'passive attitude towards the appearance of things', the Post-Impressionists were 'exploring and expressing the emotional significance which lies in things'.[2] In the catalogue to the second exhibition, which gave greater prominence to the work of Matisse and Picasso, Fry explained that the modern movement 'implied a reconsideration of the very purpose and aim as well as the methods of pictorial and plastic art … these artists do not seek to give what can, after all, be but a pale reflex of actual appearance, but to arouse the conviction of a new and definite reality'.[3] Although their writings of this period are roughly contemporaneous with the first experiments in fully abstract art being carried out in Continental Europe, it is important to note that Fry and Bell developed their ideas primarily in relation to representational painting and sculpture. Through their defence of formalism, they sought not merely to legitimize the critical priorities of the artists whose work they admired, but also to provide a universally relevant theory of art. Both Fry's theoretical essays and Bell's book *Art*, published in 1914, are thus at once polemical interventions on behalf of artistic modernism and a contribution to philosophical aesthetics.

The second Post-Impressionist exhibition was better received than the first, and although Fry and Bell did not win full acceptance for the art they promoted they did succeed in stimulating extensive debate about the ideas on which they believed it was based.[4] Bell, in particular, possessed a gift for rousing formulations, whose effectiveness as a slogan was often bought at the expense of reductivism or over-simplification. Views that had been expressed in a more tentative and exploratory form by artists and critics on the Continent were hardened into a doctrine that could easily be grasped. Bell begins *Art* by declaring that the central task of aesthetics is to identify the 'essential' feature that distinguishes artworks from other objects and artefacts, for 'either all works of visual art have some common quality, or when we speak of "works of art" we gibber'.[5] He then goes on to formulate his 'aesthetic hypothesis':

> What quality is common to Sta. Sophia and the windows at Chartres, Mexican sculpture, a Persian bowl, Chinese carpets, Giotto's frescos at Padua, and the masterpieces of Poussin, Piero della Francesca, and Cézanne? Only one answer seems possible – significant form. In each, lines and colours combined in a particular way, certain forms and relations of forms, stir our aesthetic emotions. These relations and combinations of lines and colours, these aesthetically moving forms, I call 'Significant Form'; and 'Significant Form' is the one quality common to all works of visual art.[6]

The principal constituents of Bell's theory of art are to be found compressed within this short passage. The identifying feature of works of visual art is their capacity to arouse in the viewer a unique type of response, which he terms 'aesthetic emotion'. Aesthetic emotion is distinct both from the emotions we feel in our everyday lives and from any feelings that might be awakened by an artwork's depicted content or subject matter; it is prompted exclusively by formal properties, by those non-representational relations of line, shape and colour that he designates as significant form. Bell's argument is notoriously circular: he characterizes art in terms of its power to awaken aesthetic emotion, aesthetic emotion as a response to significant form, and significant form as the property of art that arouses aesthetic emotion. Having thus closed the circuit, he rules out of consideration the 'representative element', which he dismisses as irrelevant to genuine aesthetic appreciation. To use line and colour 'to recount anecdotes, suggest ideas, and indicate the customs and manners of an age' is to meet a demand for illustration that had been rendered otiose by the 'perfection of photographic processes and of the cinematograph'.[7] A painting may be admired for the information it conveys, its psychological associations or its skilful technique, but this is not to value it as art. By contrast, aesthetic emotion allows the viewer to enter 'a world with an intense and peculiar significance of its own ... unrelated to the significance of life'.[8]

Fry's position is more equivocal; in particular, he seems to have been unwilling to accept Bell's claim that representational content is entirely irrelevant to the value we place on art.[9] In the 'Retrospect' added to his first collection of essays, *Vision and Design*, published in 1920, he envisages a spectator who, when looking at Raphael's *Transfiguration* (1516–20, Pinacoteca Vaticana, Vatican City), is 'so absorbed in purely formal relations as to be indifferent even to [the] aspect of the design as representation'.[10] Fry concedes that the ability to concentrate exclusively on the formal properties of a work of art is not only 'extremely rare' but also unduly restrictive insofar as it renders the viewer 'entirely blind to all the overtones and associations of a picture like the *Transfiguration*'.[11] Most viewers – including Fry himself, as he admits – respond not only to the 'formal design' of an artwork but also to its 'dramatic idea'. Nonetheless, he maintains that the fusion of these two 'sets of emotion', whereby each reinforces and heightens the other, is merely apparent: closer analysis of the viewer's mental state reveals that it is possible 'to isolate the elusive element of the pure aesthetic reaction from the compounds in which it occurs'.[12] Once we recognize that it is possible 'to be moved by the pure contemplation of the spatial relations of plastic volumes', we can distinguish between the various ancillary emotions that are aroused by the work's subject matter and a properly aesthetic response to its formal properties.[13]

In January and February 1910, the same year as the first Post-Impressionist Exhibition, Fry translated for the *Burlington Magazine* an article on Cézanne by the French painter and theorist Maurice Denis.[14] In his 'Introductory Note', he described the 'new conception of art' as one in which 'the decorative elements preponderate at the expense of the representative', observing that the 'great and original genius ... who really started this movement, the most fruitful and promising of modern times, was Cézanne'.[15] This assessment was echoed by Bell, who declared emphatically that 'Cézanne is the full-stop between Impressionism and the contemporary movement'.[16] Although in some measure based on a misunderstanding of Cézanne's ideas about art and his working practice – which remained indebted to the Impressionist project of capturing the artist's sensations before nature through the application of individual touches of colour – Fry came to believe that his paintings were held together by 'a kind of abstract system of plastic rhythms'.[17] The privileged position accorded to Cézanne in the evolution of modernism was based on the claim that he had established the priority of the 'plastic' and 'decorative' dimension of art over the need for mimetic accuracy. The apparent distortions and simplifications, and the unfinished or sketch-like quality of some of his work, were interpreted as sacrifices made in pursuit of greater pictorial unity and expressive power.

Writing in 1917, Fry summarized the 'revolution' that Cézanne had inaugurated as 'the re-establishment of purely aesthetic criteria in place of conformity to appearance – the rediscovery of the principles of structural design and harmony'.[18] Without going so far as Bell, who describes the period from Giotto to Leonardo as 'a long, and, at times, almost imperceptible fall', Fry contends that the pursuit of verisimilitude and technical virtuosity for its own sake, which reached its apogee in the Renaissance, had led to a neglect of the 'ideas of formal design ... in the fervid pursuit of naturalistic representation'.[19] For both thinkers, rejection of the Vasarian narrative of the progressive conquest of appearances permitted a re-evaluation not only of pre-Renaissance Italian art, including the work of so-called 'primitives' such as Cimabue and Duccio, but also the art of Byzantium and other non-Western cultures. Within this interpretative framework, Post-Impressionism could be understood as a return to purely pictorial values that had been neglected or occluded by the drive towards naturalism. In Bell's memorable phrase, the Post-Impressionists 'shake hands across the ages ... with every vital movement that has struggled into existence since the arts began'.[20] While artists at different times have been more or less sensitive to the dimension of form, resulting in a series of peaks and troughs in the history of art, the true source of aesthetic value remains constant. A painting by Cézanne moves us in the *same way* as a Persian bowl or a Chinese carpet, for it is the presence of significant form that is the source of our properly aesthetic responses.

There are a number of features that link the position defended by Fry and Bell with the views of Heinrich Wölfflin, discussed in the previous chapter.[21] Wölfflin can also be characterized as a formalist insofar as his account of the specifically visual root of style rests on a close analysis of differences in the internal structure and ordering of artworks rather than the study of external factors such as workshop practices, the development of new techniques and materials, or an investigation into the wider social, economic and political contexts in which art is made and appreciated. Similarly, the emphasis that he places on the 'decorative' dimension of the visual arts might be thought to parallel the formalist claim that line, shape and colour are to be valued primarily for their aesthetic qualities. However, it is important to distinguish Wölfflin's contention that there are general principles governing the formal organization of artworks that can be analysed independently of what is represented from the claim that form itself has independent value.[22] Although Wölffin – like Fry and Bell – decisively rejects the naturalist presuppositions underpinning Vasari's account of artistic progress, this does not lead him to separate the decorative from the imitative. Instead, as we have seen, he seeks to show that there can be a variety of different solutions to one and the same problem and that there is no overarching normative standard against which the development of art can be measured.[23] By contrast, Fry and Bell defend a strongly normative position: not only are artworks to be valued primarily for their formal properties, but greater value is to be placed on those artworks that prioritize form over content.[24]

The formalist thesis that artistic value derives exclusively from the internal relations between the formal elements of a painting, and that what is depicted therefore has little or no role to play in aesthetic appreciation, can be challenged in several ways. First, as Fry recognizes, in practice it is extremely difficult to bracket out the various ideas and associations that are prompted by a painting's subject matter. How are we to know, in any instance, whether and to what extent we are responding to an artwork's form rather than to some other feature of the painting? The concept of significant form remains highly elusive, and it is difficult to see how it can be isolated in the way Fry and Bell propose. Second, the thesis is at odds with much of what we know about the history of art, making it hard to understand why artists and viewers have devoted so much time and attention to representational content rather than focusing exclusively on abstract spatial and coloured relations.[25] Finally, and most tellingly, the thesis fails to acknowledge that in the vast majority of cases appreciation of the formal properties of an artwork is closely integrated with recognition of its representational content. Consider, for example, Tintoretto's *Presentation of the Virgin* (Plate 14). When looking at the large female figure in the foreground, we do not see an abstract form *and* a figure with an extended arm, as if these were two discrete entities; the visual dynamism of the painting, which Wölfflin describes as 'bursting with spatial energy', derives in part from the torsion of the woman's body and the invited movement of our eye into spatial depth as we follow the direction of her outstretched right hand.[26]

A more difficult case is presented by Cézanne's *Woman with a Coffee Pot* (Plate 15), whose resolutely planimetric composition, built on a scaffolding of horizontal and vertical lines, seems designed to accentuate the formal correspondences between the upright cylindrical shape of the percolator and the cup, and the simplified form of the human figure. Taken out of context, Cézanne's advice to the painter Émile Bernard to 'treat nature by means of the cylinder, the sphere, the cone' appears to support a strongly formalist reading of this painting, in which volumetric forms are set against a shallow, patterned ground.[27] Nonetheless, to view the painting exclusively as a study in significant form is to overlook its effectiveness as a portrait and thus to lose sight of

Cézanne's sustaining interest in the contrast between the physical presence of the sitter and the inanimate objects that surround her. Appreciation of the painting's formal or plastic qualities and recognition of its representational content are not independent activities that can be isolated and combined at will. Indeed, Cézanne seems to have been fascinated by the interplay of depictive and configurational aspects in his paintings and drawings, and many of his own statements about his work testify to an ongoing struggle to reconcile what he saw as two competing demands.[28]

Most philosophers agree that formalism fails as a theory of art. Budd states the consensus position when he observes that this 'counter-intuitive' doctrine 'not only lacks any plausible supporting arguments ... it is flawed both internally and externally'.[29] One last ditch strategy, pursued by Nick Zangwill, has been to undertake a 'tactical retreat' in order to 'find and secure the truth in formalism'.[30] What he terms 'moderate formalism' is the view that 'while *some* aesthetic properties of works of art are formal, others are not', and that although most works of art have non-formal aesthetic properties 'there are *some* works of art that *only* have formal properties', such as instrumental music and, in the field of visual art, fully abstract painting and sculpture.[31] Zangwill's approach is neatly captured in his reworking of Bell's declaration that 'to appreciate a work of art we need bring with us nothing but a sense of form and colour and a knowledge of three-dimensional space'.[32] He maintains that all we need to do is delete the 'nothing but' to produce a claim that is 'almost always true'.[33] Although unimpeachable, this emendation drains formalism of its philosophical interest for it reduces to the platitude that we appreciate art for its formal properties as well as for its content or subject matter. In the absence of any account of the *relation* between these two elements – such as Wollheim, Wölfflin and others have sought to provide – the theory is troublingly uninformative. Zangwill's suggestion that an exception needs to be made for the specific case of abstract art is more persuasive, but, once again, without an account of the reasons for the emergence of fully abstract painting or an explanation as to why it should be accorded special value, the theory tells us nothing more than that abstract art pleases, if it does, through its formal properties.

If we are to take formalism seriously, we need to recognize that it stands or falls as a theory that can encompass both representational and abstract works of art, for its claim on our attention rests on the assertion that art's value as depiction and its value as design are in conflict. What I shall term 'strong formalism' not only introduces an unwarranted bifurcation of pictorial value into illustration and design, it holds that these two values are antithetical: whereas the first belongs to the domain of everyday needs and experiences, the second lifts us into a higher imaginative realm that is detached from 'actual life and its practical utilities'.[34] Bell expresses this idea with characteristic force when he claims: 'Every sacrifice made to representation is something stolen from art'.[35] Fry early on entertained the possibility that, taken to its logical extreme, the 'method' that he discerned in the work of the Post-Impressionists would result in 'the attempt to give up all resemblance to natural form, and to create a purely abstract language of form – a visual music', but he insisted that the success of this project could be decided only on the basis of experience.[36] The arguments that he and Bell put forward were intended to provide a basis for identifying the source of genuinely aesthetic emotion in works of representational art as well as abstract works of craft and design, and the philosophical interest of their position is lost if it is deprived of this overarching ambition.

Bell later came to believe that although *Art* had helped to challenge the misconceptions and prejudices surrounding the work of Cézanne and other Post-Impressionist artists, the book introduced errors and exaggerations of its own. In the preface to the 1949 edition, he describes it as little more than a historical document, claiming that 'if *Art* has any value for future generations it will be as a record of what people like myself were thinking and feeling in the years before the first War'.[37] It is tempting to concur with this conclusion and to dismiss formalism as an historical phenomenon that is of limited relevance to philosophy. I would like to suggest, however, that the main problem with the theory of art put forward by Fry and Bell is that it is *insufficiently* historical. In their desire to establish the continuity of Post-Impressionism with the art of other times and places they overlook the fact that it possesses certain distinctive characteristics that make it unlike earlier forms of art practice. Similarly, they fail to acknowledge that a commitment to at least some of the tenets of formalism played an important role in the self-understanding of the artists whose work they promoted. The claim that there is an irresolvable conflict between the formal or decorative unity of a work of art and the requirement of verisimilitude is unpersuasive as a global thesis. However, once correctly interpreted as a historically specific response to the pressures under which avant-garde artists found themselves working in the late nineteenth and early twentieth centuries it acquires considerable explanatory potential.

For this reason, I now want to examine the more sophisticated version of formalism put forward by the American art critic and theorist Clement Greenberg. I aim to show that Greenberg's theory of modernism as a self-critical process makes good the historical deficit that vitiates the formalism of Fry and Bell and that his writings offer an alternative framework for understanding the significance of non-objective or fully abstract art. Greenberg's ideas are rarely discussed by philosophers, who either neglect his work entirely or present a simplified and distorted summary of his views.[38] This problem is compounded by a tendency to focus exclusively on 'Modernist Painting', which remains the most widely read and anthologized of his writings. By the time he wrote this essay, which was originally given as a radio broadcast in 1960, his identification of a retrospective logic of development had become increasingly doctrinaire and inflexible, serving as means of criticizing or excluding tendencies that did not fit with his account. The progressive breakdown of modernism in the 1960s, and the accompanying reaction against the dominance of Greenberg's views, has tended to obscure the originality of his early writings. I therefore begin by discussing what I see as the strengths of his position, drawing on his essays from the late 1930s onwards as a means of recovering the key insights underpinning his account of the development of modern art. I argue that Greenberg's historicized variant of formalism makes two important advances over the better-known version of formalism defended by Fry and Bell and that it therefore deserves independent consideration despite the well-founded objections to which it is exposed.

Greenberg's Theory of Modernism

In his first major essay, 'Avant-Garde and Kitsch', published in 1939, Greenberg set himself the task of explaining how it is that 'a part of Western bourgeois culture has produced something unheard of heretofore: – avant-garde culture'.[39] The concept of an artistic avant-garde, which attempts 'to wrest tradition away from a conformism that is about to overpower it', can be traced back to the early nineteenth century.[40] The term was coined in the 1820s by the French socialist Saint-Simon, who used it to characterize art's place in the vanguard of social change.[41] The positioning of advanced art practice in opposition to mainstream culture was consolidated in the mid-nineteenth century by Realist artists such as Gustave Courbet, who combined technical radicalism with explicit social critique. Even when artists turned away from the task of directly picturing the conditions of modern social existence – such as, for example, in the Symbolist movement that flourished in *fin-de-siècle* Europe – formal experimentation continued to retain its transgressive and subversive associations. Despite the absence of socially significant subject matter, Cubism, Expressionism and, of course, Abstraction were all seen as 'radical' movements that challenged the prevailing orthodoxy by asserting the independence of art from external constraints. Claims for the autonomy of art sat uneasily with claims for its efficacy as an agent of social change, however, resulting in periodic attempts to restore the connection between art and life, either through a return to more overt forms of picturing or by exploring alternative modes of engagement, such as those pioneered by Dada and Constructivism.

Greenberg's innovative response to this problem was to argue that the advent of the avant-garde was made possible by a 'superior consciousness of history – more precisely, the appearance of a new kind of criticism of society, an historical criticism'.[42] 'Avant-Garde and Kitsch' is ostensibly concerned with the distinction between high and low culture, but the essay's explanatory power derives from a second, more far-reaching distinction between the dynamism of the avant-garde and the decline of Renaissance naturalism in the late eighteenth and nineteenth centuries into 'a motionless Alexandrianism' in which 'the really important issues are left untouched because they involve controversy . . . all larger questions being decided by the precedent of the old masters'.[43] The result is academicism: 'the same themes are mechanically varied in a hundred different works, and yet nothing new is produced.'[44] With this diagnosis in place, Greenberg is able to advance his claim that 'the true and most important function of the avant-garde was not to "experiment" but to find a path along which it would be possible to keep culture *moving*'.[45] Since this could not be achieved through traditional methods of picturing, avant-garde artists turned their attention away from 'the subject matter of common experience' towards the 'disciplines and processes' of art itself:

> Picasso, Braque, Mondrian, Miró, Kandinsky, Brancusi, even Klee, Matisse and Cézanne derive their chief inspiration from the medium they work in. The excitement of their art seems to lie most of all in its pure preoccupation with the invention and arrangement of spaces, surfaces, shapes, colours, etc., to the exclusion of whatever is not necessarily implicated in these factors.[46]

Although the emphasis on the resources of the medium is, perhaps, distinctive to Greenberg, his account of the formalist commitments that shaped the work of the artistic avant-garde in the late nineteenth and early twentieth centuries is remarkably similar to that put forward by Fry and Bell. The key difference, at this stage, lies in his attempt to provide a historical justification for the phenomena he describes.

The ideas that Greenberg sketched out in 'Avant-Garde and Kitsch' were developed in greater detail the following year in an essay entitled 'Towards a Newer Laocoon'. Here, for the first time, he explicitly seeks to explain the 'present superiority' of abstract art.[47] This qualification is important, for he insists that if at the time of writing it is abstract rather than figurative art that meets the most advanced standards of taste, this is a result of its position in a particular tradition of art. The title of the essay refers to a book by the German philosopher, Gotthold Lessing, entitled *Laocoön: An Essay on the Limits of Painting and Poetry*, first published in 1766.[48] Drawing on Lessing's analysis of the problems that arise when one art form takes on characteristic effects that are proper to another, Greenberg claims that the rise of literature to the status of a dominant art in the post-Renaissance period resulted in a progressive 'confusion of the arts'.[49] He argues that in the course of the eighteenth and nineteenth centuries painting began to assume the narrative and anecdotal functions of literature, prioritizing subject matter at the expense of the medium, which was treated as 'a regrettable if necessary physical obstacle between the artist and his audience'.[50] Without hesitating to identify the artists he has in mind – Vernet, Gérome, Leighton, Watts, Moreau, Böcklin, the Pre-Raphaelites – Greenberg observes that 'it was not realistic imitation in itself that did the damage so much as realistic illusion in the service of sentimental and declamatory literature':

> Everything depends on the anecdote or message. The painted picture occurs in blank, indeterminate space; it just happens to be on a square of canvas and inside a frame. It might just as well have been breathed on air or formed out of plasma … Everything contributes to the denial of the medium, as if the artist were ashamed to admit that he had actually painted his picture instead of dreaming it forth.[51]

It is precisely to counter this tendency that avant-garde artists sought to draw attention to the limiting conditions of the medium in which they worked. The modernist preoccupation with formal problems is not a matter of art for art's sake – an apolitical withdrawal into aestheticism – but a 'salutary reaction' against the confusion of the arts, and thus an attempt to preserve painting by establishing its proper field of activity.[52] Similar developments are also to be found in the other arts, but the consequences for painting, according to Greenberg, have been particularly complex and rewarding.

We are now able to draw together the main strands of Greenberg's argument and to see how this relates to the better-known presentation of his views in 'Modernist Painting'. Each art is engaged in a struggle to establish its 'unique and proper area of competence', a struggle that takes place almost entirely through the progressive clarification of the resources and restrictions inherent in the medium.[53] The guarantee of art's 'standards of quality as well as of its independence' is to be found in the process of self-criticism through which each art determines the type of experience that it alone is able to afford.[54] This process involves, first, the identification and exhibition of the indispensable properties and limits that are specific to each particular art, and second, the expulsion of all effects that are borrowed from other art forms. In the case of painting, the limits include the physical properties of the pigment, the shape of the support and the 'ineluctable flatness of the surface'.[55] Whereas the old masters had treated these limitations as 'negative factors that could be acknowledged only implicitly or negatively', under modernism they 'came to be regarded as positive factors, and were acknowledged openly'.[56]

It is not possible here to discuss the full ramifications of Greenberg's account, which is likely to persuade, if at all, only at an appropriate level of detail. Instead, I want to focus on his treatment of two topics that we have already touched upon: the significance of Cézanne's innovative method of painting and the invention of Cubism by Braque and Picasso. This will help us to identify some of the strengths of Greenberg's approach as well as its potential shortcomings. In his essay 'Cézanne and the Unity of Modern Art', published in 1951, Greenberg acknowledges Cézanne's debt to Impressionism and his avowed commitment to accurately recording his 'sensations' before nature. However, he claims that the unintended result of Cézanne's attempt to establish 'a different, more emphatic, and supposedly more "permanent" kind of unity' was to draw attention to the picture plane as an independent factor.[57] His willingness to 'adjust the representation in depth to the two dimensional surface pattern', while at the same time seeking to indicate solidity and three-dimensional space through parallel and roughly rectangular brushstrokes, created 'a new and powerful kind of pictorial tension' characterized by a 'never ending vibration from front to back and back to front'.[58] Greenberg does not deny that Renaissance artists also paid careful attention to the picture surface, including properties of facture, handling and design, but he claims that they sought to avoid the sort of push-and-pull effects that result from Cézanne's emphasis on the surface pattern of the painting as an entity with its own 'equally valid aesthetic rights'.[59] In seeking to convey the potential richness and complexity of these effects, Greenberg offers a virtuoso description of Cézanne's mature technique:

> As [he] digs deeper behind his shapes with ultramarine ... he makes them oscillate, and the back and forward movement within the picture spreads and at the same time becomes more majestic in its rhythm because more unified and all-enveloping ... The image exists in an atmosphere made intenser because more pictorial, the result of a heightened tension between the illusion and the independent abstractness of the formal facts.[60]

In accordance with his claim in 'Towards a Newer Laocoon' that the 'history of avant-garde painting is that of a progressive surrender to the resistance of the medium' and that this 'consists chiefly in the flat picture's denial of efforts to "hole through" it for realistic pictorial space', Greenberg interprets Cubism as a continuation of the tendency that he identifies in Cézanne.[61] During the first, analytic period of Cubism – to which works such as Braque's *The Portuguese* (Plate 9) belong – the 'fictive depths of the painting were drained, and its action was brought forward and identified with the immediate, physical surface of the canvas'.[62] The use of pasted papers in the second, synthetic period provided a yet more radical means of focusing attention on the surface of the picture; the resolutely frontal layering of flat pieces of paper onto card or board – as in Picasso's *Violin* of 1912 (Plate 11) – emphasizes 'the identity of the picture as a flat and more or less abstract pattern rather than as a representation'.[63] Greenberg argues that the breakthrough of the collage technique lies not in the emphasis on surface pattern for its own sake – something that would be indistinguishable from a merely decorative design – but in the dynamic tension that is set up between the picture surface and the representation of depth. The resulting instability allows the different components of the picture both to recede and to come forward:

> The strips, the lettering, the charcoaled lines and the white paper begin to change places in depth with one another, and a process is set up in which every part of the picture takes its turn at occupying every plane, whether real or imagined, in it …The flatness of the surface permeates the illusion, and the illusion re-asserts itself in the flatness. The effect is to fuse the illusion with the picture plane without derogation of either – in principle.[64]

This new and powerful fusion of the literal, physical surface of the picture with its depicted content simultaneously mobilizes and undermines what for Greenberg remains the one indispensable condition of pictorial representation – the establishment of a figure–ground relationship, the presence of a mark or other pictorial element whose virtual relation to the surface is different to its physical one.

No matter how brilliant Greenberg's analysis of Cubism might be in its own terms, it is too narrowly conceived to do justice to the full range and complexity of the exploration of pictorial meaning undertaken by Braque and Picasso. In reducing Cubism to a set of formal concerns that devolve exclusively on the relation between the picture surface and the representation of depth, Greenberg overlooks their fascination with the problem of reference. His approach can thus be contrasted with the various semiotic interpretations, discussed in Chapter 4, which investigate the differences between pictorial and linguistic signs, as well as with more recent social-historical accounts that emphasize the Cubists' close engagement with popular and commercial culture, including the fragments of newspaper, posters, sheet music and other printed matter that are incorporated into their work. As we shall see, Greenberg's theory of modernism is exposed to the charge of reductivism on more than one front, for it also depends on an exclusionary and highly selective focus on certain artists and movements rather than on others. Before discussing this issue, I want to bring out a second important difference between his views and the position defended by Fry and Bell. Whereas Fry and Bell leave the notion of significant form undefined, tending to construe formalism privatively in terms of the need to abstract from a painting's representational content, Greenberg succeeds in presenting a *positive* characterization of the visual interest that is provided by the non-referential or strictly formal elements of pictorial art.

The difference between the two positions can best be explained by drawing on an argument put forward by Malcolm Budd in *Values of Art*. Budd claims that it is necessary to disambiguate the idea of representational content as this figures in the core formalist thesis that a picture's representational content is irrelevant to artistic value. He points out that it would be 'absurd' to understand this thesis as implying that the value of a picture is determined by the two-dimensional design of the picture surface, considered independently of whatever it represents, for this would be tantamount to the demand that 'pictures should be seen as if they were not pictures, as if they were non-representational structures'.[65] The concept of significant form should therefore be understood as referring not to the two-dimensional surface of the picture but to what he terms its 'analogue content'. Irrespective of whether a painting depicts a woman, a coffee jug, a landscape, or any other recognizable scene or objects, it can also be viewed as a representation of abstract volumes that are spatially related to one another. To attend to a painting's significant form is thus to disregard, as far as possible, its subject matter and to consider it 'only from the point of view of its "analogue content", that is to say, its being a spatial composition of the elements of colour (hue, brightness, saturation), shape, size and depth'.[66] The idea of analogue content thus provides a means of understanding how, on the formalist view, a picture's aesthetic value derives neither from the two-dimensional array of coloured marks on its surface nor from its illustrative content or subject matter but from the 'plastic construction' of coloured masses in space.

Although Budd's interpretation allows formalism to be presented as a positive rather than a merely negative thesis, it also brings out its major weakness. He rightly observes that the formalist division of pictorial value into illustration and plastic construction is untenable since it fails to acknowledge the phenomenon of twofoldness. As we saw in Chapter 3, the appreciation of a picture as a picture involves a dual awareness of the marked surface and the depicted content: these two forms of awareness do not merely coexist but interpenetrate and reciprocally transform each other in the viewer's experience. By drawing on Wollheim's account of the phenomenology of pictorial viewing, Budd can show that:

> it is mistaken to think of the artistic function of the picture surface . . . as either decorative or representational (plastic expression or successful illustration); for this neglects the crucial characteristic of pictorial art, namely the *interrelationship* between the marks on the surface and what is depicted in them.[67]

It is clear, however, that this charge cannot be levelled against Greenberg's version of formalism, which makes the working out of the relationship between the overt acknowledgement of the picture surface and the representation of pictorial depth central to the development of modernist painting. Greenberg is, of course, largely indifferent to the subject matter of the works he describes, focusing instead on their internal, formal relations. But whereas strong formalism issues in the claim that the viewer must abstract from a painting's representational content to attend to its plastic form, Greenberg seeks to identify an alternative source of pictorial value. Far from contradicting Wollheim's insight into the distinctive phenomenology of representational seeing, according to which the viewer is simultaneously aware both of the marked surface and of what that surface represents, Greenberg argues that the resulting tension is the source of modernist painting's most powerful and distinctively pictorial effects. The dynamic push and pull between surface and depth that he identifies in the work of Cézanne, and then in the Cubist experiments of Braque and Picasso, is carried through into his account of abstract art. However, this does not rest on a denial that the formal and the figurative interpenetrate in the experience of looking at a picture. Indeed, Greenberg's claim that the representation of pictorial depth is conditional for painting as an art anticipates ideas that Wollheim developed several decades later. Like Wollheim, he distinguishes representation from figuration, arguing that 'the first mark made on a canvas destroys its literal and utter flatness'.[68] The orientation towards flatness characteristic of modernist painting can never be absolute, for without the 'illusion' of spatial relations there would be nothing but a patterned surface.[69] Fully abstract art is therefore not to be understood as a negation of painting but as an attempt to make its limiting conditions both more explicit and more expressive.

Abstraction and the Easel Picture

Greenberg's account of an historically self-conscious avant-garde that seeks to restore the identity of painting by emphasizing the significance of the medium allows him to make a powerful case for abstract art. There are several places in which he suggests that painting may no longer be able to represent the lived reality of modern social existence and that those artists who continue to paint figure studies, still lives and landscapes are condemned to produce work that is merely derivative or lacking in ambition. Thus, for example, in an essay published in 1944 he claims that 'the techniques of art founded on conventions of representation have exhausted their capacity to reveal fresh aspects of exterior reality' and that 'instead of being aroused, the modern imagination is numbed by visual representation'.[70] However, his defence of abstract art is founded, for the most part, in an analysis of the rewards to be gained from a concentration on purely pictorial factors. He acknowledges that abstract art entails a loss of many of the satisfactions that painting has traditionally provided, but he contends that this is a 'necessary impoverishment' and that what has been abandoned in modernist painting is not so much the representation of recognizable objects as the 'representation of the kind of space that recognizable objects can inhabit'.[71] The absence of figurative content is compensated by the 'necessity that painting become … more sensitive, subtle and various, and at the same time more disciplined and objectivized by its physical medium'.[72]

Nowhere is Greenberg's sensitivity to the subtlety and variety of abstract painting more vividly revealed than in his analysis of the work that Jackson Pollock showed in a series of exhibitions in New York, beginning with his first one-man show in 1943 (see Plate 16, *Silver over Black, White, Yellow and Red*, 1948). Greenberg initially found Pollock's style 'Gothic' and 'morbid', worrying that it was marred by 'inconsistencies, ugliness, blind spots and monotonous passages', but he also claimed that Pollock was 'the most powerful painter in contemporary America' – a judgment for which he was ridiculed at the time.[73] As we might expect, Greenberg contends: 'Pollock's strength lies in the emphatic surfaces of his pictures, which it is his concern to maintain and intensify'.[74] However, the key to his interpretation lies in the claim that Pollock succeeded in imposing a formal order and discipline that derived from Cubism onto paintings that were much larger in scale and ambition that anything that had been attempted previously. Rather than compressing and tightening the space of the picture, Pollock allowed it to expand so that there were multiple centres of interest and intensity. He was thereby able to 'create a genuinely violent and extravagant art without losing stylistic control'.[75] Greenberg's insistence on the conscious and deliberate character of Pollock's method of painting distinguishes his interpretation from other, rival accounts that emphasized the spontaneity of the artist's celebrated drip technique. These include not only 'expressivist' interpretations that latched onto Pollock's unguarded claim in 1947 that 'the source of my painting is the unconscious', but also the position defended by the critic Harold Rosenberg, who maintained that abstract expressionism needs to be understood through the existential drama of the creative process rather than formal properties of the finished painting, which was nothing more than an 'arena in which to act'.[76]

Central to Greenberg's historical justification of abstract painting is his claim that it stands in a relation of continuity with the past. Rather than initiating a radical break with tradition, as both advocates and detractors of abstraction maintained, the work of Pollock and other so-called 'advanced' artists should be seen as a further stage in the progressive self-clarification of the indispensable means and limits of painting.[77] In the mid-1950s, Greenberg confidently asserted that 'the avant-garde survives in painting because painting has not yet reached the point of modernization where its discarding of inherited conventions must stop lest it cease to be viable as art'.[78] However, there are features of his analysis of abstract expressionism that cast doubt on this assumption. As early as 1941, when reviewing an exhibition by Kandinsky, he had noted 'how easy it is for the abstract painter to degenerate into a decorator', describing this as the 'besetting danger of abstract art'.[79] Once artists such as Newman, Rothko and Pollock started to paint on a large scale, producing paintings that filled the viewer's visual field, they risked divorcing abstract art from the tradition of the easel picture. The 'crucial issue' raised by the work of these painters is therefore 'where the pictorial stops and decoration begins'.[80]

Greenberg contends that no matter how much a painting is flattened, as long as there is an indication of spatial depth – so that the 'forms are sufficiently differentiated and kept in dramatic imbalance' – it will remain a picture.[81] But in Pollock's large-scale canvases from 1946 onwards he began to observe a new kind of pictorial organization in which there is no highlighting or grouping, and thus no obvious centre of dramatic interest, but rather an evenly distributed network of motifs that appears to extend beyond the boundaries of the frame. Although this tendency brought with it 'a greater concentration on surface texture and tactile qualities', Greenberg recognized that Pollock's 'decentralized', 'polyphonic' or 'all-over' style of painting threatened to initiate a radical break with the inherited conventions of the easel picture.[82] Not only did the framing edge cease to play a role in determining the painting's internal structure, there was also a danger that the painting would be seen as a 'single, indivisible piece of texture' rather than as 'the *scene* of forms'.[83] The rapid take-up of this approach by some of Pollock's contemporaries led Greenberg to suggest that the 'dissolution of the picture into sheer texture, sheer sensation, into the accumulation of similar units of sensation, seems to answer to something deep-seated in contemporary sensibility. It corresponds perhaps to the feeling that all hierarchical distinctions have been exhausted, that no area or order of experience is intrinsically or relatively superior to any other.'[84] However, in order to remain consistent with the premises of his own account, he had to acknowledge that the emergence of all-over painting also had consequences for the future of the medium: 'for in using the easel picture as they do – and cannot help doing – these artists are destroying it.'[85]

While Greenberg's account of the 'crisis of the easel picture' provided a means of addressing problems internal to painting, the real challenge to his theory of modernism came not from the latest developments in advanced painting, as he understood this term, but from the decision by other avant-garde artists to abandon painting and sculpture in favour of non-medium-specific practices. The gradual narrowing of his position, and the corresponding retreat into an increasingly doctrinaire conservativism, must be seen, at least in part, as a response to the innovations of the various neo-avant-garde movements of the 1950s, which rejected the pursuit of aesthetic autonomy in favour of a more direct engagement with the experience of modern life. The 'assemblages', 'environments' and 'happenings' of Fluxus could no more be assimilated into Greenberg's theory of modernism than the mixed-media work of artists such as Claes Oldenburg and Robert Rauschenberg, whose 'combine paintings' seemed designed to flout the very idea of purity and an orientation to flatness. By 1960, when Greenberg wrote 'Modernist Painting', with its declaration that the arts could save themselves from 'levelling down' only by 'demonstrating that the experience they provided was valuable in its own right and not to be provided by any other kind of activity', he was already fighting a rearguard action.[86] The identification of ambitious painting with the progressive isolation and testing of the cardinal norms and conventions of the easel picture bore little relation to what was happening in galleries and studios, and on the streets, of cities such as New York, Paris and London. In the context of civil rights protests, the women's liberation movement and growing opposition to the war in Vietnam, Greenberg's insistence on 'purity' began to look like a denial of art's responsibility to anything but itself. This situation was compounded by his dismissal of alternative forms of art practice as mere stunts that proceeded from the artist's intention to shock or scandalize rather than being grounded in genuine aesthetic conviction.[87]

The second major problem with Greenberg's theory of modernism derives not from its narrowing down of painting to a self-critical tradition of abstract art – with all the attendant exclusions that brings in its train – but from the very idea of an internal 'logic of development'. Greenberg first used this term in 'Avant-Garde and Kitsch' as a means of acknowledging that the developments he describes – although 'inexorable' – were not the result of a conscious programme.[88] He deploys the same argument in 'Modernist Painting' where he insists that modernist self-criticism 'has been altogether a question of practice, immanent to practice, and never a topic of theory' and that 'no artist was, or yet is, aware of it, nor could any artist ever work freely in awareness of it'.[89] It is not hard to see that such statements are ultimately self-defeating and that Greenberg's theorization of modernism as a historical process also contributed to its dissolution. He fiercely resisted the claim that the quality of a painting could be determined by its contribution to the progressive self-definition of art, insisting that aesthetic judgment is spontaneous and involuntary.[90] However, many artists and critics who were influenced by Greenberg came to believe that painting should be assessed in just these terms. Michael Fried, for example, argued that if a painting was to 'compel conviction', it had to reveal an awareness of recent developments in art.[91] Fried sought to distinguish his position from Greenberg's 'essentialism' by claiming that modernism is a 'cognitive enterprise' in which the artist seeks to discover 'not the irreducible essence of *all* painting' but rather 'that which, at the present moment in painting's history, is capable of convincing him that it can stand comparison with the painting of both the modernist and the premodernist past whose quality seems to him beyond question'.[92] Far from salvaging Greenberg's theory, Fried's revisions served to make its strong historicist presuppositions more explicit and thus more open to criticism.

As we saw in Chapter 5, historicism is the view that cultural artefacts, such as works of art, can be fully understood only by considering the specific historical circumstances in which they were produced. This weak contextualist commitment is relatively unproblematic and is adopted by most forms of historical enquiry. By contrast, strong historicism holds that there are discernible 'laws of development' that progressively unfold through history. One of the reasons for Wölfflin's focus on the art of the sixteenth and seventeenth centuries was his belief that the developmental logic underpinning the history of Western art could be more readily identified in earlier periods than in his own time, which was characterized by a kind of stylistic disorder. By contrast, modernist critics such as Greenberg and Fried sought to link past, present and future in a continuous, linear narrative, which depended in part on distinguishing ambitious or progressive art from other movements and practices that they considered stationary or regressive. This value-laden narrative – which was articulated not only through the writings of figures such as Greenberg and Fried but also through the exhibition practices of major museums such as the Museum of Modern Art in New York – allowed the work of the artists it enfranchised to gain considerable prestige and attention. However, the apparent cohesion of modernism was achieved at the cost of excluding those twentieth-century art movements and practices that did not share the same critical priorities, resulting in the marginalization and disparagement of the work of artists associated with Dada, Constructivism and Surrealism, as well as the various forms of politically engaged realism that flourished before and after the Second World War. The exclusive focus on a Western tradition of painting also served further to marginalize the work of non-Western artists that did not fit within the modernist framework.

Two further consequences served to undermine Greenberg's theory of modernism at the very moment that it achieved institutional dominance. First, the idea that painting develops through a sequence of stages – together with the corollary that to be advanced in relation to the art of the recent past was a marker of aesthetic quality – inevitably led artists and critics to seek to identify, and in some cases to realize, the next stage in the process. Rosenberg coined the term 'recipe painters' to describe artists who produced work to order, or who were more concerned with their prospective place in history than with the genuine expression of feeling.[93] As Ekaterina Morozova has shown, the problem of historical self-consciousness was at the forefront of disputes about art in the 1960s.[94] Despite Greenberg's protestations that the logic of modernism was only discernible in retrospect, he was criticized for attempting to *produce* history by determining the subsequent direction that painters should take if they were to occupy a place in the historical continuum. In an essay published in 1960, the same year as 'Modernist Painting', he claimed that the trajectory of modernism had not, after all, reached its apogee in Pollock's 'all-over painting', but was being carried forward by a new generation of artists, including Morris Louis and Kenneth Noland, whose work he vigorously promoted.[95] Although the technique of staining paint into unprimed canvas – originally developed by Helen Frankenthaler – could conceivably be interpreted as a further 'suppression of the difference between painted and unpainted surfaces', Greenberg's analysis of the supposed advances achieved by post-painterly-abstraction is dependent on his prior construction of modernism and it is hard to avoid the sense of an endgame being played out.[96]

The second unintended consequence of Greenberg's historicism is closely related to the first since the identification of an imminent logic of development inevitably points towards its own conclusion or terminus: the claim that painting had been reduced to just two 'constitutive norms or conventions:

flatness and the delimitation of flatness' left nowhere else for painting to go.[97] The problems inherent in Greenberg's account were brought to the fore by the series of 'Aluminium Paintings' that Frank Stella exhibited in the Leo Castelli Gallery in New York in 1960. By employing unusually thick stretchers, into which he cut notches both at the edges and at the centre, Stella made his paintings stand out from the wall as three-dimensional objects. These works, which were deliberately ambiguous between the conventional easel picture, with its pictorial representation of spatial depth, and the literal depth of a material object, could be understood both as a further investigation of the cardinal norms of painting and as a breakthrough that paved the way for Minimalism and other forms of art that emphasized the physical properties of 'specific objects' in relation to the space of the viewer rather than relations that are internal to the work itself.[98]

To the informed art-world insider, the meaning of the 'Aluminium Paintings' was, to a large extent, dependent upon their relation to Greenberg's theory of modernism. By producing work that was situated at the limit at which 'a picture stops being a picture and turns into an arbitrary object', Stella called into question the doctrine of medium-specificity and the idea that painting could continue to advance through a process of progressive self-delimitation.[99] It soon became clear that what Krauss termed the 'expanded field', encompassing such divergent practices as land art, performance, installation and assemblage, could not be accommodated within the developmental narrative of modernism, whose exhaustion was closely identified with the decline of painting as an ambitious art form.[100] However, the breakdown of modernism was also brought about through internal pressures, including a second-order awareness – and subsequent rejection – of Greenberg's account of historical progress. In Greenberg's own terms, we might say that once the project of historical self-criticism was extended to include its own historicist presuppositions, it could no longer fulfil a legitimating function.

The Challenge of Photography

There have been periodic claims for the obsolescence of painting ever since the artist Paul Delaroche responded to the invention of photography with the declaration 'From today, painting is dead!'[101] In the second decade of the twentieth century Duchamp announced that he was 'abandoning painting' to pursue alternative forms of art practice, including his readymades. He later insisted that 'for a period like ours ... one cannot continue to do oil painting, which, after four or five hundred years of existence, has no reason to go on eternally'.[102] More dramatically, the Russian artist Aleksandr Rodchenko stated that in 1921 he had 'reduced painting to its logical conclusion' by exhibiting three monochromatic canvases in the primary colours of red, blue and yellow, and that from this point on 'there will be no more representation'.[103] Whereas Rodchenko's position is ambiguous between declaring the end of figurative painting and announcing a new beginning through fully abstract art, there is a weary finality to Asger Jorn's observation: 'Painting is over. You might as well finish it off. Detourn. Long live Painting.'[104] These words were written to accompany an exhibition in 1959 of his 'detourned paintings', in which he took representational paintings by amateur artists that he had found in flea markets and then overpainted them with abstract gestural marks.

What are we to make of such pronouncements and how much credence should we give to the claim that painting has been rendered obsolete? From the standpoint of the twenty-first century, should we look back on painting as an outmoded form of art, of no more relevance to contemporary life than stained-glass windows and alabaster carvings? Or does painting continue to hold its place as a source of enduring value and substantive critical interest? At the risk of simplification, it is possible to identify two challenges to painting that have, if anything, become more pressing over time. The first, expressed with disarming directness in the quotation from Delaroche, derives from the invention of photography and other technologies of visual imaging. Photography, particularly in its modern, digital incarnation, is not only cheaper and faster than painting, which is a time-consuming, craft-like process, dependent on brushes, pigment, primers and stretchers; it is also more versatile, ranging from microphotography at a scale that is inaccessible to unaided vision through to satellite cameras that take us above the surface of the earth. The sheer ubiquity of photographic and digital imagery, be it through news photographs, advertisements or on our computer screens, makes it closer to contemporary experience. We are at home with photography in a way that painting cannot hope to match: it is both an integral part of the world we inhabit and the dominant mode of recording and transmitting visual information. The second challenge also has a historical dimension, since it is closely linked to the breakdown of modernism as a sustaining paradigm for the making and appreciation of art. For much of the modern period, avant-garde painting was closely associated with the pursuit of aesthetic autonomy. However, by the mid-1960s the values underpinning the modernist division of art from life had lost their hold. If Greenberg's historical defence of the 'present superiority' of abstract art had run its course, or at least no longer seemed relevant to contemporary concerns, how could artists find a way back to figuration without adopting the outmoded techniques of academic painting? After the demise of modernism, what possibilities remained open to painters who wished to make representational images, and how were they to compete with the success of photography?

That these two challenges are closely interrelated becomes clear when we recognize that the emergence of the avant-garde in the early to mid-nineteenth century was contemporaneous with the invention and dissemination of photography. It seems plausible to suggest that the ceding of the routine requirements of picturing to photography acted as a catalyst for the concentration on non-mimetic factors and that the gradual withdrawal into abstraction provided a means of diffusing the tension between photography and painting.[105] It would be wrong to assume, however, that photography and painting developed in isolation from one another: painters learned new techniques of representation from photography, just as photography drew on the vast resources of painting. From the outset, there was a productive exchange between the two practices, evinced, for example, in Degas's adoption of the photographic effect of 'cropping' – the partial occlusion of figures and objects by the frame – to present a more natural and less obviously composed view of his subject, a strategy that, in turn, has precedents in the work of Tintoretto and other Baroque artists who sought to avoid the highly ordered compositional structures utilized by their classicist predecessors.

At the other end of the historical spectrum, the engagement with mass-media images that characterizes the work of Pop artists such as Andy Warhol and Roy Lichtenstein can be identified as a direct challenge to the modernist pursuit of aesthetic autonomy. It is noteworthy that the return to figuration among avant-garde artists frequently took place through a reworking of images that were taken over from popular culture. The seemingly simple expedient of painting from pre-existing images not only offered a way of reintroducing figurative content, it also enabled artists to address some of the complex issues raised by the return to pictorial representation. The recognition that photography offered a way out of the apparent impasse of painting after modernism is eloquently expressed by the German artist Gerhard Richter, who had begun painting from photographs in 1963:

> I was surprised by photography, which we all use so massively every day. Suddenly, I saw it in a new way, as a picture that offered me a new view, free of all the conventional criteria I had always associated with art. It had no style, no composition, no judgement. It freed me from personal experience. That's why I wanted to have it, to show it – not to use it as a means to painting but to use painting as a means to photography.[106]

The paradoxical notion of using painting as a means to photography can be understood in several different ways. Initially, at least, Richter saw photopainting as a technique that enabled him to depict a wide range of subject matter without having to concern himself with the traditional requirements of invention, design, composition and pictorial unity. In his early writings and interviews, he repeatedly contrasts the artificiality of painting with the simplicity, directness and credibility of photography. He is, of course, fully aware that photographs can be subjected to manipulation, but he claims that, unlike art photography, which is fashioned in accordance with a prior idea of beauty, amateur snapshots, even when they are technically faulty or out of focus, are viewed as truthful in a way that painting is not.[107] By taking up images from newspapers, advertisements and amateur photographs, including his own, and re-presenting them in the medium of paint, he sought to give painting something of the apparent neutrality and objectivity of its source material: painting, like photography, would be a vehicle of information, a documentary record of the mediatized world, rather than a medium for expressing the artist's feelings and ideas. It quickly became clear, however, that reproducing an image is never a neutral decision and that the represented content undergoes a decisive transformation.

Consider, for example, Richter's painting *Christa and Wolfi* of 1964 (Plate 17), which is based on one of his wife's family photographs. It shows an everyday domestic scene in which two women look out at the camera, together with a dog sitting on a chair. One of the first things Richter realized was that by allowing the photographic source to determine the picture's composition, he was free to concentrate on purely 'painterly' concerns such as the texture and handling of the paint and the balance of tonal values. Although he describes his use of photography as a 'crutch' that helped him to get to reality, it also enabled him to engage with the specific technical and physical resources of painting without abandoning recognizable subject matter.[108] Ralph Rugoff has observed that one of the consequences of painting from photographs is that the artist has to pay equal attention to every part of the image, resulting in a unified consistency of detail and a levelling of hierarchical differences that echoes the 'all-over quality' that Greenberg had identified in Pollock's abstract paintings.[109] The orientation towards flatness characteristic of modernist painting, together with the absence of any determinate centre of interest, is brought into disorientating conjunction with the salience and spatial depth of the photographic original. This sophisticated variation on the vaunted push-and-pull effect of modernist painting is further complicated by the depiction of the white border around the photograph at the top and two side edges. The border is difficult to make out in a reproduction, which, paradoxically, turns the painting of a photograph back into a photographic image, with an additional border of its own. Richter's photopaintings are no more reproducible without loss through photographs than the large-scale abstracts of Jackson Pollock or any of the other artworks discussed in this volume. A photographic reproduction loses the very 'painterly' qualities that distinguish *Christa and Wolfi* from its source.

Interpreted in the context of the other paintings he made at this time, which depict a seemingly haphazard choice of objects and people, from chandeliers and folding clothes dryers through to administrative buildings and figures from newspapers, *Christa and Wolfi* appears to be yet another example of the banal and overlooked, temporarily lifted from the flood of photographic imagery by its reworking in the medium of paint. At the time he made these works, Richter insisted that his choice of subject matter was arbitrary: 'As a record of reality, the thing I have to represent is unimportant and devoid of meaning . . . All that interests me is the grey areas, the passages and tonal sequences, the pictorial spaces, overlaps and interlockings.'[110] However, he later conceded that the subject of the photographs did sometimes play an important role in his selection of images.[111] *Christa and Wolfi* is one of several paintings from this period that make more or less explicit reference to recent German history. *Uncle Rudi* (1965), for example, is based on a photograph of his uncle, Rudolph Schönfelder, wearing Nazi uniform, and the painting was first displayed at an exhibition in commemoration of the victims of Lidice. Pursuing this line of interpretation, Paul B. Jaskot has argued that the dog in *Christa and Wolfi* is 'a resonance or trace of one of *the* brutal symbols of the SS and other Nazi perpetrators, that is, the German shepherd, or police dog'.[112] It is important to recognize, however, that Richter's painterly interventions cause the image to recede or withdraw from view at the same time as they it rescue from obscurity. He frequently emphasizes the photographic effect of imprecision or 'blurring' (the result of camera shake or insufficient depth of field) by dragging the paint across the surface of the canvas. This curious conflation of the handmade and the mechanical renders the image unstable, making it difficult for the viewer to bring its subject into focus. As several critics have observed, Richter's strategy of both revealing and obscuring the photographic original evokes the processes of remembrance and forgetting that characterize our ambivalent relation to the past.[113]

How, then, are we to characterize the differences between photopainting and photography? On the one hand, it seems clear that far from simply doubling the photographic original, painting a photograph changes the way in which the source image is viewed. Insofar as we register the difference between the smooth surface of a photograph and the built-up surface of a painting, which consists of innumerable touches of paint, our attention is drawn to its handcrafted quality. Rugoff argues that painting instils 'a crucial delay' in our response to photographic imagery: it is not only that it takes time to make a painting, as opposed to the instantaneity of the photograph, painting also takes longer for the viewer to process. The 'more nuanced and variegated surface' of a painting allows for a complex layering of information that 'invites the eye to linger, to scrutinize the hundreds of contacts between brush and canvas'.[114] On the other hand, photopainting works to undermine the opposition between the unique handcrafted art object and the infinitely reproducible photographic image. Even the humblest snapshot acquires a different status once it is transposed into the medium of paint and presented in a gallery context: it is accorded a singularity that such images are normally denied, creating a space for critical reflection that is often truncated or compressed by the sheer quantity of visual information that surrounds us.

Richter's photopaintings constitute just one facet of his enormously diverse body of work, which includes abstract paintings, monochromes, colour charts and three-dimensional objects.[115] Moreover, he is just one of a number of painters who have drawn on photography as a means of engaging with the forms and structures of our highly mediatized world. As the emergence of photopainting indicates, the distinction between the handcrafted and the mechanical has started to break down. Not only have technological advances allowed photography to achieve the scale, brilliance of colour and compositional complexity of oil painting – amply demonstrated by the work of photographers such as Jeff Wall and Andreas Gursky – but the transition from photochemical to electronic and digital media permits a degree of intervention and manipulation that stretches the notion of the photographic towards the painterly. As the modernist emphasis on medium specificity recedes in significance, it is arguable that the two practices are becoming further entwined, allowing for a more open-ended range of possibilities in which painting and photography can come together on a common ground. The core themes that I have addressed in this book – the difference between a copy and a representation, the relation of surface and subject, the problem of reference and denotation, the analysis of pictorial style, and the role of historical self-consciousness – reveal the richness and complexity of painting as an art, a complexity that, so far at least, has enabled it to sustain its relevance under ever-changing historical circumstances. Richter's search for a way forward out of the impasse of modernism allows us to appreciate the remarkable resilience of painting while at the same time reminding us that it continues to face new challenges.

7

Contemporary Painting

Approaching the Contemporary

To argue against an established position is already, in some sense, to acknowledge its authority, or, at least, to allow the position one is arguing against to delimit the range of possible responses. The premises may be rejected, the inferences challenged as weak or unpersuasive, and the conclusions identified as erroneous. Nonetheless, the terms of the debate have already been established and, in rejecting what came before, the opponent is drawn back onto the same, contested ground. This, in highly schematic form, is the familiar dialectic of modernism and postmodernism. Each vaunted surmounting of modernism turns out in retrospect to have been overdetermined by the attempt to wrest free of a critical framework that continued to shape the views of even its most resolute opponents. Difference is substituted for identity, pluralism for unity, bathos for transcendence, hybridity for purity, the marginal for the mainstream, and discontinuity for historical progress. However, the inversion of values, or the substitution of the lower term for the higher, keeps the same structural oppositions in place. From this perspective, perhaps the most remarkable feature of what has come to be identified as 'the contemporary' is that it is no longer bound – even negatively – by the preoccupations of modernism. In part, this is simply a matter of historical distance. However, it is also the marker of a new-found freedom, initially hard won, but now worn with a certain lightness that is itself testament to a transformation in critical priorities.

If we are not to become entrammelled in the same contradictions, we need to begin *in medias res* and to allow our understanding of contemporary painting to be guided, at least initially, by possibilities that have been opened by recent developments in artistic practice. I therefore want to start by looking at the work of two contemporary artists whose approach to painting, in different ways, might be taken to exemplify an informed freedom from constraint: Lynette Yiadom-Boakye and Amy Sillman. Both artists are involved in an ongoing dialogue with earlier forms of art, including modernism, but the conversation is conducted on their own terms: they reach out to find points of interconnection that are valuable to them or productive, sometimes continuing, sometimes subverting or destabilizing features of the tradition, but their practice is not determined by opposition to what came before.

Two girls stand on a beach, gazing down at something we cannot see in the rocks beneath their feet, poised in momentary contemplation (Plate 18). The scene is suffused with an even, silvery light that allows the colour of their clothes and the warm tone of their skin to stand out against a largely undifferentiated ground. There is enough detail for us to recognize that each of them has her hair tied up in a bun and that they wear light-fitting clothes that leave their limbs free for movement, but we cannot read their expressions and the disclosure of interiority comes from the held posture of shared curiosity. Nothing helps us to identify where this beach might be or even when this scene might have taken place, and the image floats free of any specificity other than the unspoken companionship of the two protagonists. The title, *Condor and the Mole*, resonates with the painting but leaves us guessing as to its meaning. Equally enigmatic is the portrait of a seated young man, viewed from slightly above, with a cat lying across his left shoulder, entitled *In Lieu of Keen Virtue* (Plate 19). His dark olive-green trousers and bright orange jumper dominate the composition, which is tightly focused on the figure, cropping his legs and the edge of the chair, and excluding all other information. Unlike the two girls, his face is carefully delineated and, it would seem, instantly recognizable. He, too, is depicted in a state of contemplation, lost in thought, or looking intently at something beyond the frame of the picture. Few clues are offered to his state of mind, but the painting forcefully conveys the sense of someone who is comfortable in their own body and who, even in repose, has a physical grace that makes us glad to be in their presence.

When asked about the figures in her paintings, Yiadom-Boakye remarked, 'They're just kind of who they are. They exist in the paint.'[1] This statement, which might be taken to hold true for any painted figure, has a special meaning in this case, since although she recognizably works in the genre of portraiture, depicting figures either singly or in groups using full- and three-quarter-length formats, she does not work from models, photographs or preliminary sketches: instead, the individuals she depicts are derived entirely from her imagination. Although convincingly lifelike, they are fully imagined. To view several of her paintings alongside one another, or to visit an exhibition of her work, allows us to recognize that she does not paint generic types or construct amalgams out of disparate parts. The figures in her paintings are carefully delineated individuals, comparable in their realization to characters in novels.[2] As products of the imagination they invite our imaginative engagement, and the deliberate omission of any contextual information that might locate them in terms of period or place directs our attention towards their inner lives as well as their outer appearance. One consistent feature of her practice is that all the figures she paints are black, with widely varying skin tones and facial features. This in itself is unremarkable as Yiadom-Boakye is a British-Ghanaian artist. It is only from the perspective of someone who belongs to a different social world that she can be said to be making the invisible visible.[3] Nonetheless, there is a quiet insistence on what s he terms the 'strength' and 'moral fibre' of the figures she depicts, and the confident ease with which they inhabit their bodies, untroubled by the exigencies of work or the encroachments of everyday life, offers a compelling alternative to the dominant narrative of oppression that is so often imposed from without.[4]

Yiadom-Boakye does not disavow the wider issues that are raised by her work. However, she has observed that the breakthrough came when she stopped 'trying to push ideas into painting, to illustrate them' and instead accepted the physicality of painting and the necessity of thinking *through* the process of working paint on the canvas.[5] This is reflected in her acknowledgement that her 'starting points are usually formal ones' and that she normally begins a painting 'with something very simple that poses some kind of a problem or challenge: a color, a composition, a gesture, a particular direction of the light'.[6] Using traditional artist's materials – oil paint, rabbit-skin glue, and canvas or herringbone linen – she paints wet-on-wet, not allowing a layer of paint to dry before the next is applied, and most of her paintings are completed in a single day. There is a bravura virtuosity to this method that has parallels to improvisation in the domain of music. The resulting informality and lack of academic finish has important precedents in the work of painters Yiadom-Boakye admires such as Jean-Antoine Watteau, Walter Sickert and Edgar Degas, but her method of working and choice of subject matter is all her own. Another way of putting this is to say that there is nothing 'neo' about the return to figuration when it is informed by recognizably contemporary concerns and commitments. Her figures are not located in a specific historical moment, but they are identifiably of our own time. When placed together in an exhibition, they seem to be brought into dialogue with each other, an effect that is reinforced by the decision to hang the paintings low, so that the figures are at head height. The viewer who is conversant with the history of painting is invited to acknowledge that there is another conversation taking place, one that takes place in what Hilton Als terms an 'undefined space' that offers 'a new kind of beginning'.[7]

In her book on the philosophy of curation, Sue Spaid contends: 'Philosophers working in the analytic tradition have tended to treat visual art experiences as distinct experiences with discrete objects (singletons), something that is rarely true since spectators typically experience artworks in particular contexts, whether specific sites or exhibitions.'[8] This point can be carried further, for although it is empirically the case that our experiences of artworks rarely take place in isolation, it doesn't necessarily follow that viewing several works alongside one another is preferable or that this has positive benefits. Paintings, in particular, can easily get lost in group exhibitions, failing to hold their own against larger and more assertive artworks or finding themselves overwhelmed by the context of display. By contrast, there are normally positive gains that arise from viewing a painting as part of an individual painter's practice. Indeed, in most cases, it is possible to defend the normative view that rather than treating each painting as a discrete object, we should endeavour to understand individual artworks in relation to the larger practice of which they form a part. This holds true for the work of Yiadom-Boakye, as I have suggested above. However, Spaid's proposal that it is misleading to conceive artworks as singletons is particularly apposite in relation to the work of the American artist Amy Sillman. Although each of her paintings has its own internal coherence, they can also be viewed as stages or moments in the working out of an idea that takes place within and across several works, often heading in multiple directions at once. Here the part cannot be taken for the whole, for the practice to which the individual paintings belong is internally diverse and constantly changing, driven by what Sillman terms her 'devotion to a procedure of transformation.'[9]

Finger x 2 (Plate 20), now in the collection of the Metropolitan Museum of Art, was first shown at Sillman's exhibition *stuff change*, held at Sikkema Jenkins & Co., New York, in 2016. The title of the exhibition is a literal translation of the German term *Stoffwechsel*, normally translated as 'metabolism'. The capacity to derive energy from breaking down ingested materials to create a new synthesis offers a metaphor for Sillman's relation to the inherited tradition of Abstract Expressionism, a movement that she affectionately terms 'Ab Ex' to signal both proximity and distance.[10] However, the term 'stuff change' also provides a means of characterizing her own approach to painting, which is unusually labour-intensive. An exhibited painting will normally have gone through a series of quite radical changes before she decides it is finished. Sillman is characteristically open about this process, sometimes sharing slides of the various stages undergone by a painting before it reaches its final state.[11] The transitions are often highly discontinuous, characterized by unexpected leaps and reversals as new shapes and colour combinations displace earlier configurations, which may be completely erased. As Sillman notes, 'The result is a complicated surface that has been touched in many ways, with a strong sense of attachment and antagonism. It's not a nice, polite way of making art, where you plan and then execute some kind of model – this is foreign to me.'[12]

Viewed in isolation, *Finger x 2* might be taken for a study in the inherited visual language of an earlier generation of artists and it is not difficult to identify oblique references to the work of figures such as Hans Hoffman, Philip Guston and Richard Diebenkorn. The composition, however, is slightly off-kilter: traces of the previous stages still push through to the surface and the relation between the parts is kept adroitly unsettled. The apparent solemnity of the contrasting blocks of colour is also undermined by the mordant humour of the extended finger, wedged between abstract shapes but recognizably pointing at something we cannot see. Familiarity with Sillman's practice is likely to sensitize us to the presence of humour in her work or what Nicholas Hattful terms its 'total lack of contrivance'.[13] It also allows us to identify the re-emergence of certain tropes and motifs, such as the representation of an extended arm that appears in many of her early paintings, and the consistency of her engagement with the idea of splitting, doubling and repetition through the device of painting ones and twos. David Salle perceptively links this to the 'goofy, self-deprecating world of cartoons', with whose restless energy her work shares so much.[14] Among the paintings shown in the *stuff change* exhibition were a series of gestural abstract paintings that employ a freer, more expressive idiom, helping to correct the misapprehension that any one of the works on display might be considered definitive. However, the large-scale oil paintings were also accompanied by numerous smaller works, including over one hundred drawings, two stop-start video animations, and a 'zine', created by cutting and pasting together texts and images. These various outputs all form part of Sillman's practice and there is no reason to assume that they stand in a hierarchical relation to one other. This is consistent with her willingness to share her working methods with the viewer, but it also reflects her fascination with the different temporalities that belong to media such as film and animation. In some of her exhibitions she has displayed multiple inkjet prints pulled from animations made on her iPhone, utilizing its low-budget resources as an investigative means of working out ideas quickly and effectively.[15] Even the finished oil paintings have a provisional or arrested quality that allows them to retain something of the sustained 'awkwardness' of their process of making. While it is not necessarily wrong to view *Finger x 2* as evidence for the continued vitality of abstraction, this is achieved through a mode of working that refuses to 'aggrandize' painting and instead embraces 'the intimate and discomforting process of things changing as they go awry'.[16] The individual paintings are, in some sense, the results of this process, but they cannot stand in for it, and they remain connected to the larger practice of which they form a part.

The conceptual neatness prized by analytic philosophers is very hard – if not impossible – to achieve in relation to a field as diverse, vibrant and disordered as contemporary art.[17] Proximity also prevents the kind of clarity that comes with historical distance. Both Yiadom-Boakye and Sillman are established artists, whose work has been written about and discussed over an extended period. However, there is an inevitable risk of distortion in selecting just two painters working today to introduce the concerns of this chapter, and the sheer profusion of practices and approaches can make any such choices appear arbitrary or merely subjective. It might seem retrograde in this context to refer to the work of the nineteenth-century novelist Charles Dickens, but the following passage by David Trotter helps to capture something of the contemporary situation:

> What most distinguishes Dickens's novels from those by almost any other writer, and from life, is that hardly anything in them ever recedes entirely into the background. Dickens fought long and hard against the human tendency to focus exclusively on what is of immediate pressing concern in any given situation. His often anodyne protagonists have to compete for our attention with the idiosyncratic vitality possessed by the dozens of minor characters who surround them (hundreds, if there's a riot in progress). After a while a glazed expression seems to settle on their faces, as it dawns on them that they will never become the sort of person their creator most liked to describe.[18]

As Trotter suggests, in life as in art we are constrained by the need for selectivity, and this has the effect of pushing into the background things (and persons) that are equally deserving of attention. Another consideration is that anything that is said about contemporary art is likely to date quickly, serving perhaps as a useful commentary but without lasting significance. This is surely one of the reasons why few analytic philosophers have ventured to write on the subject. The existing literature is correspondingly thin, particularly as regards painting and its place in the contemporary art world, with the limited forays into answering this question tending towards a highly conservative defence of the 'privileged status' of representational painting.[19] In the absence of an established context of philosophical debate, there is much to be gained from turning instead to the writings of critics and art theorists, who have helped to shape the terms in which contemporary art is understood. It is sometimes the brilliance of a particular formulation that is convincing rather than the overall position that an author defends, but there is a rigour and seriousness of commitment towards contemporary art that is yet to be matched by analytic philosophy.

Despite this unusual degree of uncertainty, I believe that contemporary painting raises a number of questions that can usefully be considered from a philosophical perspective. The term 'contemporary' itself invites further investigation. Is it a neutral term, used simply to designate art that is being made today? Or does it fulfil an evaluative function – analogous to the term 'modernism' – enabling those who employ it to distinguish certain kinds of art from others that continue to flourish but are not singled out for the same critical attention? Some theorists have argued that 'the contemporary' constitutes a new and distinctively organized period of art and that it is separated from the modern era by a radical break or caesura.[20] If there has been some kind of rupture or transformation, how should this be characterized and on what grounds might it be understood as definitive of the contemporary situation? Another related question concerns the continued viability of the category of 'painting' in today's multimedia art world. Does the designation of a work of art *as* a painting hold any special significance or does it simply identify the use of certain materials and procedures in preference to others? Another way of putting this is to ask whether there is anything to be gained from seeking to preserve the identity of painting in relation to other art forms or whether we should accept that medium-specific distinctions have, for the most part, ceased to matter.

One of the few uncontroversial observations that can be made about contemporary art is that it is decisively shaped by the advent of new digital technologies and the seemingly limitless proliferation of images and information that circulate through digital networks. Whereas painting in the late twentieth century developed in part through its relation to the dominant medium of photography, contemporary painting has had to come to terms with the pre-eminence of the digital image. I shall argue that – contrary to what we might expect – the prevalence of digital media and digitization has helped to establish the specificity of painting, providing a new context for understanding its distinctive characteristics. This provides the basis for a non-conservative defence of painting, one that acknowledges its place in a highly mediatized world without relying on a forced contrast between analogue and digital ways of working. I conclude by addressing the issues raised by the emergence of so-called 'spatial painting' practices, which emphasize the material properties of painting as a physical entity that occupies the same spatio-temporal world as the viewer.

The Post-Medium Condition

Is it possible that the central organizing categories of art – many of which have been in place for several hundred years or longer – simply ceased to have further relevance at a certain point in history? Consider, for example, the category of sculpture. In an essay written in 1979, Rosalind Krauss noted:

> Over the last ten years rather surprising things have come to be called sculpture: narrow corridors with TV monitors at the ends; large photographs documenting country hikes; mirrors placed at strange angles in ordinary rooms; temporary lines cut into the floor of the desert. Nothing, it would seem, could possibly give to such a motley of effort the right to lay claim to whatever one might mean by the category of sculpture. Unless, that is, the category can be made to become almost infinitely malleable.[21]

Krauss points out that although the category has been 'kneaded and stretched and twisted in an extraordinary demonstration of elasticity', it cannot have a fully open extension without collapsing in on itself.[22] Even if we accept that the term 'sculpture' functions as an 'open concept', responsive to new developments and hence emendable in its conditions of application, unless it serves to demarcate certain kinds of objects from others it ceases to be informative.[23] A genealogical or evolutionary account, whereby something is identified as a sculpture because it recognizably engages with or moves forward from established examples, can only carry us so far, for at a certain point we have to ask whether what we are looking at can still be accommodated under the same unifying category. Krauss dramatizes this moment of recognition with reference to land art and the practice of artists such as Mary Miss and Michael Heizer, whose large-scale earthworks involved excavating rock and soil from the ground: 'we stare at the pit in the earth and think we both do and do not know what sculpture is.'[24] Krauss's imaginary viewer comes to realize that the conventions she had thought immutable are themselves subject to change. The use of the third person plural invites us to share this insight and to acknowledge our own lack of certainty about the correct extension of the term.

Compared to the vicissitudes of sculpture, painting appears to be far more secure as an art form. The waning influence of modernism and the corresponding loss of conviction in medium-specificity as a means of securing the identity of the individual arts also raised searching questions about the category of painting. However, the main challenge came not from the blurring of boundaries between different forms of art but from the assumption that to continue to work within an established medium was inherently conservative. This view is expressed with uncompromising directness by the artist Joseph Kosuth:

> Being an artist now means to question the nature of art. If one is questioning the nature of painting, one cannot be questioning the nature of art. If an artist accepts painting (or sculpture) he is accepting the tradition that goes with it. That's because the word art is general and the word painting specific. Painting is a *kind* of art. If you make paintings you are already accepting (not questioning) the nature of art.[25]

Kosuth wrote these words in 1969 at the height of the conceptual art movement and they posed a direct challenge to artists working at the time. One response was to seek to 'expand' the practice of painting by incorporating it into other art forms or even to incorporate other art forms into painting. As early as 1961 the artist Niki de Saint Phalle had produced a series of paintings entitled *Tirs*, created by hanging containers of liquid paint on a wooden support and then firing at them with a gun, a strategy that was anticipated even earlier by artists belonging to the Gutai group in Japan such as Shimamoto, whose *Throws of Colour* (1956) was made by shattering glass jars filled with coloured pigment that had been placed on canvas. The fusion of painting with performance was carried forward by Yoko Ono with her series of 'Instructional Paintings': *Painting to Hammer a Nail* (1961) invites viewers to hammer a nail into the work, while *Painting to be Stepped On* (1960) consists simply of the instruction: 'Leave a canvas or finished painting on the floor or in the street.' As these examples show, despite the absolutism of Kosuth's pronouncement, painting, too, had good claim to be considered a form of conceptual art. In the early 1960s Lawrence Weiner produced a series of 'Propeller Paintings', based on television test patterns, and many of the iconic text-based pieces of conceptual art, including works by John Baldessari and Mel Ramsden, were made using acrylic on canvas.

Perhaps the most sustained attempt to enlist painting in the service of conceptualism was carried out by On Kawara. He began his series of 'Date Paintings' in 1966 and continued working on it for five decades, producing nearly three thousand acrylic paintings. Each 'Date Painting' consists of a monochrome canvas in red, blue or grey, with the month, day and year inscribed on it in white sans serif, without the use of stencils. Although he didn't succeed in producing a painting every day, he would destroy any painting that wasn't completed by midnight, imposing a discipline that structured his life as well as his work. The continuation of the same thing over and over again, with the most minimal of variations, taking place over time but not changing through time, establishes a correlation between temporality and transience that is figured in each work but is only fully comprehensible through our awareness of the constraints imposed by the project as a whole. The critic Peter Schjeldahl has observed that at the heart of On Kawara's 'multitudinous production' there is a 'wintry vacancy; the content is as uniform as death'.[26] The correlation between renunciation and withdrawal is also to be found in the work French-Polish artist Roman Opalka, who from 1965 until his death in 2011 dedicated himself to a single piece entitled *Opalka 1965/1 – ∞*. The work consists of a large number of canvases, which Opalka termed *Détails*, all the same size, on which he painted by hand the numerical sequence of whole numbers from 1 to a projected infinity, using acrylic paint and a O-size brush, moving from left to right from the top of the canvas to the bottom, and then continuing the sequence at the top of the next canvas. Opalka was aware, of course, that the project could never be completed, declaring: 'It is very important that my last *Détail* will not be finished by me but by my life.'[27] As in the case of On Kawara, each painting invites us to consider the relation between transience and permanence, but it does so at the cost of a monastic disengagement from anything other than its own predetermined structure.

In retrospect, it now seems clear that, in the wake of modernism, painting suffered a kind of 'legitimation crisis', a term used by the German philosopher Jürgen Habermas to characterize the decline in confidence in the economic, political-administrative and sociocultural systems that regulate late capitalist societies.[28] The beleaguered condition of painting had much to do with the loss of its earlier position at the vanguard of modern art and it was widely held that to engage seriously with painting as an art form was to seek to reverse the gains made by the upheavals of the 1960s and 70s. Articles with titles such as 'Last Exit: Painting' (Thomas Lawson), 'The End of Painting' (Douglas Crimp), 'Figures of Authority, Ciphers of Regression' (Benjamin Buchloh) and 'Signs Taken for Wonders' (Hal Foster), all published in the early to mid-1980s, sought to establish that any return to painting was inherently conservative, driven by expediency and a cynical subservience to the requirements of the art market.[29] The task of these critics was made easier by the terms in which painting was defended. Crimp, for example, responds directly to the arguments deployed in the catalogue text for Barbara Rose's exhibition *American Painting: The Eighties*, where she identifies painting as 'a transcendental, high art, a major art, an art of universal as opposed to topical significance' and claims that 'only painting [is] genuinely liberal in the sense of free'.[30] For Crimp it is clear that:

> [t]he rhetoric which accompanies this resurrection of painting is almost exclusively reactionary: it reacts specifically against all those art practices of the sixties and seventies which abandoned painting and coherently placed in question the ideological supports of painting, and the ideology which painting, in turn, supports.[31]

These disputes were rooted in the specific circumstances of the time, including the emergence of a brash form of neo-expressionism in both Europe and North America, exemplified by the work of artists such as Sandro Chia and Julian Schnabel, whose large and brightly coloured canvases proved highly popular among dealers and collectors but were received with opprobrium by left-leaning critics, for whom the return to expression in painting could only be seen as a parody or pastiche of earlier art forms, without real significance, which 'performed' authenticity and sincerity as a means of catering to the demands of the market.[32]

The resulting polarization of views continues to shape contemporary debates. Some critics point to the resilience of painting and its capacity to adapt to changing circumstances, either by assimilating new developments, such as the emergence of digital media, or by expanding to accommodate rival art forms, a process traced back to the 1960s when it 'embraced ready-made objects, linguistic propositions and performative elements in its pictorial sphere'.[33] On this account, by learning to go 'beyond itself', painting has successfully adapted to the expanded field of art.[34] The trope of going 'beyond painting' has been in play since the early twentieth century, long predating the turn away from the modernist focus on medium-specificity. It was already used as the title for an essay published by Max Ernst in 1935, and many of the innovations of Dada, Surrealism and Constructivism – including, above all, the use of collage – can be seen as an attempt to open painting to other forms of representation, linguistic as well as visual. Once this alternative trajectory is acknowledged, it is possible to identify painting as a 'success medium' that has survived into the twenty-first century through its openness to challenge and its ability to accommodate seemingly contradictory tendencies.[35]

The opposing line of argument accepts that painting retains its prominence in commercial galleries, commanding high prices and, in virtue of its portability and durability, providing a more secure form of investment than performance-based or multimedia artworks, but it draws attention to the fact that market success is frequently accompanied by critical indifference. It is telling that in the vast survey, *Art Since 1900*, written by Foster, Krauss, Bois and Buchloh, all associated with the journal *October*, painting almost entirely drops out of view after the 1970s, with the exception of Gerhard Richter.[36] Painting still finds itself at the margins of a museum and biennale culture that is centred on installation, moving image and digital media, and there have been correspondingly few exhibitions dedicated to new painting in major museums.[37] However, the survival of painting is not like that of a rare animal species or a language spoken by a diminishing number of people. Those who see it as essentially past acknowledge that it continues to flourish commercially, but they argue that it persists only as a reshuffling or recycling of familiar motifs without genuine invention. This argument is clearly a reprise of Hegel's notorious thesis of the 'end of art'. Just as the composer Felix Mendelssohn was shocked that Hegel could proclaim art 'dead as a door nail' (*mausetot*) in the late 1820s when Beethoven was only recently deceased and Goethe still alive, it is tempting to rebut any insistence on the demise of painting with a list of names of contemporary painters, many of whom have worked steadily through the period in question.[38] While the sheer quality and variety of contemporary painting should suffice to allay such concerns, this doesn't answer the central challenge, which is that the present has been cut off from the past by a fundamental shift in values. Once again, it is Krauss who has provided the terms in which this shift has come to be understood and many critics now accept that we have entered what she identifies as 'the post-medium condition'.[39]

In the essays that she wrote in the 1970s and 80s, many of which were contemporaneous with the developments that she sought to comprehend, Krauss willingly acknowledged the difficulties of subsuming a heterogenous diversity of practices under a single description. Her essay 'Notes on the Index', published in 1977, begins with the declaration:

> Almost everyone is agreed about '70s art. It is diversified, split, factionalized. Unlike the art of the last several decades, its energy does not seem to flow through a single channel for which a synthetic term, like Abstract-Expressionism, or Minimalism, might be found. In defiance of the notion of collective effort that operates behind the very idea of an artistic 'movement', '70s art is proud of its own dispersal.[40]

By contrast, her book *A Voyage on the North Sea: Art in the Age of the Post-Medium Condition*, published in 1999, attempts to impose a retrospective sense of order on this period. Through a detailed analysis of Marcel Broodthaers's 1972 exhibition, *Musée d'Art Moderne – Département des Aigles*, she seeks to show that the emergence of conceptual art irrevocably altered the relation between art and individual artistic media. Broodthaers's installation contained more than three hundred different representations of eagles, spanning both high art and popular culture, and in an enormous variety of different media, no one of which was privileged over any other: pictures, texts and objects were placed indiscriminately alongside one another. Krauss maintains that the eagle functioned for Broodthaers as an emblem for conceptual art and that the installation successfully established the absolute equality or levelling of all the items it contained. What was important was the artist's concept or idea and it was therefore a matter of indifference which medium or media were used. According to Krauss, 'the triumph of the eagle announces not the end of Art but the termination of the individual arts as medium-specific; and it does so by enacting the form that this loss of specificity will now take'.[41] Krauss's analysis is double-edged, for the levelling she identifies also undermines the distinction between artworks and commodities, allowing works of art to be treated as pure exchange value. Far from celebrating this transformation, she maintains that 'all over the world, in every biennial and at every art fair, the eagle principle functions as the new Academy. Whether it calls itself installation art or institutional critique, the international spread of the mixed-media installation has become ubiquitous'.[42] Krauss maintains that the liberation of art from dependency on the medium has resulted in a new kind of dependency, a dependency on the powerful art institutions that control the selection and display of art.[43]

Jan Verwoert has helpfully reconstructed the ensuing controversy in a way that brings out the consequences of Krauss's position for the medium of painting. If we ask the question 'why painting should be considered in isolation from other media?' or 'does it make sense to make a single medium the subject of a single text or exhibition?', there seem to be two radically opposed responses.[44] Those who agree with Krauss's diagnosis will answer in the negative. Artists are no longer bound by the requirement to work in a specific medium: it is the conceptual project that has primacy, and even if an artist elects to use paint or canvas, this holds no greater significance than the decision to use coloured plastic or pieces of plywood. The choice is purely strategic, and artists can move freely between different media, turning to sculpture, video, installation or performance if this provides a better means of presenting their ideas. The second answer is affirmative, insisting that the artist's choice of medium does still matter. To overlook the significance of the medium is to view art as concerned above all with the presentation of transferable content for which the materials employed are simply a vehicle of communication. Advocates of this view argue that art is not a matter of illustrating pre-existing ideas, which could, in any case, potentially be articulated in non-artistic form, but should instead be understood as a sustained process of engagement with the resources of the medium. The art of painting necessarily involves dialogue with the inherent constraints and possibilities of the medium, and the proposal that it is only the artist's 'idea' that matters is troublingly superficial.

Although Verwoert does not use this term, the two arguments are presented in the form of an antinomy: depending upon the starting point, both positions seem equally compelling, and yet they cannot both be right. The impasse arises, I believe, from the way in which Krauss sets up the problem in the first place. The rejection of medium-specificity within conceptual art is identified not as one artistic strategy among a competing plurality of different approaches, but as an irreversible historical transformation that subsequently limits the possibilities available to other artists. In Verwoert's telling phrase, it 'represents a threshold that no one can step back over'.[45] The result is a Manichean dualism in which the range of available options is restricted to just two directly opposed alternatives. However, nothing constrains us to adopt this perspective. At a certain point in recent history, it may have seemed to artists and critics that they had to choose between medium-specificity and an expanded form of art practice informed by the innovations of conceptual art, but subsequent developments have shown that these alternatives are neither binding nor productive. Krauss's analysis of the 'eagle principle' purports to establish a framework for understanding the structures that distinguish contemporary art from earlier periods. However, as the choice of the term 'post-medium condition' already reveals, her account is locked into a binary relation with the contested inheritance of modernism, displacing medium-specificity but still according it negative primacy in the ordering of the available alternatives. As I have already suggested, the best way forward is simply to step sideways from this seemingly intractable dispute and to acknowledge that the scope of the artist's freedom to engage with both ideas and materials is considerably greater than either Krauss or her opponents are willing to concede. Not only has the category of painting retained its 'elasticity' but this is something that has come to be valued over any attempt to determine its limits or to confine it within a larger theoretical framework.

Confronting the Digital Divide

The mere advent of new technology doesn't render older technology redundant, unless it is replaceable without loss. Consider the example of contemporary music. Despite the availability of a wide range of digital music-making technologies – including synthesizers, digital pianos, drum machines, samplers, sequencers and multitrack systems – composers continue to score work for traditional string, woodwind, brass and percussion instruments without this seeming in any way conservative or retrograde. The touch, weight, feel and even the distinctive timbre of instruments made from materials such as wood, bone, metal and animal hides has proved worth preserving, and this suggests that it has not yet been fully replicated or superseded by advances in technology. In the work of composers such as Kaija Saariaho and Olga Neuwirth analogue and digital technologies are employed alongside one another, while a composer such as Thomas Adès is not considered any less original or innovative simply because much of his work is scored for instruments that could be found in an eighteenth-century orchestra. It is arguable that the choice of instrumentation provides a means both of sustaining continuity and signalling any intended breaks with earlier traditions of music making. However, the forces for which a piece of music is scored appear to be far less invested than in the parallel case of the visual arts, where the use of analogue technologies carries different connotations and is often directly pitted against the encroachments of digitization.

The lines are, perhaps, most clearly demarcated for artists who work in moving image and photography, where the technological advances of digital media appear to outstrip any residual attachment to older and more cumbersome ways of working. If an artist choses to use analogue media, this is a strategic decision that has a bearing on the meaning of the work. Tacita Dean, for example, acknowledges that her decision to continue using 16mm film is an attempt to hold on to the past and to preserve connections that are at risk of being lost through the convenience of digital media. Even in films with apparently neutral content such as *The Green Ray* (2001), which records the slowest setting ray of the sun just before the descent of darkness, the use of photochemical filmstock is charged with significance, allowing the artist to dwell on the elusiveness and transience of optical phenomena. For Dean, 'analogue implies a continuous signal—a continuum and a line, whereas digital constitutes what is broken up, or rather, broken down, into millions of numbers'.[46] The correlation between the passing of a former way of life and the attempt to capture this process through the use of analogue media is also to be found in the work of Zoe Leonard, whose photographic project *Analogue* consists of several hundred square-format prints of shopfronts photographed with an old Rolleiflex camera, taken over a decade in the Lower East Side of New York. Leonard has observed that although 'new technology is usually pitched to us as an improvement ... progress is always an exchange. We gain something, we give something else up. I'm interested in looking at some of what we are losing.'[47]

It would seem, then, that in the visual arts, at least, there is a 'digital divide' that separates those artists who chose to work in analogue media from those who embrace the use of new technologies.[48] Painting, as an analogue medium, appears to lie unambiguously on one side of the divide. This conviction provides the basis for a conservative defence of the enduring value of painting in the digital age whose constituent features are repeated with only minor variations in innumerable catalogue entries and exhibition reviews. The expressive warmth and subjectivity of painting is opposed to the cold functionality of the digital image, which serves primarily as a vehicle of information. In contrast to the rapidity, ubiquity and ease of digital reproduction, the labour of painting and the comparative slowness of execution gives it a singularity that lifts it out of the unending flow of media images. Painting requires powers of close observation and sensitivity to materials, directly combining vision and touch in a way that is unmatched by other media. To turn away from pixels to pigment is to commit to the 'old, slow art of the eye and the hand, united in service of the imagination'.[49] The physicality of painting – the movement of the brush against the texture of the support – leaves an expressive trace that cannot be captured by digital technology. The art of painting therefore provides a means of resisting the flattening effects of digitization and it stands in a relation of opposition to the digital revolution.

I hope to have already jolted loose some of the assumptions underpinning this account through my discussion of the work of Lynette Yiadom-Boakye and Amy Sillman at the start of this chapter. However, there are several other considerations that can be brought to bear. As Clare Bishop has pointed out in her searching analysis of the role of digital media in contemporary art, even when artists do not directly make digital art, they frequently employ new technology in one or more stages of the production, distribution and presentation of their work. The medium of painting is supported by what she terms a 'digital apparatus': JPEGs are placed on gallery and museum websites, PDFs are sent to the press and to potential buyers, and it is often the case that we first get to know an artist's work through images viewed on a computer screen.[50] Many painters also work from digital imagery, either as source material or as a first stage in developing their ideas, and there are celebrated instances of artists, such as Sillman and David Hockney, who have embraced readily available technologies such as the iPhone to produce 'digital paintings' alongside their work in traditional media. Bishop contends that when we look more closely at the art that has come to prominence in museums, galleries and art fairs since the invention of the World Wide Web in 1989 – including performance, installation, assemblage and participatory art – the anticipated wholesale shift to the digital turns out not to have taken place or at least not in the form that might have been expected: so-called 'new media' art occupies its own specialized domain, largely separate from the mainstream art world, and few artists overtly address the transformations wrought by digital technology.[51] Bishop concludes that the effects of the digital revolution are to be found at a deeper, structural level rather than simply in the adoption of new media, and that the digital is 'the shaping condition – even the structuring paradox – that determines artistic decisions to work with certain formats and media'.[52]

The tendency to disavow the role played by digital media is perhaps less marked in contemporary painting than in the other forms of art discussed by

Bishop, but her argument provides an important corrective to the simplifications that sustain the conservative defence of painting. The seemingly effortless creation, manipulation, distribution and reproduction of images that is enabled by new digital technologies places a kind of pressure on painting. It is only by addressing the currency of the digital image that we can understand the value that has come to be placed on analogue forms of art and the position they occupy in the contemporary art world. This proposal can be presented in the form of a question: why does painting continue to be made and appreciated in the digital age when images can be created and disseminated with such facility using readily available technologies? To answer this question, we cannot simply contrast analogue painting and digital image: instead, we need to examine the connections that link them together. These connections can be forged through the positive embrace of new technologies, as is the case for both Wade Guyton and Julie Mehretu, whose work I shall discuss below. However, they can also be established through a negative process of definition, in which the transformations wrought by digital technology cast a raking light on the traditional practice of painting, helping to bring out saliencies that might otherwise have been overlooked.

Guyton's *Untitled* (Plate 21) was made for his exhibition, *Das New Yorker Atelier, Abridged,* which travelled in slightly modified form in 2017 from the Museum Brandhorst in Munich to the Serpentine Gallery in London. The exhibition belongs to a long tradition in which artists have used their work to reflect on the studio space as a subject in its own right – in this case Guyton's studio in downtown Manhattan – and the title of the show refers to a painting by the Swiss artist Hans Jakob Oeri, *Das Pariser Atelier* [The Paris Studio] (1807), in the collection of the Kunstmuseum Winterthur. At over 2 metres tall, *Untitled* invites comparison with some of the statement works of Abstract Expressionism, whose visual language it appears to share: the line down the middle is reminiscent of one of Barnett Newman's 'zips' and the ragged edges recall the work of Clyfford Still. However, although the work is on linen, stretched over a support, it was made not with a brush or any other means of applying paint by hand, but with a commercial grade Epson 11880 printer using UltraChrome HDR ink. Guyton's signature technique begins with a modified digital file, based on a photograph, screenshot or bitmap, which he sends to the large Epson printer in his studio. He then folds a sheet of linen in half and tapes it together so that it will fit inside the printer and feeds each side slowly through the machine, allowing any stutters or pulls to determine the appearance of the work when it is opened up, with the longitudinal line of the fold still clearly visible. A second work in the exhibition was evidently made using the same digital image – identifiable through the tip of the artist's shoe, visible in the bottom left-hand corner – but it was printed using UltraChrome K3 ink, and there are marked differences in the colour, ink density, striations, marks and smudges. These two paintings are based on a photograph of the interior of Guyton's studio. However, the range of imagery in the exhibition extends from buildings on the New York skyline that can be seen from the studio windows through to screenshots taken from the computer that sits on his desk, resulting in surprising dislocations of scale and resolution.

The withdrawal of direct physical contact in the application of paint and the delegation of the painting process to a machine might suggest that Guyton's work is best understood in terms of 'appropriation' and that his aim is simply to underscore the redundancy of painting in the digital age. This interpretation was, perhaps, encouraged by the title of his first one-person show at the Whitney Museum of American Art in New York in 2012: *Wade Guyton OS*. The use of the familiar initials for a computer 'Operating System' carries unmistakeable connotations of impersonality, as if his unorthodox technique were designed to eliminate any residue of subjectivity. However, Guyton takes far too much care over the appearance of the finished paintings for this interpretation to be remotely plausible and the sensuousness of the marked surface, with its strange glitches, shifts, disruptions and imperfections, belies the suggestion that he is engaged in a parodic display of deskilling. The hyperbolic claim by the critic Jerry Salz, 'In 2002 Wade Guyton invented a new paintbrush. Its name was the Epson printer', starts out from the other extreme, and it is unsurprising that Guyton's work has given rise to strongly contrasting evaluations.[53] Attention to the process through which the paintings are made is clearly important, but other critics contend that the 'back-story of their manufacture' is of little significance since the finished works so clearly cater to established canons of taste. Dan Fox – in equally hyperbolic mode – contends that 'even if these [paintings] were made with potato prints, the result is still an historically sanctioned modernist aesthetic that reinforces its authority each time it's repeated'.[54] Fox also points out that for all Guyton's reliance on new digital technology – iPhones, scanners, computers, printers, and so forth – his paintings 'are essentially analogue objects for an industry still far more comfortable with the physical than the digitally immaterial'.[55] What both of these assessments appear to overlook is the way in which Guyton carefully positions his work precisely at this critical juncture: the ability to inhabit both registers simultaneously is central to the effect of his paintings, which are located in the territory between the virtual and the physical without this seeming in the least uncomfortable.

Julie Mehretu's vast and complex paintings provide an alternative way of approaching these issues. Her highly politicized practice as an artist stands in marked contrast to the self-referentiality of Guyton's work, which remains studiously neutral towards any surviving content. *Mogamma, A Painting in Four Parts: Part 3* (Plate 22) is one of a quartet of paintings conceived as a single work that was made in response to the protests against the regime of Hosni Mubarak that took place in Tahrir Square in Cairo in 2011.[56] The title refers to the Mogamma building, a large administrative centre constructed in modernist style in the late 1940s, that was identified by many of the protestors as a symbol of government oppression. Architectural drawings of the Mogamma form the starting point for the painting, but these are overlaid with drawings of other buildings on the square, which were constructed at different periods in its rich and varied past, which extends from the Mamluk Sultanate through to the period of colonial occupation and the Egyptian Revolution. Working with a team of assistants, Mehretu researched into the history of the square and established a network of associations with other sites of protest, including Zócalo in Mexico City, Zuccotti Park in New York, and Meskel Square in Addis Ababa, Ethiopia, the country in which she was born and raised until her parents were forced to flee to America by political unrest. Digital images of plans and elevations of buildings from these multiple sites were projected onto the surface of the canvas and traced over by hand, creating an extraordinarily dense weave of references. The architectural drawings remain visible in the finished work, but they can no longer be separated out or fully comprehended. Further layerings of marks, created using ink and acrylic, were made by Mehretu without the help of assistants. As in previous works, such as *Retopistics: A Renegade Exploration* (2001), in which she examined transit systems and migration movement patterns, and *Black City* (2007), in which she explored the history of fortifications and security infrastructure, Mehretu employs a vocabulary of abstract shapes that draws on the visual devices used in maps and diagrams to suggest the directional movement of people and things, and the ways in which this is regulated and controlled by systems of power. Some of the shapes are reminiscent of early modernist abstraction, obliquely referring back to the utopian promise of Suprematism and the work of artists such as Lissitzky and Malevich, while other marks have a free-form quality that is more agitated and disruptive. Finally, Mehretu employs silk-screen printing to incorporate eight-bit characters and small grids of circles and squares, which seem to float like digital code across the surface of the canvas.

What are we to make of this enormous work, which at more than 4.5 metres tall and 3.5 metres wide fully envelops the viewer? The density of allusions and references built up through the painstaking process of research carried out by Mehretu and her assistants has a kind of counterpart in the density of the mark-making and the multiplicity of separate layers. However, this makes it extremely difficult to read the relevant information off the surface of the painting. While the work is clearly political in its content and orientation, the resources employed by Mehretu consist almost entirely of abstract marks and shapes. This includes the architectural drawings that form its starting point, for not only are the tracings frequently rendered upside down, predominantly in the upper part of the painting, they are so intermingled and compacted that only fragments can be discerned, preventing any coherent grasp of the whole of which they originally formed a part. The extent to which the work taxes – and arguably exceeds – the comprehension of the viewer through its sheer scale and level of intricacy has a parallel in certain works of music such as Messiaen's *Turangalîla Symphony*, whose length, size of orchestration, and complexity of intertwining rhythmic and melodic motifs makes it almost impossible to follow the separate lines of musical argument. One way of making sense of this is to view the painting as deliberately disorientating: the discontinuous articulation of different temporalities and different locations through a bewildering variety of schemata allows Mehretu to model in the work itself the challenges of apprehending complex phenomena in a single synoptic overview. T. J. Demos has persuasively argued that the *Mogamma* paintings 'render their viewing points similarly compound – even structurally impossible – always incomplete when viewed from any location' and that the 'structural stability and symbolic power of the Mogamma building is consequently undone from within'.[57] There is no overt conflict between Mehretu's willingness to employ the latest advances in digital technology alongside silk-screen printing and drawing by hand. However, the different elements of the work are kept discrete rather than fused together, and the viewer is required to negotiate the multiple orders of organization that coexist on the surface of the canvas.

The strongly experiential character of the effects that Mehretu seeks to realize through her paintings would suggest that any form of digital reproduction that failed to match the scale and the level of detail of the original work would necessarily constitute an impoverishment. However, the assumption that lower resolution images are simply inferior copies without any intrinsic value of their own has been challenged by the artist and writer Hito Steyerl in her brilliantly provocative essay 'In Defence of the Poor Image'.[58] Steyerl accepts that digital images are often degraded through reproduction and that as they are compressed, reformatted, uploaded and otherwise modified, their quality deteriorates even further. Nonetheless, she contends that the poor image – or what she terms the 'copy in motion' – possesses countervailing virtues that arise from its accessibility and its potential for reuse.[59] Steyerl's analysis of the ways in which images are shared and reproduced provides a means of destabilizing the 'contemporary hierarchy of images', in which high-resolution images such as original photographs and films are located at the top and low-resolution images at the bottom. Once we recognize that images gain other kinds of value through 'replication, remediation and dissemination', the impoverishment that arises from compression and reformatting can be identified as a gain that allows images to travel quickly and to be adapted for use in other contexts.[60] Here we might think, for example, of mobile phone images taken at the pro-democracy protests in Egypt and other countries during the Arab Spring and the extent to which these gained in political reach and effectiveness through being uploaded to social networking sites and distributed to media agencies. As Steyerl acknowledges, the category of the 'poor image' also encompasses surveillance footage and other means of government control, and there is no guarantee that the wider circulation of an image will be put to progressive ends. Nonetheless, the redeployment of images in the service of state suppression can be identified as yet another manifestation of the phenomenon she identifies: the seemingly paradoxical reversal of the relation between resolution and power.

There is a process of levelling at work here, since analogue artworks such as paintings, sculptures and original photographic prints also have a second life as digital images. However, the pervasiveness of digital imagery and the multiplicity of platforms on which it can be viewed and distributed also has consequences for artists who work primarily in digital media. Some artists seek to exercise control through the production of numbered limited editions, with other copies – designated as 'viewing copies' – declared devoid of monetary value even if they are identical in every other respect.[61] Many digital artworks also have specified viewing conditions, such as two-channel videos that are meant to be shown on different screens, and there are some works, such as Douglas Gordon's *Between Darkness and Light (After William Blake)*, that depend entirely on their installation in the gallery space.[62] In other instances, the curator has to decide how the digital image is to be displayed and viewed. Boris Groys has drawn attention to the some of the challenges that arise from showing digital artworks in the context of museums and galleries rather than allowing them to circulate freely through information networks. He contends that the 'digitalization of the image was initially thought of as a way to escape the museum or, generally, any exhibition space – to set the image free', but the result has been 'a new confinement inside the museum and the exhibition walls'.[63] The very heterogeneity of the devices and platforms through which digital artworks such as photographs and videos can be viewed accords the gallery space a new role as the guarantor of the authenticity of the work and the conditions under which it is meant to be experienced. This includes decisions about the hardware through which the image is shown or projected. Some older works are dependent on outdated technology such as TV monitors or VHS recorders that require considerable care and expense to maintain, further reinforcing the dependence of digital art on the apparatus of the museum.

Viewed from this perspective, the analogue art of painting possesses several advantages. Despite the circulation of digital copies, there is no uncertainty about the size, format or resolution of the original and there are no correlative worries about the need to stabilize the identity of the artwork through exhibition in a gallery or the intervention of a curator. As a singular physical object, a painting secures its own identity, and any doubts about its constituent (non-aesthetic) properties can be put to rest by returning to the original work. The technology of painting also makes it comparatively easy to conserve. Counter-intuitively, its sheer longevity as a medium means that even works produced several hundred years ago do not seem as dated to us as early works of video art: a painting by Dürer or Rembrandt is less conspicuous in a gallery setting than a black and white video shown on a bulky monitor from the 1960s or 70s. The stability of painting is clearly one reason why it continues to be favoured by investors. However, the comparison with digital art also helps us to understand why painting continues to hold an important place in the contemporary art world alongside – and sometimes in conjunction with – the latest advances in technology. Rather than opposing analogue and digital as if these were two disjunctive alternatives, we need to acknowledge that painting now belongs to the digital age and that it is both sustained and enriched by the ongoing exchange with other media and the new possibilities this creates.

The Two Spaces of Painting

One conclusion that might be drawn from these reflections is that a painting is not an image, or at least, not merely an image, and that its material properties anchor it in the same physical world that we inhabit as its viewers. We can develop this idea further by distinguishing between two different spaces of painting. The first of these, which I have discussed in some detail throughout this book, is the space within the picture or what is normally termed pictorial space. Through the making of marks on a surface, the painter opens up a virtual relation of depth, which is capacious enough to accommodate almost any depicted content, but which can also be narrowed down or flattened until there is only the barest sense that one mark recedes or advances in relation to another. The second of the two spaces is the actual space that is occupied by the painting itself, determined not only by the dimensions of the picture surface but also by the depth of the support. A painting is a physical object that – in most cases – can be moved from one place to another, possesses a certain weight and has qualities of shape, texture, durability, and so forth, that are often overlooked but that are nonetheless constitutive of its existence as a material entity that endures through time and is also changed by the passage of time. It is this second space of painting that has become the focus of attention for many contemporary artists, whose work explores what happens to painting when its condition as a physical thing in the world is properly acknowledged.

Angela de la Cruz's *Larger than Life (Knackered)* was originally made for the ballroom of the Royal Festival Hall in London in 1998. It was recreated by the artist in 2004 and it has subsequently been displayed in a variety of different locations, including the Galerie Thomas Schulte in Berlin, where it was installed in 2015 (Plate 23). Measuring over 14 x 10 metres, it is probably one of the largest moveable paintings ever made, but it is resolutely anti-monumental, and the effect of being bent and twisted to fit the available space is tragicomic rather than grandiose. Initially, the painting appears to have been crushed or broken by its immurement within the confines of the gallery. However, it can also be seen as folding out to occupy the surrounding space, extending across the floor and up the walls, taking over the gallery and making it impossible for someone to step inside without climbing over it. The work is situated between painting and sculpture, destabilizing the familiar conception of a painting as flat surface that hangs on a wall and instead asserting its own material presence.

One of the striking features of *Larger than Life (Knackered)* is that although the painting is fully abstract – starting out as a colossal brown monochrome with a yellow border – it nonetheless seems to take on human characteristics: hunched, contorted, perhaps even cowering or squatting, it is hard not to see the canvas as enduring vicissitudes and displaying a capacity for resistance. These projections are supported by our sense that the basic anatomy of the painting has been broken: the stretcher over which the canvas is normally pulled tight to produce a flat surface has been damaged in several places, causing the painting to slump in on itself. Other works by De La Cruz explore what happens to painting when it comes down from the wall: canvases are wedged into chairs, unstitched from their supports and crumpled on the floor.[64] Each of these paintings has a strong corporeal presence, evoking the human body without the use of figuration. *Larger than Life (Knackered)* is perhaps unusual insofar as it is site-specific, adapted each time to the different locations in which it is displayed. As De La Cruz has noted, the work bears traces of its travels and it is now cracked in places and worn, like a suitcase or an old leather jacket, further reinforcing the anthropomorphic associations.[65] However, there remains something unruly about its presence in the gallery space: an immense painting that is scarcely containable within four walls, it forsakes the virtual realm of pictorial space and challenges us to acknowledge its obdurate existence in the same physical world as ourselves.

I have consistently referred to *Larger than Life (Knackered)* as a painting, a designation that is also adopted by the artist. In the work of De La Cruz, it is clear that something is being done to painting, or perhaps being done with painting, rather than a concerted attempt to leave painting behind. This also holds true for a number of other contemporary artists – such as Simon Callery, Guillermo Mora and Jost Münster – whose work has been described as 'breaking the pact around flatness as a technical-aesthetic rule'.[66] The commitment to what has come to be termed 'spatial painting' brings new considerations into play: an object in the round cannot secure a relation of frontality to the viewer in the same way as a flat canvas, for example, and a work in three dimensions will cast its own shadow. However, for the most part, the resulting technical problems are addressed by these artists from within the practice of painting, whose status is secured rather than undermined by the exploration of its neglected spatial characteristics.

There are other cases, however, in which the identification of an object as a painting is far from straightforward. This is not a matter simply of establishing the appropriate sortal category so that the artwork can be categorized correctly. The provisional allocation of an artwork to one art kind rather than another potentially changes the way in which it is viewed and interpreted. The resulting shift in perspective can be generative or conflictual, depending on the specific case. For the spatial painting practices that I have been considering here, the recognition that a work identified as painting also possesses qualities in common with other art forms such as sculpture or installation – and, inversely, that a work identified as a sculpture or an installation possesses qualities in common with painting – provides a mean of enriching our appreciation. Just as De La Cruz's paintings can be appreciated for their sculptural qualities, so works by mixed-media and installation artists such as Isa Genzken and Cosima von Bonin can be appreciated for their rich palette of colours and the way in which shapes and forms are combined to form an ordered composition.[67] Von Bonin's *Total Produce (Morality)*, from 2010, for example, is made from various fabrics, foam materials, rubber, wood and neon tubes rather than pigment on canvas. Nonetheless, the placement of the sprawling legs of the octopus against the brightly patterned base provides a sculptural variation on the familiar relationship between figure and ground, giving the work a strongly pictorial character.

More problematic, and hence deserving of further consideration, is the claim that any artwork in which the dispersal of paint or pigment plays a role, no matter how secondary or accidental that may be to the artist's practice, can still be categorized as a painting. Consider, for example, *Green River* (1998–2001) by the Danish-Icelandic artist Olafur Eliasson, who is best known for his large-scale sculptures and installations employing natural elements such as light, water and air. For this project, he poured uranine, a water-soluble dye used to test ocean currents, into rivers in six different locations, including the Strömmen waterway in the centre of Stockholm, Sweden. The dye itself is red but once in the water it turns bright green. No announcement was made, and anyone present at the time would have seen the river transformed. The photograph of the Stockholm iteration of the project on the artist's website reveals the brilliance of the pigmentation against the dark blue of the water and the way it traces the main current of the river as it flows through the centre of the channel. Daniel Birnbaum has argued that 'for a few minutes the vast surface appeared as a huge monochromatic canvas; synthetic and completely artificial'.[68] Although this interpretation lies ready at hand, I believe that it is a misreading and that the identification of *Green River* as a painting does little to further our understanding of the work. Key factors here are the transitory status of the piece, which lasted only for a few minutes, the fact that the artist had no control over the dispersion of the colour on the surface of the river once the dye had been poured into the water, and the absence of any stable or fixed form, since its appearance was constantly changing in response to the flow of the current. It is arguable that each of these factors could, potentially, be recruited in the service of an expanded practice of painting. However, the attempt to align *Green River* with this cause fails to acknowledge that it is primarily directed towards our understanding of natural processes – making us aware that even the stately progression of the Strömmen, which is contained and controlled by the built environment, has a powerful current below the surface. Eliasson's work is in direct dialogue not with the medium of painting, and its long and complex history, but with scientific knowledge and the positive and negative benefits that arise from human intervention in the natural world. *Green River* may, for a short period of time, have taken on the appearance of a purposely marked surface, but it is miscategorized by being subsumed into the genre of painting.

This argument can be clarified by considering another example, which initially appears to be subject to similar considerations, but for which a positive case can be made that our understanding of the work is enhanced by placing it in the category of painting. The Belgian artist Francis Alÿs has an exceptionally wide-ranging practice and his works comprise a remarkable diversity of different activities: these range from pushing a melting block of ice through the streets of Mexico City (*Paradox of Praxis 1, Sometimes making something leads to nothing*, 1997), to releasing a fox at night into London's National Portrait Gallery (*The Nightwatch*, 2004), and working with a team of five hundred volunteers to move a sand dune a couple of inches on the outskirts of Lima, Peru (*When Faith Moves Mountains*, 2002). Many of these action and performance pieces are documented as videos, which are presented as artworks in their own right and exhibited in galleries and placed on the artist's website. Alÿs has also created a series of works that are directly concerned with painting or, perhaps more accurately, with the action of painting. His video piece *The Leak* (2002) shows the artist piercing a tin of blue paint and then walking along a planned itinerary of streets in Paris with the tin held upside down, so that it leaves a trail of paint behind him. Originally performed in 1995 in São Paolo, Brazil, this seemingly absurdist take on Paul Klee's well-known recommendation that the artist should 'take a line for a walk', took on additional significance when it was reprised in Jerusalem in 2004.[69] Alÿs walked along parts of the Green Line, the armistice border that separated Israel from its neighbours after the 1948 Arab-Israeli War, trailing green paint behind him as a reminder of the border that was erased by the Six Day War in 1967 and Israel's subsequent expansion into Palestinian territories (*The Green Line*, 2004). The resulting video shows footage of Alÿs's action, and there are multiple versions with different commentaries by invited participants from both sides of the conflict. Another work by Alÿs, *Painting/Retoque* (2008), involved the artist repainting by hand sixty yellow meridian strips that had nearly faded away in the former American Panama Canal Zone. Each of these works falls under multiple categories: action, performance, video and painting. The reason for including painting in this list is that *The Leak*, *The Green Line* and *Painting/Retoque* – albeit in different ways – all make explicit reference to the traditional conception of the artist as a mark-maker. The implied contrast between the safely bounded space of the canvas and Alÿs's real-world interventions provides a means of drawing attention to the significance of lines and borders, both visible and invisible, and their capacity to regulate human conduct. Painting may only be one strand of Alÿs's practice, but his use of the medium is not indifferent. Once located in the context of these other works, *The Leak* can be identified as a carefully thought-through intervention that engages with the possibilities of painting while also connecting it with wider geopolitical issues that are situated beyond the confines of the gallery.

The second space of painting – the position it occupies in the real world – turns out to be far more extensive than we might initially have thought. This is vividly realized in the work of Katharina Grosse, whose painterly interventions are unconstrained by pre-existing boundaries, extending not only across the walls, floors and ceilings of buildings, but also out into the natural world, encompassing trees, plants, grass and sand. Grosse first developed her signature spray-paint technique in 1998, when she used a spray gun and an air compressor to paint directly onto the walls and ceiling of the Kunsthalle Bern (*Untitled*, 1998).[70] Although other artists – including Hans Hartun and Jules Olitski – had employed the technique of spraying paint before, Grosse was the first to recognize that it allowed the artist to treat any object, whether natural or artificial, as a surface for painting, and that she could thereby shift and even erase the 'dividing lines' that separate painting from the wider environment.[71] Her museum installations sometimes involve first creating structures, using materials such as Styrofoam, soil and sawn logs, which are then sprayed over with paint, but she also applies paint directly onto pre-existing buildings and objects, including natural objects such as trees and bushes. For her work *psycholustro* (2014), she painted seven sites along the railway tracks leading into Philadelphia, covering walls, warehouses, shrubs, trees, foliage and the earth on the ground with orange, pink, green and other vivid colours that contrasted sharply with the run-down and neglected character of this stretch of urban corridor. *Rockaway* (Plate 24) was made in 2016 in the Gateway National Recreation Area on the Rockaway Peninsula in Queens, New York, which had been badly hit by Hurricane Sandy in 2012. As part of a series of public art projects commissioned by MoMA PS1, Grosse was invited to produce a work on the site. Over a period of several days, she used a crane and an industrial spray gun to transform a former aquatics building for soldiers stationed at Fort Tilden that had been decommissioned and fallen into a state of disrepair, spraying paint not only on the interior walls and ceiling, but also on the exterior of the structure and outwards onto the dunes. Grosse's characteristically vibrant and intense use of colour reconfigures the site, turning it into an extraordinary painting-installation that is nonetheless responsive to the specific features of the location and its history.

In the first chapter of this book, I put forward a provisional definition of painting – the purposive marking of a surface through direct bodily movement to create a meaningful visual image – while also acknowledging that it might be necessary to expand the scope of the enquiry to accommodate a broader class of objects than are traditionally accommodated under the term. Each of the components of this definition has been placed under pressure by developments in contemporary painting. However, I believe that it can still serve as a useful point of reference. *Rockaway* clearly conforms to the first three requirements: it is the result of a deliberate or intentional sequence of actions; it involves the marking of a surface, even if that surface is extended through three dimensions and out into the surrounding world; and it is made through direct bodily movement, albeit in a weakened or attenuated manner, since the paint is applied with a spray gun rather than with a brush, and thus also involves a degree of reliance on a mechanical process. The fourth requirement, as I have already indicated, is the most problematic. Captured in a photograph, as it is in Plate 24, *Rockaway* is brought back into the domain of images. However, it is hard to determine with any degree of clarity whether the painting-installation itself should be viewed as a visual image. This, in turn, raises the question whether *Rockaway* is able sustain the distinctive phenomenology of pictorial seeing. Wollheim maintains that all that is required for representation – as distinct from figuration – 'is that we see in the marked surface things three-dimensionally related'.[72] As is the case with any painted surface, it is possible to see one area of colour in *Rockaway* advancing or receding in relation to another. Yet on a macro level this does not result in the opening up of a virtual pictorial space that is distinct from the real space occupied by the building and its surrounding environment. Similarly, although the work can be viewed as having a foreground and background, this relation shifts depending upon the position of the spectator: there is no privileged vantage point either inside or outside of the structure from which it is intended to be seen.[73]

One way of responding to this issue is to observe that the term 'painting-installation' is equivocal and that we need to decide whether the work should be viewed as a painting or as an installation. Since *Rockaway* permits the viewer to step inside and walk through the building, it meets the basic requirement of installation art, which is that the viewer can physically enter the work.[74] Entering the work allows it to be experienced as an immersive environment rather than as a discrete object or a plurality of objects located alongside one another. However, there seems to be a trade-off, and perhaps even a fundamental incompatibility, between the expansion of painting on an environmental scale and the ability to sustain the distinctive phenomenology of pictorial seeing. It is not simply that *Rockaway* lacks the frontality characteristic of easel painting, the work as a whole is no longer viewed – or perhaps even viewable – as presenting a 'virtual' world that is distinguishable from the real world. What, then, might legitimate the extension of the term 'painting' to this work? The answer lies, I believe, in the sheer painterliness of Grosse's use of colour and her refusal to relinquish the most basic constituent of painting as an art: the transformation of a surface by marking it with colours. It is this that has awakened a sense of wonder in the viewer since the earliest times. Unlike Krauss's perplexed observer in the late 1970s, who stares down at a pit in the earth and realizes that she is no longer certain what sculpture is, we have little difficulty identifying Grosse's large-scale installations as paintings. This is, perhaps, a matter of intuition rather than reasoned argument. However, I would like to essay the tentative conclusion that the fourth component of the definition is not essential to painting or, more persuasively, that it needs to be understood in a different way. Grosse's work possesses the same mysterious alchemy that makes painting so rewarding as an art: mere physical things – whether this be oil on canvas or clouds of atomized acrylic settled on walls, leaves, sand and concrete – are transfigured into something other than themselves, allowing us to see what lies before us as belonging to the world of the mind and not just to the material world.

Notes

1 Philosophical Questions

1 This idea can be traced back to Plato's *Thaetetus* (155d), where Socrates observes that a 'sense of wonder is the mark of the philosopher. Philosophy indeed has no other origin' (Plato 1989: 860).
2 Gombrich (1977). This book is based on Gombrich's A. W. Mellon Lectures in the Fine Arts, which he gave in 1956.
3 See Goodman (1960b) and Goodman (1976): 7 and 10.
4 Gombrich (1977): 7.
5 Lopes (1996): 7. Cf. Lopes's observation: 'In my view, a theory of depiction should take demotic pictures as fundamental, while also providing the basis for an explanation of how pictures can transcend the commonplace and enter the realm of the aesthetic' (1996: 7). He takes up the question of the aesthetic value of pictures in Lopes (2005). The extension of the field of study to include posters, advertising, cartoons, optical illusions and other images from popular culture was pioneered by Gombrich (1977).
6 Lopes (1996): 7.
7 Newman (1990): 247. In an interview with Emile de Antonio given in 1970, Newman observed: 'even if you can build an aesthetic analysis or an aesthetic system that will explain art or painting or whatever it is, it's of no value really, because aesthetics is for me like ornithology must be for the birds' (1990: 304).
8 Newman's two most important essays, 'The First Man Was an Artist' (1947) and 'The Sublime is Now' (1948), were published in *The Tiger's Eye*, a periodical for which Newman was an associate editor. They are reprinted in Harrison and Wood (2003): 575–7 and 580–2.
9 Newman is now identified alongside Jackson Pollock and Mark Rothko as one of the leading figures of Abstract Expressionism, but his work originally met with incomprehension and bafflement, including the charge that it was nothing more than a calculated attempt to shock. For Newman's own uncertainty about the meaning of *Onement I*, see Harrison (2003).
10 Lewis (1982): 100; Kahnweiler (1971): 43.
11 Adorno's *Ästhetische Theorie* was left unfinished at the time of his death in 1969. His most concise statement on the relation of art and philosophy is to be found, somewhat surprisingly, in the section on natural beauty where he discusses the 'aporia of aesthetics as a whole': 'Its object is determined negatively, as indeterminable. It is for this reason that art requires philosophy, which interprets it in order to say what it is unable to say, whereas art is only able to say it by not saying it' (1997: 72).

12 In an interview published in 1946 under the title 'The Great Trouble with Art
   in this Century', Duchamp declared: 'this is the direction art should turn: to
   an intellectual expression, rather than to an animal expression. I am sick of
   the expression "bête comme un peintre" – stupid as a painter' (1989: 126). For
   a discussion of Duchamp's criticisms of merely 'retinal painting', see Gaiger
   (2003).
13 For further discussion of these issues, see Feagin (1995) and Gaiger (2009).
14 The first position is defended by Munro (1967) and the second by Weitz
   (1956).
15 Pliny, *Natural History* 35.43, translated in Pliny (1857) Vol. 6: 283.
16 For a detailed treatment of these issues and a defence of the 'new theory of
   photography', which shifts attention to the 'photographic event' and thus
   allows a greater role for individual agency, see Phillips (2009) and Costello
   (2018).
17 Savedoff (2000) provides a richly informative analysis of the ways in which
   photography 'complicates' painting, and the historically changing relation
   between the two practices in response to technological developments.
18 Podro (1987): 4.

2 A Window onto the World

1 Piles (1993): 14–15. In the original French, de Piles's definition is 'un Art, qui
   par le moyen du dessein & de la couleur, imite sur une superficie plate tous
   les objets visibles'. This essay was originally published as part of a larger work
   entitled *Abregé de la vie des peintres*, Paris, 1699, revised edition 1715.
2 Dickie (1992): 109.
3 Dickie (1992): 109.
4 Pliny, *Natural History* 35.36, translated in Pliny (1857) Vol. 6: 251.
5 Xenephon, *Memorabilia* 3.10.6, translated in Sörbom (1966): 85.
6 The *Greek Anthology* (*Anthologia Graeca*) was compiled by Meleager of
   Gadara in the first century BC and was subsequently added to by other
   scholars. For a selection translated into English, see Jay (1981). The most
   comprehensive collection of primary sources on ancient Greek art is Pollitt
   (1990). See, too, Pollitt (1974). There is renewed art-historical and
   philosophical interest in the idea of 'living presence'. See, for example, Gaiger
   (2011b), Eck, Gastel and Kessel (2014), and Eck (2015).
7 Alberti (1991): 60.
8 Vasari (1987) Vol. 1: 252.
9 Vasari (1987) Vol. 1: 266.
10 Vasari (1987) Vol. 1: 58 and 90.
11 Vasari (1987) Vol. 1: 124.
12 Vasari (1987) Vol. 1: 124–5.
13 Vasari (1987) Vol. 1: 88.

14 Braque, 'Thoughts on Painting' (1917), trans. Edward Fry, in Harrison and Wood (2003): 214.

15 Plato, *Cratylus* 432 b–d, in Plato (1989): 466. For a detailed overview of Plato's theory of art, see Janway (1995), and for a thought-provoking collection of essays, see Denham (2012).

16 Alberti (1991): 35.

17 Alberti (1991): 54. Cf., too, Alberti's comparison of a painting with the reflective surface of water: 'What is painting but the art of embracing by means of art the surface of the pool?' (Alberti 1991: 61).

18 Alberti (1991): 67.

19 Puttfarken claims: 'From the beginning, Alberti's notion of a composition is neither derived from, nor is it concerned with, the picture as an entity, as a structured whole. It is derived from the observation of a single, individual object in nature and the way in which this object is visually made up of its surfaces' (2000: 54). The opposing view is defended by Michael Baxandall, who claims: 'Composition, in the sense of a systematic harmonization of every element in a picture towards one total desired effect, was invented by Alberti in 1435' (1988: 135).

20 Alberti (1991): 67–8.

21 Alberti (1991): 75.

22 Alberti (1991): 75.

23 Plato, *Cratylus* 432 b–d, in Plato (1989): 466.

24 See Sörbom (1966). For a comprehensive discussion of the concept of mimesis, see Halliwell (2002).

25 The classic discussion of the difference between the modern concept of art and the concepts employed in earlier periods is Kristeller (1951) and (1952). For more recent work on the topic, see Mortensen (1997) and Shiner (2001).

26 Plato, *Republic* 595b, in Plato (1989): 820.

27 Plato *Republic* 597b, in Plato (1989): 821.

28 Plato, *Republic* 597e, in Plato (1989): 822.

29 Plato, *Republic* 598b, in Plato (1989): 823.

30 Plato, *Republic* 602b, in Plato (1989): 827.

31 Plato, *Republic* 602c–d, in Plato (1989): 827.

32 Plato, *Republic* 602d, in Plato (1989): 827.

33 Plato, *Republic* 606b, in Plato (1989): 831.

34 Plato, *Republic* 605a–b in Plato (1989): 830.

35 Plato, *Republic* 605b, in Plato (1989): 830.

36 Plato, *Republic* 603b, in Plato (1989): 828.

37 Plato, *Sophist* 268d, in Plato (1989): 1017.

38 Plato, *Sophist* 240a–b, in Plato (1989): 983.

39 Plato, *Sophist*, 235d–236e, in Plato (1989): 978.

40 Plato, *Sophist* 266c, in Plato (1989): 1014.

41 See Ijseeling (1997): 16–21.

42 See Plato, *Statesman* 288c, in Plato (1989): 1056–7.

43 Plato, *Ion* 534b, in Plato (1989): 220. Cf., too, Plato's observation that 'it was not wisdom that enabled [poets] to write poetry, but a kind of instinct or inspiration, such as you find in seers and prophets, who deliver all their sublime messages without knowing in the least what they mean' (*Socrates' Defence (Apology)* 22c, in Plato 1989: 8).

44 Plato, *Symposium* 210–11, in Plato (1989): 561–3. Diotima's words are recounted by Socrates.

45 See Plato, *Republic* 598b, in Plato (1989): 823.

46 Johann Joachim Winckelmann, for example, in his *Reflections on the Imitation of Greek Works in Painting and Sculpture* (1755) claims: 'In the masterpieces of Greek art, connoisseurs and imitators find not only nature at its most beautiful but also something beyond nature, namely certain ideal forms of its beauty, which, as an ancient interpreter of Plato tells us, come from images created by the mind alone' (1987: 6). The ancient interpreter to whom Winckelmann refers is believed to be Plotinus.

47 Reynolds (1997): 44–5. This quotation is taken from the 3rd Discourse, which Reynolds delivered in 1770.

48 Alberti (1991): 91.

49 Alberti (1991): 90.

50 Alberti (1991): 37.

51 Alberti (1991): 38.

52 Alberti (1991): 39–40. These insights form the basis for contemporary resemblance accounts of depiction. Sophisticated versions are defended by Hagen (1986), Hopkins (1998), Hyman (2006) and Abell (2009). For a critical analysis, see Gabriel Greenberg (2013), who argues that although depictions in linear perspective can be characterized in terms of resemblance, other perspective systems such as curvilinear perspective present intractable counterexamples.

3 Surface and Subject

1 This point is made by Budd (1992): 257.

2 Gombrich (1977): x.

3 Plato, *Sophist*, 235d–236e, in Plato (1989): 978.

4 Gombrich (1977): 108. Gombrich is referring to book 10 of Plato's *Republic*, 602c–603c, in Plato (1989): 827–8.

5 Gombrich (1977): 7.

6 Gombrich (1977): 30 and 99.

7 In Michael Podro's succinct formulation, the medium is 'material in use' (Podro 1993: 45).

8 The puzzle of how a static surface can depict movement is addressed in Aasen (2021).

9 Plato, *Cratylus* 432b–d, in Plato (1989): 466.

10 Gombrich (1973): 240.

11 Gombrich (1977): 304. See, too, Gombrich (1973), where he quotes this passage and emphasizes its importance for understanding his claim that 'stimulation can, but need not, rely on the imitation of the trigger' (200).

12 Gombrich cites as an example the research of Aby Warburg, who succeeded in showing that Italian Renaissance artists who 'had previously been regarded as the champions of pure observation ... frequently took recourse to a borrowed formula' and that their borrowings from classical sculpture 'were not haphazard' (1977: 19–20). Compare, too, Gombrich's observation: 'Even Dutch genre paintings that appear to mirror life in all its bustle and variety will turn out to be created from a limited number of types and gestures ... There is no neutral naturalism. The artist, no less than the writer, needs a vocabulary before he can embark on a "copy" of reality' (75).

13 Gombrich (1977): 72.

14 Gombrich (1977): 76.

15 See Gombrich (1977): 123 and Gombrich (1982): 11.

16 Gombrich (1977): 3.

17 Gombrich (1982): 21. See, too, Gombrich (1977): 125.

18 Gombrich (1982): 23. Gombrich makes a similar observation in relation to the development of Greek naturalism: 'as soon as the Greeks looked at the Egyptian figure type from the aspect of an art which wants to "convince", it undoubtedly raised the question why it looks convincing ... it was the Greeks who taught us to ask "*How* does he stand?" or even "Why does he stand like that?"' (1977: 114).

19 Gombrich (1982): 27.

20 Gombrich (1977): 29.

21 Gombrich (1977): 246.

22 Lopes contends that the failure to satisfy what he calls the 'diversity constraint' is sufficient reason to reject Gombrich's illusion theory (Lopes 1996: 39).

23 Gombrich (1973): 180.

24 Gombrich (1977): 233.

25 Goodman (1976): 35.

26 Gombrich (1973): 206.

27 For a sophisticated defence of Gombrich's theory of pictorial perception, see Bantinaki (2007). According to Bantinaki, Gombrich does not deny that 'when one sees what a picture represents the medium can be somehow part of one's visual awareness'. Rather, what his theory excludes 'is the possibility of seeing the picture's design as a *meaningless* design – as *just* marks on a surface – while seeing what the picture represents' (272). I am broadly sympathetic with Bantinaki's approach, which avoids attributing to Gombrich the implausible claim that the viewer has no awareness of the medium, and would thus be unaware that she is looking at an engraving, say, rather than an oil painting. However, even on this modified interpretation, Gombrich's theory of pictorial perception does not allow for what has come

to be termed 'inflected pictorial experience': those cases in which the viewer's awareness of the materiality of the medium enters into and transforms her awareness of the depicted subject. For a detailed discussion of 'inflection', see Hopkins (2010) and Nanay (2010).

28 Wittgenstein (1958): 193. Wittgenstein's account of seeing aspects and the various ways in which this has been taken up by later philosophers is addressed in Kemp and Mras (2016).

29 Budd argues: 'The independent philosophical importance of the concept of noticing an aspect is due to its location at a crucial point in our concept of mind ... this point ... is the juncture of the sensory and the intellectual' (1987: 1–2).

30 Wittgenstein (1958): 193.

31 Gombrich (1977): 198.

32 'The Beholder's Share' is the title of Part Three of *Art and Illusion*. See Gombrich (1977): 153–244.

33 Gombrich (1977): 198.

34 Gombrich (1977): 5.

35 Clark (1960): 36–7.

36 Gombrich (1977): 211.

37 See Wollheim, (1973): 277–80; Podro (1993): 44–6; Budd (1992): 263–4; and Lopes (1996): 41.

38 Gombrich (1977): 24.

39 This argument is made in Wollheim (1973): 279–80.

40 Adorno (1997): 101.

41 *Las Meniñas* has given rise to a rich philosophical debate. See, for example, chapter 1 of Foucault (1994) and Searle (1980).

42 Wollheim (1987): 21. 'On Drawing an Object' is reprinted in Wollheim (1973): 3–30; see especially 27–30. For a valuable collection of responses to Wollheim's work, see Gerwen (2001), together with Wollheim's 'A Reply to the Contributors' in the same volume (Wollheim 2001).

43 Wollheim (1980): 217.

44 Wollheim (1980): 15.

45 Wollheim (1987): 21.

46 Wollheim (1987): 62. Wollheim claims that some abstract paintings, such as Barnett Newman's *Vir Heroicus Sublimis* (1950–1, Museum of Modern Art, New York), cancel out this effect and hence are non-representational. I return to this issue in the final section of this chapter.

47 Wollheim (1987): 46.

48 Wollheim (1987): 48. Gombrich pursues similar historical speculations in Gombrich (1977): 91.

49 Wollheim (1987): 48.

50 Wollheim (1987): 48. See, too, Wollheim (1980): 205.

51 Wollheim (1987): 22.

52 Podro (2004): 217. For criticism of Wollheim's claim that there is a 'standard of correctness' for each painting that is set by the intentions of the artist, see Hyman (2006): 136–9.

53 Wollheim (1987): 46.

54 Wollheim's review, 'Reflections on *Art and Illusion*', is reprinted in Wollheim (1973): 261–89; this citation, 277.

55 Wollheim (1980): 216.

56 For a wide-ranging collection of responses to this issue, see Pelletier and Voltolini (2019).

57 This position is defended by Budd, who argues: 'An alternation in the spectator's visual attention would seem to be sufficient for the recognition of and consequent admiration for the artist's artistry' (1992: 267). According to Budd, since it is possible to admire the 'how' of representation by alternating between surface and subject, aesthetic appreciation cannot be used to show that twofoldness is essential to pictorial experience.

58 Lopes (1996): 48.

59 Levinson (1998): 228–9.

60 See Nanay (2005): 249.

61 Wollheim (1980): 213.

62 Wollheim (1980): 218.

63 See Wollheim (1980): 217 and Gombrich (1997): 24–5.

64 Wollheim (1987): 62.

65 Lopes, for example, argues that 'the existence of *trompe l'oeil* pictures – pictures, experience of which are experiences of their subjects, but which typically preclude experiences of their design properties – is incompatible not only with strong twofoldness but also with the hope that pictures always have a distinctive phenomenology' (1996: 49).

66 Lopes (1996): 50.

67 Lopes (1996): 50. Cf., too, Lopes's claim: 'In truth, experiences of pictures may or may not be twofold. They can be arranged along a spectrum, with twofoldness at one pole and illusionism at the other' (1996: 76). Those who follow Lopes on this issue have sought to develop a taxonomy of different types of depiction, thereby abandoning the attempt to provide a unified theory in favour of a pluralist approach. See Cavedon-Taylor (2011) and Bradley (2014).

68 Hyman (2006): 132. Susan Feagin usefully distinguishes between those forms of *trompe l'oeil* in which something is 'presented as being' something else, such as painted surfaces in churches and palaces that are made to look like marble pilasters and columns – which she terms 'presentations' – and examples of *trompe l'oeil* painting, such as the work of Leroy de Barde, that are 'pictorial representations'. Feagin notes that these two forms of *trompe l'oeil* can even coexist within one and the same work and that 'not only paintings but *portions* of paintings may function repesentationally and presentationally' (1998: 238). See, too, Bantinaki (2010): 144–6.

69 Goodman (1976): 35.

70 See Lopes (1996): 3.

71 Kandinsky (1982): 197. Kandinsky's *Über das Geistige in der Kunst* [On the Spirtual in Art] was first published in late 1911.

72 Nanay (2010): 185–6, my emphases added.
73 Nanay (2010): 190.
74 I borrow the term 'thread of recognition' from Podro (1998): vi. See, too, Podro (1987) and Podro (1993) for an analysis of the interdependence of the viewer's awareness of surface and subject and the various ways in which the drawn line or paint surface can be 'recruited' in the service of the subject. Hopkins takes Podro's account to be controversial and offers a cautious defence of inflected pictorial experience in Hopkins (2010).

4 Resemblance and Denotation

1 Kahnweiler (1971): 57. Originally published as *Mes galeries et mes peintres. Entretiens avec Francis Crémieux* in 1961.
2 See Cox (2000): 43.
3 Bois (1987): 40. The recent interest in Kahnweiler's interpretation of Cubism is largely due to Bois's reconstruction of his views. I discuss Bois's position in more detail below.
4 Plato, *Cratylus* 383a– 384d, in Plato (1989): 422.
5 The first three books of Augustine's treatise *De Doctrina Christiana* [On Christian Doctrine] were published in AD 397. At the start of the second book, where the discussion of natural and conventional signs is to be found, he is primarily concerned with problems of biblical hermeneutics – that is to say, with the interpretation of scripture.
6 Augustine, *De Doctrina Christiana* 2.1, in Augustine (1971): 636.
7 Augustine, *De Doctrina Christiana* 2.2, in Augustine (1971): 637.
8 Peirce developed his theory of signs over a period stretching from 1866 through to his death in 1914, frequently modifiying and revising his ideas. For a helpful overview, see Short (2004).
9 Peirce (1955): 102.
10 Peirce (1955): 105. According to Peirce, 'it is a familiar fact that there are such representations as icons. Every picture (however conventional its method) is essentially a representation of that kind. So is every diagram, even though there be no sensuous resemblance between it and its object, but only an analogy between the relation of parts of each' (1955: 105).
11 Peirce (1955): 102.
12 Peirce (1955): 102.
13 Peirce (1955): 112.
14 Peirce (1955): 114.
15 Bryson (1991): 65.
16 Bryson (1991): 65.
17 Krauss, (1992): 273. For criticism of the semiotic approach to Cubism as 'cryptoformalism', see Leighten (1994).
18 Bryson (1991): 62.

19 See Goodman and Elgin (1988): 4.

20 Hyman (2006): 164. Hyman claims that *Languages of Art* 'contains the only serious attempt to explain precisely what system of conventions a general theory of depiction must postulate, if it is committed to these popular ideas' (2006: 164).

21 Goodman (1976): xii.

22 Goodman (1976): 231.

23 Goodman (1976): 3–4.

24 Goodman (1976): 5.

25 Lopes (1996): 57.

26 Budd (1993): 156.

27 See Goodman's essay 'Representation Re-Presented' in Goodman and Elgin (1988): 121–31. For Goodman's identification of the resemblance theory as a 'dogma', see Goodman and Elgin (1988): 121.

28 For an analysis of the different 'routes of reference', see Goodman (1984): 55–71.

29 I do not discuss Goodman's theory of fictional representational. Goodman holds that pictures that represent fictional objects, such as a unicorn, have 'null denotation'. To avoid hypostatizing a realm of non-existent objects, he employs the one-place predicate 'unicorn-picture' rather than the usual 'picture of a unicorn'. Pictures that have a generic subject – and thus do not represent a particular person, thing or scene – have multiple denotation. See Goodman (1976): 21–6.

30 Goodman (1976): xi.

31 Goodman (1976): 156.

32 Goodman (1976): 143.

33 Goodman and Elgin (1988): 125; see, too, Goodman (1976): 135–7. Goodman specifies the requirement of finite differentiation as follows: 'For every two characters K and K' and every mark m that does not actually belong to both, determination either that m does not belong to K or that m does not belong to K' is theoretically possible' (1976: 135–6).

34 Goodman (1976): 152.

35 A pitch intermediate between two semitones can of course be produced on a non-keyed instrument such as a violin or through the human voice. But since the system for denoting pitch in Western music is syntactically and semantically disjoint and differentiated it allows only for determinate pitches. A different system – such as that developed by some twentieth-century composers – is needed to denote pitches intermediate between half-tone intervals.

36 Goodman (1976): 185.

37 Goodman (1976): 231.

38 Goodman (1976): 35.

39 Goodman (1976): 226.

40 Goodman (1976): 230.

41 Goodman (1976); 228. Goodman's structuralist account of depiction has been taken up and developed by John Kulvicki, who has identified a further structural feature, which he terms 'transparency'. See Kulvicki (2006) and Kulvicki (2014).

42 Goodman (1976): 47. See, too, Goodman and Elgin (1988), where Goodman claims: 'The terms "convention" and "conventional" are flagrantly and intricately ambiguous. On the one hand, the conventional is the ordinary, the usual, the traditional, the orthodox as against the novel, the deviant, the unexpected, the heterodox. On the other hand, the conventional is the artificial, the invented, the optional, as against the natural, the fundamental, the mandatory' (1988: 93).

43 Goodman (1976): 5.

44 Goodman notes: 'Labelling seems to be free in a way that exemplification is not. I can let anything denote red things, but I cannot let anything be a sample of redness' (1976: 8–9). Examples of reference through exemplification include using a tailor's swatch to refer to certain properties of a fabric such as its colour, texture and pattern (but not, for example, its size), and a chip of paint on a sample card to refer to a specific colour. According to Goodman, 'The swatch exemplifies only those properties that it both has and refers to' (1976: 53). By contrast, denotational reference does not require that the sign possesses or instantiates the properties to which it refers. For an ingenious attempt to rectify Goodman's theory by showing that pictures combine these two forms of reference, see Arrell (1987).

45 The anecdote is recounted in Gulyga (1985): 73.

46 Peirce (1995): 112.

47 See Goodman (1976): 41.

48 Goodman (1976): 38.

49 Danto (1981): 72–3.

50 Goodman (1976): 231.

51 Goodman (1976): 41–2.

52 Goodman (1976): 252.

53 Goodman (1976): 252–3. Goodman characterizes syntactic and semantic density and relative repleteness as 'symptoms of the aesthetic' rather than as criteria for identifying aesthetic experience: 'A symptom is neither a necessary nor a sufficient condition for, but merely tends in conjunction with other such symptoms to be present in, aesthetic experience' (1976: 252).

54 Hyman (2006): 161 and 167.

55 Goodman and Elgin (1988): 110. An important exception is Dominic Lopes, who observes: 'Goodman's symbol theory is not a convention theory of depiction. Conventions are rules, and Goodman is sceptical about pictorial practices (or any symbolic practices) being rule-governed. What is habitual resists codification' (1996: 65). See, too, Lopes (2000). I discuss Lopes's views below.

56 Goodman (1984): 57.

57 Goodman (1984): 10.

58 Lopes (2000): 227. Cf. Goodman's observation: 'Routes of reference are quite distinct from roots of reference. I am concerned here with the various relationships that may obtain between a term or other sign or symbol and what it refers to, not with how such relationships are established' (1984: 55).

59 Goodman (1975): 43.

60 Lopes (2000). Cf., too, his observation: 'Nothing in the symbol model rules out pictures being correlated with, and standing for, their subjects because they resemble them or provide for illusionistic experiences of them or enable us to see things in them ... A theory of depiction may, without inconsistency, explain pictures as both symbolic and perceptual' (1996: 57).

61 Goodman and Elgin (1988): 115.

62 Goodman and Elgin (1988): 112. In his essay 'Seven Strictures on Similarity', Goodman points out that 'any two things have exactly as many properties in common as any other two' and that 'comparative judgments of similarity often require not merely a selection of relevant properties but a weighting of their relative importance' (1972: 443 and 445). Thus, for example, determining which two pieces of baggage at an airport are alike 'depends not only on what properties they share, but upon who makes the comparison, and when' (445). A spectator might select: size, shape, colour, material, etc.; a passenger: destination and ownership; and the ground crew: weight. Goodman concludes that 'similarity is relative and variable, as undependable as indispensable. Clear enough when closely defined by context and circumstance in ordinary discourse, it is hopelessly ambiguous when torn lose' (444).

63 Goodman (1960a): 52.

64 Goodman (1976): 10.

65 Useful overviews are provided by Valberg (2005), Kowler (2011) and Carrasco (2011); current research is published in journals such as *Visual Cognition* and *Vision Research*. For accounts of depiction that are informed by recent work in vision science, see, for example, Briscoe (2016) and Nanay (2013).

66 Gombrich (1977): 78.

67 For a conventionalist interpretation of Gombrich's early writings – and the accusation that he subsequently went back on his own insights – see Krieger (1984). See, too, Gombrich's reply, in Gombrich (1984).

68 Key passages are to be found in Gombrich (1977): x–xi, 77–8, 121, 211–17 and 252. As well as the reply to Krieger cited above, Gombrich explicitly distinguishes his position from conventionalism in 'Standards of Truth: The Arrested Image and the Moving Eye' and 'Image and Code: Scope and Limits of Conventionalism in Pictorial Representation', both reprinted in Gombrich (1982). For clarification of Gombrich's position and his criticisms of what he takes to be Goodman's conventionalism, see Gombrich (1972).

69 Gombrich contends: 'Perspective is the necessary tool, if you want to adopt what I now like to call the "eye-witness principle", in other words, if you want

to map precisely what anyone could see from a given point, or, for that
matter, what the camera could record' (1982: 281).
70 Gombrich (1977): 33–4.
71 Gombrich (1982): 271. Gombrich's subjectivist starting point does not rule
out the identification of objective properties such as outline shape, occlusion,
and gradation from light to shade that can be observed in the motif and
deployed by the artist. However, since there is never a one-to-one
correspondence between the marks on the canvas and what they stand for or
represent, these features must be compressed, accommodated and recast
within the medium of representation. Gombrich insists even a photograph 'is
not a replica of what is seen but a transformation which has to be re-
translated to yield up the required information' (1982: 282). For a
sophisticated defence of objectivism that acknowledges that 'the basic
principles of pictorial art reveal how exiguous the relationship between the
marks on a picture's surface and the kinds of objects they depict can be', see
Hyman (2006): 141.
72 I take the term 'object-presenting experiences' from Lopes (2000). It usefully
avoids many of the problems that beset Gombrich's illusion theory of
representation. As Lopes observes, to have an object-presenting experience is
to see in a picture the scene it represents, but 'such an experience need not
and usually will not dispose one to believe one is seeing the scene
represented' (231).
73 Goodman maintains: 'Realism is relative, determined by the system of
representation standard for a given culture or person at a given time'
(1976: 37).
74 Gombrich (1982): 19.
75 Goodman (1976): 3.
76 Goodman (1978): 102.
77 Goodman (1984): 5 and 6.
78 Cf. Goodman's observation: 'Practice palls; and a new mode of representation
may be so fresh and forceful as to achieve what amounts to a revelation'
(1984: 127).
79 Apollinaire, *The Cubist Painters*, trans. Edward Fry, in Harrison and Wood
(2003): 189.
80 Rivière, 'Present Tendencies in Painting', trans. Edward Fry, in Harrison and
Wood (2003): 190.
81 The 'higher truth' revealed by Cubism was generally taken to be the object's
essence or form, but it was also identified with the notion of a fourth
dimension and even X-ray photography. For a good discussion of these
various theories, see Antliff and Leighten (2001), especially chapter 2,
'Philosophies of Time and Space'.
82 Kahnweiler (1949), unpaginated.
83 Kahnweiler (1949), unpaginated. Picasso is reported by Leo Stein as saying:
'A head ... was a matter of eyes, nose, mouth, which could be distributed in
any way you like – the head remained the head.' Cited in Bois (1987): 90.

84 The term 'Analytic Cubism' is used to describe the period from c. 1908 to 1912, when Braque and Picasso sought to 'analyse' the object through multiple viewpoints and overlapping planes, using a reduced palette of colours, while the term 'Synthetic Cubism' is used to describe the period from c. 1912 to 1914, characterized by the introduction of pasted papers, textured surfaces and brighter colours. See Cox (2000): 145–6.

85 See, for example, Picasso, *Guitar, Sheet Music and Glass* (1912, McNay Art Museum, San Antonio), which combines a cutting from a newspaper containing the words 'Le Jou' and 'La bataille c'est engagé' with sheet music, *faux bois*, coloured paper and a schematic charcoal drawing of a glass.

86 Bois (1987): 40 and 52.

87 Krauss (1998): 27. Krauss first presented her interpretation of *Violin* in Krauss (1992).

88 Krauss (1998): 27–8.

89 Krauss (1998): 28.

90 Krauss (1992): 264.

91 Braque employed this device in two paintings: *Violin and Palette* (1909, Guggenheim Museum, New York) and *Violin and Pitcher* (1910, Öffentliche Kunstsammlung Basel).

92 Greenberg (1993b): 62.

93 Bois derives the term 'relative motivation' from Saussure in order to correct 'the vulgar notion of the arbitrariness of the sign, which often simply remains the conventionalist view'. He acknowledges that Picasso reduced his 'plastic system' to a 'handful of signs, none referring univocally to a referent' but he points out that 'the "system of values" governing Picasso's art . . . remained figurative' (1987: 53).

5 The Specifically Visual

1 Alberti (1972): 99.

2 See Lopes (1996): 3.

3 Wollheim (1987): 73.

4 See Podro (1993): 47, and Podro (1998): 6–17.

5 Goodman (1976): 252–3.

6 Goodman (1960a): 53. Goodman distinguishes his position – the view that 'there are many ways the world is, and every true description captures one of them' – from the position of the mystic or the obscurantist, who believes that 'there is some way the world is and that this way is not captured by any description' (1960a: 55)

7 The concept of style is conspicuously absent from *Languages of Art*. Goodman takes up the topic in a later essay, 'The Status of Style', first published in 1975, and reprinted as chapter 2 of *Ways of Worldmaking* (1978: 23–40). A central theme of this book is that acknowledgment of the plurality

of worlds does not imply that 'all right alternatives are equally good for every
or indeed for any purpose' (21).

8   See Sauerländer (1983): 254.

9   In his *Institutiones Oratoriae* 12.10, published c. AD 95, Quintilian draws a
parallel between various forms of oratory and the stylistic strengths of
specific painters and sculptors, including Zeuxis and Parrhasius (who are
praised for their attention to light and shadow and the treatment of line).

10 Gombrich (1977): 3.

11 Winckelmann (2006).

12 Hegel (1975): 14. For a detailed discussion of these issues, see Gaiger
(2011a).

13 See Gombrich (1979): 24–59, this citation 28.

14 Gombrich (1966): 81. I address Gombrich's argument at the end of this
chapter.

15 Wölfflin (1996): 231. Wölfflin's book *Klassische Kunst* [Classic Art] was first
published in 1899.

16 The term 'Romanesque', for example, was coined in the early nineteenth
century to describe pre-Gothic Western European art and architecture that
revealed a knowledge of classical Roman buildings and monuments.

17 Alpers (1987): 139.

18 Ackermann (1962): 232. See, too, Schapiro (1994): 51–102 and the essays
collected in Gombrich (1979).

19 Ackermann (1962): 228.

20 Alpers (1987): 137.

21 Wollheim (1987): 9. Wollheim goes on to observe that 'given the small
progress that art history has made in explaining the visual arts, I am inclined
to think that the belief that there is such a feature is itself something that
needs historical explanation: it is an historical accident' (1987: 9).

22 Wollheim first presented his ideas on style in the Power Lecture at the
University of Sydney in 1972. His two major articles on the subject are
Wollheim (1979) and Wollheim (1995). He also discusses pictorial style in
Wollheim (1987): 25–36.

23 Wollheim (1979): 189.

24 Wollheim (1979): 199–200.

25 Wollheim (1995): 38.

26 Wollheim (1979): 194.

27 Wollheim (1987): 27.

28 Wollheim (1995): 46–7.

29 Wollheim (1995): 38.

30 See Alpers (1987): 137.

31 Wollheim (1979): 190.

32 See Wollheim (1987): 26, and Wollheim (1995): 47–8.

33 James D. Carney has argued that art historians 'follow what W. V. Quine has
called the principle of minimum mutilation. They begin with a provisional
set of beliefs, those held by the highly regarded historians and other

individuals, though they anticipate augmentations and revisions in light of good reasons' (1991: 15).

34 Wollheim (1979): 195.

35 Goodman (1978): 38. See, too, Goodman (1976): 99–112.

36 I am referring, of course, to Leonardo's fresco *The Last Supper* of c. 1495–7, in the Refectory of S. Maria delle Grazie, Milan. Giotto's fresco of the same subject in the Scrovegni Chapel dates from c. 1305. Leonardo's composition allows the viewer to see the faces and gestures of all the figures, but it would be a highly unusual dinner that seated the guests in this way: the composition is clearly arranged for the benefit of the spectator.

37 Panofsky (1993): 59. For an excellent discussion of Panofsky's argument, see Robinson (1981). Robinson concludes that 'if we cannot link a painting to other paintings in history, then neither the art critic nor the art historian can decipher it' (1981: 14).

38 Panofsky (1993): 59–60.

39 Wölfflin (1950): vii.

40 Wölfflin maintained an extensive correspondence with Burckhardt (see Gantner 1948), and succeeded to Burckhardt's chair in Basel in 1893. In a lecture delivered in 1930, he acknowledged that his own ideas had, to a certain extent, been anticipated by the older historian: 'one can find evidence in several places for his view that art history is never simply co-extensive with cultural history, but follows its own laws, which we must try to formulate exactly' (1941: 154).

41 Burckhardt (1995). For an analysis of the Hegelian elements of Burckhardt's theory of history, see Gombrich (1979).

42 The term 'inner development' is taken from a later essay, '*Über Formentwicklung*' [On the Development of Form], published in 1941, which offers a concise summary of Wöllflin's views: 'There is in art an inner development of form. No matter how valuable it may be to relate the never-ceasing changes of form to the changing conditions of the artist's environment, and no matter how indispensable the character of the artist and the intellectual and social structure of the age may be to explaining the physiognomy of the artwork, it should not be overlooked that art, or rather the formative imagination (*bildnerische Formphantasie*) in its most general possibilities possesses a life and development of its own' (8).

43 Wölfflin (1950): 9.

44 Wölfflin (1950): 13; translation modified.

45 Wölfflin (1950): 12.

46 Wölfflin (1950): 12.

47 Wölfflin (1915): v. In a defence of his position, 'In eigener Sache', published in the journal *Kunstchronik* in 1920, Wölfflin sought to clarify his approach as follows: 'What I offer is not a new art history that is intended to take the place of the old: it is merely an attempt to look at the subject from a different perspective in order to discover guidelines for the writing of history that can guarantee a degree of certainty' (1941: 16).

48 Wölfflin (1950): 17 and 231–3.
49 For discussion of Riegl's work, see Podro (1982) and Iverson (1993).
50 See Eckl (1993) and (1996), and Wiesing (1997).
51 See Wölfflin (1950): 227. I discuss Wölfflin's indebtedness to a broadly Kantian account of the mind in the final section of this chapter.
52 Eckl (1993): 31.
53 Wiesing (1997): 44. Wiesing identifies Johann Friedrich Herbart, Robert Zimmerman and Konrad Fiedler as the key figures in the tradition of formalist aesthetics, alongside art historians such as Wölfflin and Riegl.
54 Wiesing (1997): 66.
55 Wiesing (1997): 66.
56 Wiesing (1997): 83.
57 Wölfflin (1950): 21.
58 Wölfflin (1950): 18.
59 I focus here exclusively on the formal differences between these two celebrated self-portraits. For a philosophical discussion of the art of portraiture that examines the conflict between 'the *revelatory* aim of faithfulness to the subject, and the *creative* aim of artistic expression' with specific reference to Rembrandt, see Freeland (2007). For a wide-ranging collection of essays that gathers recent philosophical thought on portaiture, see Maes (2020), and for a searching analysis of the expression of emotion in art, see Robinson (2005) and Robinson (2017).
60 Wölfflin (1950): 124.
61 Wölfflin (1950): 124.
62 Wölfflin (1950): 126.
63 Wölfflin (1950): 198.
64 Wölfflin (1950): 97–8. See, too, Puttfarken (2000): 30–1.
65 Wölfflin (1950): 208.
66 Eckl (1993): 42.
67 Wiesing (1997): 65.
68 This observation was made by Edgar Wind back in 1925: 'the purely optical, deprived of everything haptic, i.e., of all formal limits, would be as amorphous as mere light', while 'the purely haptic, deprived of all optical determination, would be completely abstract, a geometric figure' (449). See, too, Panofsky (1964): 52.
69 Wiesing (1997): 97.
70 Wiesing (1997): 98.
71 Wiesing (1997): 95–6 and 97.
72 Wollheim (1995): 46 and Wollheim (1987): 26.
73 Wölfflin (1950): 30. Wölfflin goes on to observe: 'Grünewald is certainly more painterly than Dürer, but beside Rembrandt he is recognisable as an artist of the sixteenth century, that is to say, a man of the silhouette' (30).
74 See Gombrich (1966).
75 The final section of this chapter reworks material originally presented in Gaiger (2015).

76 Wölfflin (1950): 13 and 11.
77 Wölfflin (1950): 16.
78 Wölfflin (1950): 11 (translation modified).
79 Wölfflin (1991): 277.
80 See, for example, Wölfflin (1950): vii, 16 and 226.
81 Hyman (2006): 161.
82 See Gregory (2013).
83 Wölfflin (1950): 11.
84 Wölfflin (1915): v. This foreword was omitted from later editions of the book. Wölfflin was later forced to concede that the theme of 'a universal history of vision and representation (a history of form)' had ramified in different directions and that he was unable to give it definitive shape. See the foreword to the 8th edition, published in 1943 (Wölfflin 1991: 7).
85 Wölfflin (1915): v.
86 Kant (1998): 136 [B1]. The quotation is from the Introduction to the second edition, published in 1787.
87 Fiedler (1991). Fiedler's *Über den Ursprung der künstlerischen Tätigkeit* [On the Origins of Artistic Activity] was originally published in 1887. For his account of the 'process of seeing' (*Sehprozess*), see Fiedler (1991): 176.
88 Wölfflin (1950): 226.
89 Wölfflin (1950): 226.
90 See Kant (1998): 398–9 [A319–20/B376–7].
91 Wölfflin (1950): vii.
92 See Kant (1998): 398 [A320/B376].
93 See Cassirer (2020). Cassirer's *Philosophie der symbolischen Formen* [The Philosophy of Symbolic Forms] was originally published in three volumes between 1923 and 1929.
94 Wölfflin (1950): 227.
95 A promising starting point is to be found in Robert Hanna's observation: 'Kant's explicatively useful contrast between the spontaneous conceptual functions of the understanding and the receptive perceptual functions of sensibility has one quite misleading apparent implication ... It seems to suggest that sensibility is wholly passive or non-generative and non-productive. But sensory receptivity is in no way a representational *inertness* ...' (2001: 36).
96 Wölfflin (1950): 16.
97 Wölfflin (1950): 18.
98 Wölfflin (1950): 9.
99 Wölfflin (1950): 45–6. The Infanta Margarita wears the same white and silver dress in the portrait as in *Las Meninas* (Plates 6 and 7), and both were painted in the same year.
100 Wölfflin (1950): 46.
101 For a presentation of this view, see Nanay (2012). Nanay also develops his argument with reference to Wölfflin's discussion of Bronzino and Velásquez. See, too, Nanay (2015).

102 Wölfflin (1950): 18.

103 See Danto (2001) and Carroll (2001) These two essays form part of a symposium in *Journal of Aesthetics and Art Criticism* on 'The Historicity of the Eye'.

104 With reference to Huttenlocher (2002), Nanay argues: 'Recent findings about the neural plasticitity of the brain in general and of our perceptual processes in particular show that while much of the way our perceptual processes function is in fact determined by evolution, there is a lot of room for adjustments and changes that are part of our developmental processes' (2015: 261).

105 Wölfflin (1950): 27.

106 Wölfflin (1950): 27 (translation modified).

107 Wölfflin (1950): 28.

108 Wölfflin (1950): 231. In the German original the claim is even more specific: 'Darum ist die Geschichte der Malerei nicht nur nebenbei, sondern ganz wesentlich auch eine Geschichte der Dekoration' (1991: 268).

109 Matisse (2003): 70.

110 See Wölfflin (1888), especially chapter 1, 'Der Malerische Stil' [The Painterly Style].

111 Wölfflin (1950): 28.

112 Wölfflin (1950): 146.

113 Wölfflin (1950): 125.

114 Wölfflin (1950): 134.

115 Wölfflin (1950): 134.

116 Wölfflin (1950): 16.

117 Gombrich (1966): 92.

118 Gombrich (1966): 83.

119 Gombrich (1966): 95–6.

120 Wölfflin (1950): 18.

121 Wölfflin (1950): 28.

122 Wölfflin (1950): 29.

123 Cf. Goodman (1960a): 53.

124 In *Ways of Worldmaking*, Goodman acknowledges that many of the themes he addresses in the book – 'the multiplicity of worlds, the speciousness of "the given", the creative power of the understanding, the variety and formative function of symbols' – are already to be found in the writings of Ernst Cassirer. See Goodman (1978): 1.

6 Modernism and the Avant-Garde

1 Variants of formalism in relation to other arts, especially music, were developed earlier. For a discussion of these issues, see Hamilton (2007).

2 The catalogue to the first Post-Impressionist Exhibition was written by Desmond McCarthy, based on notes by Roger Fry. See Falkenheim (1980): 16.

3 Fry (1937): 195.
4 See Falkenheim (1980): 15–32.
5 Bell (1987): 7.
6 Bell (1987): 8.
7 Bell (1987): 18.
8 Bell (1987): 26.
9 Fry (1937): 238.
10 Fry (1937): 241. The book gathers a selection of Fry's essays published over the previous two decades.
11 Fry (1937): 241.
12 Fry (1937): 241–2.
13 Fry (1937): 241. Fry's position seems to have gradually hardened into formalism. This can be seen from the note that he added to his 'Giotto: The Church of S. Francesco at Assisi' when he included it in *Vision and Design*. Fry observes that whereas when he wrote the essay in 1901 he had assumed that 'the value of the form for us is bound up with recognition of the dramatic idea', he now believes that it is possible 'by a more searching analysis of our experience in front of a work of art to disentangle our reaction to pure form from our reaction to its implied associated ideas' (Fry 1937: 112).
14 Denis's essay on Cézanne was originally published in 1907 in *L'Occident*. Fry's translation, together with his 'Introductory Note', is reprinted in Harrison and Wood (2003): 39–46. Twenty-one paintings by Cézanne were included in the first Post-Impressionist Exhibition.
15 Fry, 'Introductory Note', in Harrison and Wood (2003): 40.
16 Bell (1922): 11.
17 Fry (1927): 78.
18 Fry (1937): 19.
19 Bell (1987): 44 and Fry (1937): 234. Bell devotes a section of *Art* to 'The Classical Renaissance and its Diseases' (Bell 1987: 156–80).
20 Bell (1987): 44. Bell contends: 'A good Post-Impressionist picture is good for precisely the same reasons that any other picture is good. The essential quality is permanent' (1987: 41).
21 Wölfflin's *Principles of Art History* was not published until 1915, but Fry was familiar with his earlier writings, including *Classic Art* (1899). He reviewed the fourth German edition of *Principles of Art History* for the *Burlington Magazine* in 1921. For a discussion of Fry's indebtedness to the ideas of Wölfflin and other German art historians, see Falkenheim (1980) and Maginnis (1996).
22 Puttfarken rightly observes that in his descriptions of individual paintings Wölfflin 'fully acknowledged the interaction of formal arrangement and narrative meaning' (2000: 45). See, too, Wollheim (1995): 45.
23 See Wölfflin (1950): 18 and 28.
24 This point is made by Krukowski (1998): 215–16.
25 See Budd (1995): 54–5.

26 Wölfflin (1950): 211. Compare Budd's observation: 'Formalism neglects depicted movement, depicted force and resistance, depicted energy and lassitude, and other features that are obviously relevant to a picture's unity, balance, harmoniousness, or impressive organisation' (1995: 56).

27 Cézanne, letter to Emile Bernard, 15 April 1904, translated by J. Rewald in Harrison and Wood (2003): 33.

28 Cf., for example, Cézanne's observation, recorded by the poet Léo Larguier: 'Painting does not mean slavishly copying an object. The artist must perceive and capture harmony from among many relationships. He must transpose them in a scale of his own invention while he develops them according to a new and original logic' (Doran 2001: 18).

29 Budd (1995): 50.

30 Zangwill (2001): 55.

31 Zangwill (2001): 58–9. Zangwill develops his account of moderate formalism by drawing on Kant's distinction between free and adherent beauty in the *Critique of Judgment* (§16). See Kant (2000): 114–16.

32 Bell (1987): 27.

33 Zangwill (2001): 66.

34 Fry (1937): 244.

35 Bell (1987): 44.

36 Fry (1937): 195–6. Fry observes that artists who pursue full abstraction 'may or may not be successful in their attempt. It is too early to be dogmatic on the point, which can only be decided when our sensibilities to abstract forms have been more practiced than they are at present' (Fry 1937: 196).

37 Bell (1987): xv.

38 See, for example, Hyman (2006): 110 and 206–7. Budd (1995) does not discuss Greenberg. An exception is Zangwill (2001): 66, and, more recently, Newall (2011), who offers a careful analysis of Greenberg's position but focuses quite narrowly on his later writings.

39 Greenberg (1986a): 7. For an analysis of Greenberg's ideas in relation to Kant, see Gaiger (1999).

40 The quotation is from Walter Benjamin's 'Theses on the Philosophy of History' (1940) as cited in Gibson (1996): 205.

41 Relevant sections from Saint-Simon's *Opinions Littéraires* of 1825, are translated by Jonathan Murphy in Harrison, Wood and Gaiger (1998): 37–41.

42 Greenberg (1986a): 7.

43 Greenberg (1986a): 6.

44 Greenberg (1986a): 6.

45 Greenberg (1986a): 8.

46 Greenberg (1986a): 8–9.

47 Greenberg (1986a): 37.

48 See Lessing (1984). For a discussion of the twentieth-century reception of Lessing's ideas, see Gaiger (2013a).

49   Greenberg (1986a): 26.

50 Greenberg (1986a): 27.

51 Greenberg (1986a): 27 and 29.

52 Greenberg (1986a): 23.

53 Greenberg (1993b): 86.

54 Greenberg (1993b): 86. Greenberg contends that 'the essence of Modernism lies ... in the use of characteristic methods of a discipline to criticize the discipline itself, not in order to subvert it but to entrench it more firmly in its area of competence' (1993b: 85).

55 Greenberg (1993b): 87.

56 Greenberg (1993b): 86.

57 Greenberg (1993a): 84. Greenberg argues that even though Cézanne was 'committted ... to the motif in nature, he still felt that it could not of its own accord provide a sufficient basis of pictorial unity; that had to be read into it by a combination of thought and feeling – thought that was not a matter of extra-pictorial rules, but of consistency, and feeling that was not a matter of sentiment, but of sensation' (1993a: 84–5).

58 Greenberg (1993a): 85–6.

59 Greenberg (1993a): 87.

60 Greenberg (1993a): 89.

61 Greenberg (1986a): 34.

62 Greenberg (1986b): 260.

63 Greenberg (1986b): 261.

64 Greenberg (1993b): 63.

65 Budd (1995): 51. Bell contends: 'Pictures which would be insignificant if we saw them as flat patterns are profoundly moving because, in fact, we see them as related planes' (1987: 27), while Fry holds: 'It is doubtful whether a purely flat surface, without suggestions of significant value, can arouse any profound emotion' (1926: 26).

66 Budd (1995): 51.

67 Budd (1995): 58.

68 Greenberg (1993b): 90.

69 Greenberg contends that even for Mondrian 'the result of the marks made on [the canvas] is still a kind of illusion that suggests a kind of third dimension. Only now it is a strictly pictorial, stricly optical third dimension' (1993b: 90).

70 Greenberg (1986a): 203.

71 Greenberg (1993a): 189 and (1993b): 87.

72 Greenberg (1986a): 204. According to Greenberg, the real achievement of the avant-garde therefore lies not in the 'deliverance of painting from representation' but in its 'recapture of the literal realization of the physical limitations and conditions of the medium and the positive advantages to be gained from the exploitation of those limitations' (1986b: 5).

73 Greenberg (1986b): 166.

74 Greenberg (1986b): 166.

75 Greenberg (1986b): 75.

76 Pollock's remark is cited in Wood (2003): 164. Rosenberg's interpretation of abstract painting was first developed in his 1952 essay 'The American Action

Painters', in Rosenberg (1959): 23–39. Greenberg points out that Rosenberg's theory of 'action painting' cannot explain 'why the painted left-overs of "action," which were devoid of anything but autobiographical meaning in the eyes of their own makers, should be exhibited by them and looked at and even acquired by others' (1993b: 136).

77 In his essay, '"American-Type" Painting', published in 1955, Greenberg identifies 'advanced' art with 'ambitious art today', characterized by 'testing the limits of the inherited forms and genres, and of the medium itself' (1993a: 235).

78 Greenberg (1993a): 217.

79 Greenberg (1986a): 65.

80 Greenberg (1993a): 232.

81 Greenberg (1986b): 222.

82 Greenberg (1986b): 202 and (1986b): 224.

83 Greenberg (1986b): 223.

84 Greenberg (1986b): 224.

85 Greenberg (1986b): 225.

86 Greenberg (1993b): 86.

87 See, for example, 'Counter-Avant-Garde', originally published in 1971, in Greenberg (2003): 5–18.

88 Greenberg (1986a): 37.

89 Greenberg (1993b): 91.

90 Greenberg addressed this issue directly in a note added to the 1978 reprint of 'Modernist Painting': 'There have been some further constructions of what I wrote that go over into preposterousness: That I regard flatness and the inclosing of flatness not just as the limiting conditions of pictorial art, but as criteria of aesthetic significance; that the further a work advances the self-definition of art, the better that work is bound to be' (1993b: 94).

91 Fried, 'Art and Objecthood', originally published in 1967, in Fried (1998): 169. With reference to Greenberg, Fried argues that 'flatness and the delimitation of flatness ought not to be thought of as the "irreducible essence of pictorial art" but rather as something like *the minimal conditions for something's being seen as a painting*; and that the crucial question is not what these minimal and, so to speak, timeless conditions are, but rather what, at a given moment, is capable of compelling conviction, of succeeding as painting. This is not to say that painting *has no* essence; it is to claim that that essence – i.e., that which compels conviction – is largely determined by, and therefore changes continually in response to, the vital work of the recent past' (1998: 169).

92 Fried, 'Shape as Form: Frank Stella's New Paintings', originally published in 1966, in Fried (1998): 99.

93 Rosenberg, cited in Morozova (2004): 26.

94 See Morozova (2004).

95 Greenberg (1993b): 94–100.

96 Greenberg (1993b): 97.

97 Greenberg (1993b): 131.

98   The first interpretation is put forward by Michael Fried in his 'Three American Painters' of 1965, in Fried (1998): 213–65, and the second by Donald Judd in his 'Specific Objects', published the same year. Relevant extracts from Judd's essay are reprinted in Harrison and Wood (2003): 824–8. For photographs of Stella's 'Aluminium Paintings' *in situ*, and a critical discussion of the issues surrounding the exhibition, see Day and Riding (2004).

99   Greenberg (1993b): 90.

100 Krauss (1979).

101 Although Delaroche's words are frequently cited, there is no identifiable source for the attribution.

102 Cabanne (1971): 93.

103 Rodchenko made this claim retrospectively in his 'Working with Mayakovsky' of 1935. His remarks are cited in Buchloh (1986): 44.

104 Asger Jorn, 'Detourned Painting', originally published in 1959, in Harrison and Wood (2003): 708.

105 See Foster (2007): 6 and Rugoff (2007): 10–17.

106 Richter (1995): 72–3.

107 See Richter (1995): 31, 66, 73 and 93.

108 Richter (1995): 66.

109 Rugoff (2007): 14.

110 Richter (1995): 37.

111 See Richter's 'Interview with Benjamin H. D. Buchloh, 1986' in Richter (1995): 132–56, especially 143–53. For an informative analysis of this issue, see Smythe (2014).

112 Jaskot (2005): 474.

113 These issues are considered in greater detail in Gaiger (2004) and Storr (2002).

114 Rugoff (2007): 16.

115 See Foster (2003) and Gaiger (2004) for a discussion of Richter's simultaneous exploration of different kinds of painting.

7 Contemporary Painting

1   Cited in Mitter (2020).

2   The novelist Zadie Smith is particularly attentive to this feature of Yiadom-Boakye's work: 'Yiadom-Boakye's people push themselves forward, into the imagination—as literary characters do—surely, in part, because these are not really portraits. They have no models, no sitters. They are character studies of people who don't exist.' See Smith (2017).

3   'Black selfhood has always existed and is not invisible to black people' (Smith 2017). See, too, Als (2015): 101–3.

4   Cited in Schlieker (2020): 13. In an interview with Antwaun Sargent, Yiadom-Boakye addresses this issue directly: 'One of the things people assume about my stance is that I don't want to talk about race and that

somehow this isn't political. It's never been that. I just don't like being told who I am, how I should speak, what to do and how to do it . . . It isn't so much about placing anyone in the canon as it is about saying that we've always been here, we've always existed, self-sufficient, pre- and post-discovery, and in no way defined by who sees us' (Sargent 2020: 39).

5 Sargent (2020): 34.

6 Cited in Laster (2017).

7 Als (2015): 101 and 102.

8 Spaid (2020): 3. Taken out of context, Spaid's claim here is easily misunderstood. She is drawing attention to the relative neglect by analytic philosophers of the conditions of display, and the relations this establishes between different works of art. Feagin (1995) is an important exception here. However, as Spaid notes, philosophical investigation of the curation of artworks is still at a relatively early stage.

9 Cited in Hatfull (2018).

10 Sillman (2020): 113–24.

11 For an informative discussion, see Smith (2019): 9–10.

12 In Saunders (2010).

13 Hatfull (2018).

14 Salle (2010).

15 See Smith (2019): 51. Sillman's first iPhone work, *Pinky's Rule*, made in 2011, formed the basis for an exhibition at Capitain Prezel in Berlin that same year in which she showed hundreds of inkjet prints taken from the 7-minute animation.

16 The terms in inverted commas are Sillman's own. See Sillmann (2020): 36 and 147; the citation is from Sillman (2020): 151.

17 It is noteworthy that contemporary artists rarely draw on the resources of analytic philosophy and that the interests of philosophers working in this tradition seldom align with the concerns that animate the contemporary art world. By contrast, there are a number of philosophers working in the Continental tradition whose writings form a frequent point of reference. I am thinking here of well-known figures such as Giorgio Agamben, Jacques Rançiere and, above all, Gilles Deleuze. In asking why the ideas of Deleuze, in particular, have proved so stimulating to artists, it would be rewarding to investigate whether there is an underlying affinity between his way of thinking about problems in philosophy and the approaches that artists, including painters, sometimes adopt in their work.

18 Trotter (2020).

19 See, for example, the essays collected in Freeman and Matravers (2015). Ed Winters, in his contribution to this volume, argues that paintings belong to a discrete 'pictorial economy', different from other kinds of pictures, and that 'the longevity of painting as an aesthetic endeavour' is secured by its position in a 'tradition'– conceived in the conservative terms established by T. S. Eliot – as opposed to membership of the broader category of visual culture. See Winters (2015): 45 and 52–3.

20 The most prominent defender of this view is Terry Smith. See Smith (2011).
21 Krauss (1979): 30.
22 Krauss (1979): 30.
23 See Weitz (1956). Weitz proposes: 'A concept is open if its conditions of application are emendable and corrigible; i.e., if a situation or case can be imagined or secured which would call for some sort of *decision* on our part to extend the use of the concept to cover this, or to close the concept and invent a new one to deal with the new case and its new property' (1956: 31).
24 Krauss (1979): 33.
25 Kosuth (2003): 855. Kosuth goes on to argue: 'The "value" of particular artists after Duchamp can be weighed according to how much they questioned the nature of art; which is another way of saying "what they *added* to the conception of art" or what wasn't there before they started' (2003: 856).
26 Schjeldahl (2015b).
27 Cited in Morgan (2014). Opalka discusses the sustaining ideas behind his work in Panek (2004).
28 Habermas (1973).
29 See Lawson (1981), Crimp (1981), Buchloh (1981) and Foster (1986).
30 Cited in Crimp (1981): 74.
31 Crimp (1981): 74.
32 Lawson, for example, with reference of the work of 'pseudo-expressionists' such as Schnabel and Chia, claims: 'Their enterprise is distinguished by homage to the past, and in particular by nostalgia for the early days of modernism. But what they give us is a pastiche of historical consciousness, an exercise in bad faith' (1981: 147).
33 Graw, Birnbaum and Hirsch (2012): 6.
34 See Graw and Lajer-Burcharth (2016).
35 For the identification of painting as a 'success medium', see Graw (2018).
36 Foster, Krauss, Bois and Buchloh (2016).
37 This observation holds true even for the Museum of Modern Art (MOMA) in New York, which under Alfred H. Barr had supported the work of emerging painters through its acquisition policies. Peter Schjeldahl observes in his review of 'The Forever Now: Contemporary Painting in an Atemporal World', held in 2015, that it was the first large-scale survey exhibition dedicated to contemporary painting at MOMA since 'The New American Painting' in 1958, a hiatus of over fifty years. See Schjeldahl (2015a).
38 See Gaiger (2011a): 188.
39 Krauss (1999).
40 Krauss (1977): 68,
41 Krauss (1999): 12.
42 Krauss (1999): 20.
43 This argument is also put forward in Buchloh (1990).
44 Verwoert (2005).
45 Verwoert (2005). A comparable position is defended by Arthur Danto, who claims that the exhaustion of the great master narrative of medium-specificity

brought about the 'end of art' – or, rather, the end of the history of art – and that this 'inaugurates the greatest era of freedom art has even known' (Danto 1997: 114). For a critical response to Danto's relaxed or tolerant pluralism and the identification of potential sources of value conflict for contemporary art, see Gaiger (2013b).

46 Dean (2006): 8. See, too, Iversen (2012).
47 Leonard insists: 'There is something more here than quaintness, or nostalgia. It is a feeling of connectedness to the rest of the world' (2002: 90 and 91).
48 I take up the phrase 'digital divide' from Bishop (2012).
49 Schjeldahl (2015a).
50 Bishop (2012): 442.
51 Bishop (2012): 436.
52 Bishop (2012): 436
53 Salz (2012).
54 Fox (2016). A similar point is made by John Yau, who observes: 'Guyton may have invented a paintbrush, but the only thing he has done with it is to allude to a lot of works by other artists' (Yau 2012).
55 Fox (2016).
56 The four paintings were first exhibited in 2012 at documenta 13 in Kassel, Germany.
57 Demos (2013): 57.
58 Steyerl (2009).
59 Steyerl (2009).
60 Joselit (2013): xiv.
61 See Lütticken (2009).
62 The work pairs two films about adolescent girls driven by external forces – Henry King's *The Song of Bernadette* (1943) and William Friedkin's *The Exorcist* (1973) – by projecting them onto opposite sides of a semi-transparent screen so that the images are seen to overlap each other.
63 Groys (2008): 82.
64 See, for example, *Self* (1997), *Ready to Wear* (1999) and *Nothing* (1998).
65 In Swenson (2016).
66 Smythe (2013): 8.
67 I owe this observation to Sharon (Ran) Shi, who first drew my attention to the pictorial qualities evident in the work of artists such Genzken and Von Bonin.
68 Birnbaum (2002): 60. Birnbaum defends the view that painting is 'a zone of contagion, constantly branching out and widening its scope' (2002: 61).
69 The phrase comes from the title of the first section of Klee's *Pedagogical Sketchbook*, originally published in 1925. See Klee (1973): 16–17.
70 For an insightful discussion of this work and its significance for the development of Grosse's practice, see Volk (2020): 41–3.
71 See Loock (2014).

72 Wollheim (1987): 21.
73 In an interview with Gregory Volk, Grosse declared: 'It is very important
    for me to show that there is no one vantage point from which you can see the
    work. Every corner, every bit of the painting that you see will move and
    change your understanding of what you see' (Volk 2020: 20).
74 See Bishop (2005): 6.

Bibliography

Aasen, S. (2021), 'Depicting Movement', *Australasian Journal of Philosophy*, 99 (1): 34–47.

Abell, C. (2009), 'Canny Resemblance', *Philosophical Review*, 118 (2): 183–223.

Abell, C. and K. Bantinake, eds (2010), *Philosophical Perspectives on Depiction*, Oxford: Oxford University Press.

Ackermann, J. S. (1962), 'A Theory of Style', *Journal of Aesthetics and Art Criticism*, 20 (3): 227–37.

Adorno, T. W. (1997), *Aesthetic Theory*, trans. R. Hullot-Kentor, London: Athlone Press.

Alberti, L. B. (1991), *On Painting*, trans. Cecil Grayson, London: Penguin.

Alpers, S. (1987), 'Style Is What You Make It: The Visual Arts Once Again', in B. Lang (ed.), *The Concept of Style*, 137–62, Cambridge: Cambridge University Press.

Als, H. (2015), 'Face to Face', in *Verses After Dusk: Lynette Yiadom-Boakye*, exh. cat., 101–3, London and Vienna: Serpentine Galleries and Koenig Books.

Antliff, M. and P. Leighten (2001), *Cubism and Culture*, London: Thames & Hudson.

Arrell, D. (1987), 'What Goodman Should Have Said About Representation', *Journal of Aesthetics and Art Criticism*, 46 (1): 41–9.

Augustine (1971), *On Christian Doctrine*, trans. J. F. Shaw, Chicago: William Benton.

Bantinaki, K. (2007), 'Pictorial Perception as Illusion', *The British Journal of Aesthetics*, 47 (3): 268–79.

Bantinaki, K. (2010), 'Pictorial Perception as Twofold Experience', in C. Abell and K. Bantinaki (eds), *Philosophical Perspectives on Depiction*, 128–50, Oxford: Oxford University Press.

Baxandall, M. (1988), *Painting and Experience in Fifteenth Century Italy*, Oxford: Oxford University Press.

Bell, C. (1922), *Since Cézanne*, London: Chatto & Windus.

Bell, C. (1987), *Art*, ed. J. B. Bullen, Oxford: Oxford University Press.

Birnbaum, D. (2002), 'Where is Painting Now?', *Tate: International Arts and Culture*, 1: 60–3.

Bishop, C. (2005), *Installation Art: A Critical History*, London: Tate Publishing.

Bishop, C. (2012), 'Digital Divide', *Artforum*, 51 (1): 434–42.

Bois, Y.-A. (1987), 'Kahnweiler's Lesson', *Representations*, 18: 33–68.

Bois, Y.-A. (1993), *Painting as Model*, Cambridge, MA and London: MIT Press.

Bradley, H. (2014), 'Reducing the Space of Seeing-In', *The British Journal of Aesthetics*, 54 (4): 409–24.

Briscoe, R. (2016), 'Depiction, Pictorial Experience, and Vision Science', *Philosophical Topics*, 44 (2): 43–81.

Bryson, N. (1991), 'Semiology and Visual Interpretation', in N. Bryson, M. A. Holly and K. Moxey (eds), *Visual Theory: Painting and Interpretation*, 61–73, Cambridge: Polity Press.

Buchloh, B. H. D. (1981), 'Figures of Authority, Ciphers of Regression: Notes on the Return of Representation in European Painting', *October*, 16: 39–68.

Buchloh, B. H. D. (1986), 'Primary Colours for the Second Time: A Paradigm Repetition of the Neo-Avant-Garde', *October*, 37: 41–52.

Buchloh, B. H. D. (1990), 'Conceptual Art 1962–1969: From the Aesthetics of Administration to the Critique of Institutions', *October*, 55: 105–43.

Budd, M. (1987), 'Wittgenstein on Seeing Aspects', *Mind*, 96: 1–17.

Budd, M. (1992), 'On Looking at a Picture', in J. Hopkins and A. Savile (eds), *Psychoanalysis, Mind and Art: Perspectives on Richard Wollheim*, 257–79, Malden, MA and Oxford: Blackwell.

Budd, M. (1993), 'How Pictures Look', in D. Knowles and J. Skorupski (eds), *Virtue and Taste: Essays on Politics, Ethics and Aesthetics*, 154–75, Oxford and Cambridge, MA: Blackwell.

Budd, M. (1995), *Values of Art: Pictures, Poetry and Music*, London: Penguin.

Burckhardt, J. (1995), *The Civilization of the Renaissance in Italy*, trans. S. Middlemore, London: Phaidon.

Cabanne, P. (1971), *Interviews with Marcel Duchamp*, trans. Ron Padgett, New York: Da Capo Press.

Carney, J. D. (1991), 'Individual Style', *Journal of Aesthetics and Art Criticism*, 49 (1): 15–22.

Carrasco, M. (2011), 'Visual Attention: The Past 25 Years', *Vision Research*, 51: 1484–525.

Carroll, N. (2001), 'Modernity and the Plasticity of Perception', *Journal of Aesthetics and Art Criticism*, 59 (1): 11–17.

Cassirer, E. (2020), *The Philosophy of Symbolic Forms*, trans. S. G. Lofts, London and New York: Routledge.

Cavedon-Taylor, D. (2011), 'The Space of Seeing-In', *The British Journal of Aesthetics*, 51 (3): 271–8.

Clark, K. (1960), *Looking at Pictures*, London: John Murray.

Costello, D. (2018), *On Photography: A Philosophical Inquiry*, London and New York: Routledge.

Cox, N. (2000), *Cubism*, London: Phaidon.

Crimp, D. (1981), 'The End of Painting', *October*, 16: 69–86.

Danto, A. (1981), *The Transfiguration of the Commonplace: A Philosophy of Art*, Cambridge, MA and London: Harvard University Press.

Danto, A. (1997), *After the End of Art: Contemporary Art and the Pale of History*, Princeton: Princeton University Press.

Danto, A. (2001), 'Seeing and Showing', *Journal of Aesthetics and Art Criticism*, 59 (1): 1–9.

Day, G. and C. Riding (2004), 'The Critical Terrain of "High Modernism"', in P. Wood (ed.), *Varieties of Modernism*, 188–213, Newhaven and London: Yale University Press.

Dean, T. (2006), 'Analogue', in T. Vischer and I. Friedli (eds), *Analogue: Drawings 1991–2006*, 8–10, Basel: Schaulager.

Demos, T. J. (2013), 'Painting and Uprising: Julie Mehretu's Third Space', in *Julie Mehretu: Liminal Squared*, exh. cat., 54–61, White Cube, London, and Marian Goodman Gallery, New York.

Denham, A. E., ed. (2012) *Plato on Art and Beauty*, Basingstoke: Palgrave Macmillan.

Dickie, G. (1992), 'Definition of "Art"', in D. Cooper (ed.), *A Companion to Aesthetics*, 109–13, Oxford: Blackwell.

Doran, M., ed. (2001), *Conversations with Cézanne*, trans. J. L. Cochran, Berkeley: University of California Press.

Duchamp, M. (1989), *The Writings of Marcel Duchamp*, ed. M. Sanouillet and E. Peterson, New York: Da Capo Press.

Eck, C., J. Gastel and E. Kessel, eds (2014), *The Secret Lives of Artworks: Exploring the Boundaries between Art and Life*, Leiden: Leiden University Press.

Eck, C. (2015), *Art, Agency and Living Presence: From the Animated Image to the Excessive Object*, Leiden: Leiden University Press.

Eckl, A. (1993), 'Zum Problem der kategorialen Funktion von Wölfflins "Kunstgeschichtlichen Grundbegriffen". Erläuterungen an einem Beispiel ihrer Anwendung', *Zeitschrift für Ästhetik und Allgemeine Kunstwissenschaft*, 38: 29–52.

Eckl, A. (1996), *Kategorien der Anschauung: Zur transzendentalphilosophischen Bedeutung von Heinrich Wölfflins 'Kunstgeschichtlichen Grundbegriffen'*, Munich: Wilhelm Fink.

Falkenheim, J. (1980), *Roger Fry and the Beginnings of Formalist Art Criticism*, Ann Arbor: UMI Research Press.

Feagin, S. L. (1995), 'Paintings and their Places', *Australasian Journal of Philosophy*, 73 (2): 260–8.

Feagin, S. L. (1998), 'Presentation and Representation', *Journal of Aesthetics and Art Criticism*, 56 (3): 234–40.

Fiedler, K. (1991), *Über den Ursprung der künstlerischen Tätigkeit*, in G. Boehm (ed.), *Schriften zur Kunst*, Vol. 1: 111–220, Munich: Wilhelm Fink.

Foster, H. (1986), 'Signs Taken for Wonders', *Art in America*, 74 (6): 81–91.

Foster, H. (2003), 'Semblance According to Gerhard Richter', *Raritan*, 23 (3): 159–77.

Foster, H. (2007), 'At the Hayward: "The Painting of Modern Life"', *London Review of Books*, 29 (1). Available online at: https://www.lrb.co.uk/the-paper/v29/n21/hal-foster/at-the-hayward.

Foster, H., R. Krauss, Y.-A. Bois and B. H. D. Buchloh (2016), *Art Since 1900: Modernism, Antimodernism, Postmodernism*, 3rd edn, London: Thames & Hudson.

Foucault, M. (1994), *The Order of Things: An Archaeology of the Human Sciences*, trans. A. Sheridan, New York: Random House.

Fox, D. (2016), 'Review of Wade Guyton at the Petzel Gallery, New York', *Frieze*, 164. Available online at: https://www.frieze.com/article/wade-guyton-0.

Freeland, C. (2007), 'Portraits in Painting and Photography', *Philosophical Studies*, 135 (1): 195–209.

Freeman, D. and D. Matravers, eds (2015), *Figuring Out Figurative Art: Contemporary Philosophers on Contemporary Paintings*, London: Routledge.

Fried, M. (1998), *Art and Objecthood: Essays and Reviews*, Chicago and London: The University of Chicago Press.

Fry, R. (1926), *Transformations: Critical and Speculative Essays on Art*, London: Chatto & Windus.

Fry, R. (1927), *Cézanne: A Study of His Development*, London: L. & V. Woolf.

Fry, R. (1937), *Vision and Design*, Harmondsworth: Penguin.

Gaiger, J. (1999), 'Constraints and Conventions: Kant and Greenberg on Aesthetic Judgment', *The British Journal of Aesthetics*, 39 (4): 376–91.

Gaiger, J. (2002), 'The Analysis of Pictorial Style, *The British Journal of Aesthetics*, 42 (1): 20–36.

Gaiger, J. (2003), 'Interpreting the Readymade: Marcel Duchamp's *Bottlerack*', in J. Gaiger (ed.), *Frameworks for Modern Art*, 57–103, New Haven and London: Yale University Press.

Gaiger, J. (2004), 'Post-Conceptual Painting: Gerhard Richter's Extended Leave-Taking', in G. Perry and P. Wood (eds), *Themes in Contemporary Art*, 88–135, New Haven and London: Yale University Press.

Gaiger, J. (2006), 'Catching up with History: Hegel and Abstract Painting', in K. Deligiorgi (ed.), *Hegel: New Directions*, 159–76, Chesham: Acumen.

Gaiger, J. (2009), 'Dismantling the Frame: Site-Specific Art and Aesthetic Autonomy', *British Journal of Aesthetics*, 49 (1): 43–58.

Gaiger, J. (2011a), 'Hegel's Contested Legacy: Rethinking the Relation Between Art History and Philosophy', *The Art Bulletin*, 93 (2): 178–94.

Gaiger, J. (2011b), 'Participatory Imagining and the Explanation of Living-Presence Response', *British Journal of Aesthetics*, 51 (4): 363–81.

Gaiger, J. (2013a), 'The Contemporaneity of Lessing's Aesthetics', in R. Robertson (ed.), *Lessing and the German Enlightenment*, 97–117, SVEC: Voltaire Foundation.

Gaiger, J. (2013b), 'Value Conflict and the Autonomy of Art', in O. Hulatt (ed.), *Aesthetic and Artistic Autonomy*, 65–88, London: Bloomsbury.

Gaiger J. (2015), 'Intuition and Representation: Wölfflin's Fundamental Concepts of Art History', *Journal of Aesthetics and Art Criticism*, 33 (2): 164–71.

Gantner, J. (1948), *Jacob Burckhardt und Heinrich Wölfflin: Briefwechsel und andere Dokumente ihrer Begegnung, 1882–1897*, Basel: Benno Schwaabe.

Gerwen, van R., ed. (2001), *Richard Wollheim on the Art of Painting: Art as Representation and Expression*, Cambridge: Cambridge University Press.

Gilmore, J. (2000), *The Life of a Style: Beginnings and Endings in the Narrative History of Art*, Ithaca and London: Cornell University Press.

Gibson, A. (2003), 'Avant-garde', in R. S. Nelson and R. Shiff (eds), *Critical Terms for Art History*, 2nd edn, 202–16, Chicago and London: The University of Chicago Press.

Gombrich, E. H. (1966), 'Norm and Form: The Stylistic Categories of Art History and their Origin in Renaissance Ideals', in E. H. Gombrich, *Norm and Form: Studies in the Art of the Renaissance*, 81–98, London: Phaidon.

Gombrich, E. H. (1972), 'The "What" and the "How": Perspective Representation and the Phenomenal World', in R. Rudner. and I. Scheffler (eds), *Logic and Art: Essays in Honour of Nelson Goodman*, 129–49, Indianapolis: Bobbs-Merrill.

Gombrich, E. H. (1973), 'Illusion and Art', in R. L. Gregory and E. H. Gombrich (eds), *Illusion in Nature and Art*, 193–243, London: Duckworth.

Gombrich, E. H. (1977), *Art and Illusion: A Study in the Psychology of Pictorial Representation*, 5th edn, London: Phaidon.

Gombrich, E. H. (1979), *Ideals and Idols: Essays on Value and History in Art*, Oxford: Phaidon.

Gombrich, E. H. (1982), *The Image and the Eye: Further Studies in the Psychology of Pictorial Representation*, London: Phaidon.

Gombrich, E. H. (1984), 'Representation and Misrepresentation', *Critical Inquiry*, 11 (2): 195–201.

Goodman, N. (1960a), 'The Way the World Is', *The Review of Metaphysics*, 14: 48–56.

Goodman, N. (1960b), 'Review of Gombrich's *Art and Illusion*', *Journal of Philosophy*, 57: 595–9.

Goodman, N. (1972), *Problems and Projects*, Indianapolis and New York: Bobbs-Merrill.

Goodman, N. (1976), *Languages of Art: An Approach to the Theory of Symbols*, 2nd edn, Indianapolis: Hackett.

Goodman, N. (1978), *Ways of Worldmaking*, Indianapolis: Hackett.

Goodman, N. (1984), *Of Mind and Other Matters*, Cambridge, MA and London: Harvard University Press.

Goodman, N. and C. Z. Elgin (1988), *Reconceptions in Philosophy and other Arts and Sciences*, London: Routledge.

Graw. I, D. Birnbaum and N. Hirsch, eds (2012), *Thinking Through Painting: Reflexivity and Agency Beyond the Canvas*, Berlin: Sternberg Press.

Graw, I. and E. Lajer-Burcharth, eds (2016), *Painting Beyond Itself: The Medium in the Post-Medium Condition*, Berlin: Sternberg Press.

Graw, I. (2018), *The Love of Painting: Genealogy of a Success Medium*, Berlin: Sternberg Press.

Greenberg, C. (1986a), *The Collected Essays and Criticism, Volume 1: Perceptions and Judgments, 1939–1944*, ed. J. O'Brian, Chicago and London: The University of Chicago Press.

Greenberg, C. (1986b), *The Collected Essays and Criticism, Volume 2: Arrogant Purpose, 1945–1949*, ed. J. O'Brian, Chicago and London: The University of Chicago Press.

Greenberg, C. (1993a), *The Collected Essays and Criticism, Volume 3: Affirmations and Refusals, 1950–1956*, ed. J. O'Brian, Chicago and London: The University of Chicago Press.

Greenberg, C. (1993b), *The Collected Essays and Criticism, Volume 4: Modernism with a Vengeance, 1957–1969*, ed. J. O'Brian, Chicago and London: The University of Chicago Press.

Greenberg, C. (2003), *Clement Greenberg: Late Writings*, ed. R. C. Morgan, Minneapolis: University of Minnesota Press.

Greenberg, G. (2013), 'Beyond Resemblance', *Philosophical Review*, 122 (2): 215–87.

Gregory, D. (2013), *Showing, Sensing and Seeming: Distinctively Sensory Representations and their Contents*, Oxford: Oxford University Press.

Groys, B. (2008), *Art Power*, Cambridge, MA: MIT Press.

Gulyga, A. (1985), *Immanuel Kant*, trans. S. Bielfeldt, Frankfurt am Main: Suhrkamp.

Habermas, J. (1973), *Legitimationsprobleme im Spätkapitalismus*, Frankfurt am Main: Suhrkamp.

Hagen, M. A. (1986), *Varieties of Realism: Geometries of Representational Art*, Cambridge: Cambridge University Press.

Halliwell, S. (2002), *The Aesthetics of Mimesis: Ancient Texts and Modern Problems*, Princeton: Princeton University Press.

Hamilton, A. (2007), *Aesthetics and Music*, London and New York: Continuum.

Hanna, R. (2001), *Kant and the Foundations of Analytic Philosophy*, Cambridge: Cambridge University Press.

Harrison, C. (2003), 'Abstract Art: Reading Barnett Newman's *Eve*' in J. Gaiger (ed.), *Frameworks for Modern Art*, 105–51, Newhaven and London: Yale University Press.

Harrison, C. and P. Wood, eds (2003), *Art in Theory: 1900–2000. An Anthology of Changing Ideas*, Malden, MA and Oxford: Blackwell.

Harrison, C., P. Wood, and J. Gaiger, eds (1998), *Art in Theory: 1815–1900. An Anthology of Changing Ideas*, Malden, MA and Oxford: Blackwell.

Hatfull, N. (2018), 'The Vicarious Warmth of Amy Sillman's Paintings', *Frieze*, 200. Available online at: https://www.frieze.com/article/vicarious-warmth-amy-sillmans-paintings.

Hegel, G. W. F. (1975), *Aesthetics: Lectures on Fine Art*, trans. T. M. Knox, 2 vols, Oxford: Clarendon Press.

Hopkins, J. (1998), *Picture, Image and Experience*, Cambridge: Cambridge University Press.

Hopkins, R. (2010), 'Inflected Pictorial Experience: Its Treatment and Significance', in C. Abell and K. Bantinaki (eds), *Philosophical Perspectives on Depiction*, 151–80, Oxford: Oxford University Press.

Huttenlocher, P. R. (2002), *Neural Plasticity: The Effects of the Environment on the Development of the Cerebral Cortex*, Cambridge, MA: Harvard University Press.

Hyman, J. (2006), *The Objective Eye: Color, Form and Reality in the Theory of Art*, Chicago and London: The University of Chicago Press.

Ijseeling, S. (1997), *Mimesis: On Appearing and Being*, trans. H. Ijsseling and J. Bloechl, Kampen: Kok Pharos.

Iverson, M. (1993), *Alois Riegl: Art History and Theory*, Cambridge, MA: MIT Press.

Iverson, M. (2012), 'Analogue: On Zoe Leonard and Tacita Dean', *Critical Inquiry*, 38: 796–818.

Joselit, D. (2013), *After Art*, Princeton: Princeton University Press.

Kahnweiler, D. H. (1949), *The Sculptures of Picasso*, trans. A. B. Sylvester, London: Rodney Phillips & Co.

Kahnweiler, D. H. (1971), *My Galleries and Painters*, interviews with F. Crémieux, trans. H. Weaver, London: Thames & Hudson.

Kandinsky, W. (1982), *On the Spiritual in Art*, in K. C. Lindsay and P. Vergo (eds), *Kandinsky: Complete Writings on Art*, Vol. 1: 119–219, London: Faber & Faber.

Kemp, G. and G. M. Mras, eds (2016), *Wollheim, Wittgenstein and Pictorial Representation: Seeing-as and Seeing-in*, London and New York: Routledge

Kowler E. (2011), 'Eye Movements: The Past 25 Years', *Vision Research*, 51: 1457–83.

Janaway, C. (1995), *Images of Excellence: Plato's Critique of the Arts*, Oxford: Clarendon Press.

Jaskot, P. B. (2007), 'Gerhard Richter and Adolf Eichenmann', *Oxford Art Journal*, 28 (3): 457–78.

Jay, P. (1981), *The Greek Anthology: Selections*, Harmondsworth: Penguin.

Kant, I. (1998), *Critique of Pure Reason*, trans P. Guyer and A. W. Wood, Cambridge: Cambridge University Press.

Kant, I. (2000), *Critique of the Power of Judgment*, trans. P. Guyer and E. Matthews, Cambridge: Cambridge University Press.

Klee, P. (1973), *Pedagogical Sketchbook*, trans. Sybil Moholy-Nagy, London: Faber & Faber.

Kosuth, J. (2003), 'Art after Philosophy', in C. Harrison and P. Wood (eds), *Art in Theory: 1900–2000. An Anthology of Changing Ideas*, 852–61, Malden, MA and Oxford: Blackwell.

Krauss, R. (1977), 'Notes on the Index: Seventies Art in America', *October* 3: 68–81.

Krauss, R. (1979), 'Sculpture in the Expanded Field', *October* 8: 30–44.

Krauss, R. (1992), 'The Motivation of the Sign', in L. Zelevanksy (ed.), *Picasso and Braque: A Symposium*, 261–86, New York: Museum of Modern Art.

Krauss, R. (1998), *The Picasso Papers*, New York: Farrar, Strauss and Giroux.

Krauss, R. (1999), *A Voyage on the North Sea: Art in The Post-Medium Condition*, London: Thames & Hudson.

Krieger, M. (1984), 'The Ambiguities of Representation and Illusion: An E. H. Gombrich Retrospective', *Critical Inquiry*, 11 (2): 181–94.

Kristeller, P. O. (1951), 'The Modern System of the Arts: A Study in the History of Aesthetics I', *Journal of the History of Ideas*, 12: 496–527.

Kristeller, P. O. (1952), 'The Modern System of the Arts: A Study in the History of Aesthetics II', *Journal of the History of Ideas*, 13: 17–46.

Krukowski, L. (1998), 'Formalism' in M. Kelly (ed.), *Encyclopedia of Aesthetics*, Vol. 2: 213–17, Oxford: Oxford University Press.

Kulvicki, J. V. (2006), *On Images: Their Structure and Content*, Oxford: Oxford University Press.

Kulvicki, J. V. (2014), *Images*, London and New York: Routledge.

Lang, B., ed. (1987), *The Concept of Style*, Cambridge: Cambridge University Press.

Laster, P. (2017), 'Lynette Yiadom-Boakye Talks about Creating Fictional Characters Through Portraiture', *Time Out New York*, 2 May. Available online at: https://www.timeout.com/newyork/blog/lynette-yiadom-boakye-talks-about-creating-fictional-characters-through-portraiture-050217.

Lawson, T. (1981), 'Last Exit: Painting', *Artforum*, 20 (2): 40–7.

Leighten, P. (1994), 'Cubist Anachronisms, Cryptoformalism, and Business-as-Usual in New York', *Oxford Art Journal*, 17 (20): 91–102.

Leonard, Z. (2002), 'Out of Time', *October*, 100: 90–7.

Lessing, G. E. (1984), *Laocoön: An Essay on the Limits of Painting and Poetry*, trans. E. A. McCormick, Baltimore: The Johns Hopkins University Press.

Levinson, J. (1998), 'Wollheim on Pictorial Representation', *Journal of Aesthetics and Art Criticism*, 56 (3): 227–33.

Lewis, W. (1982), *Blasting and Bombadeering*, London: John Calder.

Loock, U. (2014), 'Dividing Lines', in *Katherina Grosse: Inside the Speaker*, exh. cat., 98–109, Museum Kunstpalast, Düsseldorf.

Lopes, D. (1996), *Understanding Pictures*, Oxford: Clarendon Press.

Lopes, D. (2000), 'From *Languages of Art* to *Art in Mind*', *Journal of Aesthetics and Art Criticism*, 58 (3): 227–31.

Lopes, D. (2005), *Sight and Sensibility: Evaluating Pictures*, Oxford: Clarendon Press.

Lütticken, S. (2009), 'Viewing Copies: On the Mobility of Moving Images', *E-flux Journal*, 8. Available online at: https://www.e-flux.com/journal/08/61380/viewing-copies-on-the-mobility-of-moving-images/.

Maes, H., ed. (2020), *Portraits and Philosophy*, London and New York: Routledge.

Maginnis, H. (1996), 'Reflections on Formalism: The Post-Impressionists and the Early Italians', *Art History*, 19 (2): 191–207.

Mitter, S. (2020), 'A Portraitist Whose Subjects Are All In Her Head', *The New York Times*, 16 December. Available online at: https://www.nytimes.com/2020/12/16/arts/design/lynette-yiadom-boakye.html.

Morgan, R. C. (2014), 'Roman Opalka's Numerical Destiny, *Hyperallergic*, 6 October. Available online at: https://hyperallergic.com/153559/roman-opalkas-numerical-destiny/.

Morozova, E. (2004), 'American Art Criticism and the Crisis of Art History Writing', PhD diss., The Open University, Milton Keynes.

Mortensen, P. (1997), *Art in the Social Order: The Making of the Modern Concept of Art*, Albany: State University of New York Press.

Munro, T. (1967), *The Arts and their Representations*, Cleveland: Case Western Reserve Press.

Myers, T. R. ed. (2011), *Painting: Documents of Contemporary Art*, Cambridge, MA: MIT Press.

Nanay, B. (2005), 'Is Twofoldness Necessary for Representational Seeing?', *British Journal of Aesthetics*, 45 (3): 248–57.

Nanay, B. (2010), 'Inflected and Uninflected Experience of Pictures', in C. Abell and K. Bantinaki (eds), *Philosophical Perspectives on Depiction*, 181–207, Oxford: Oxford University Press.

Nanay, B. (2012). 'The Macro and the Micro: Andreas Gursky's Aesthetics', *Journal of Aesthetics and Art Criticism*, 70 (1): 91–100.

Nanay, B. (2013), *Between Perception and Action*, Oxford: Oxford University Press.

Nanay, B. (2015), 'The History of Vision', *Journal of Aesthetics and Art Criticism*, 73 (3): 259–71.

Newall, M. (2011), *What is a Picture? Depiction, Realism, Abstraction*, New York: Palgrave Macmillan.

Newman, B. (1990), *Selected Writings and Interviews*, ed. J. P. O'Neill, New York: Alfred A. Knopf.

Panek, A. (2004), 'Roman Opalka, ici et maintenant – interview with Aneta Panek', *Artpress*, 301: 20–6.

Panofksy, E. (1993), 'Iconography and Iconology: An Introduction to the Study of Renaissance Art', in E. Panofsky, *Meaning in the Visual Arts*, 51–81, Harmondsworth: Penguin.

Panofksy, E. (1964), *Aufsätze zu Grundfragen der Kunstwissenschaft*, ed. H. Oberer and E. Verheyen, Berlin: Bruno Hessling.

Peacocke, C. (1987), 'Depiction', *Philosophical Review*, 96 (3): 383–410.

Peirce, C. S. (1955), *Philosophical Writings*, ed. J. Buchler, New York: Dover.

Pelletier, J. and A. Voltolini, eds (2019), *The Pleasure of Pictures: Pictorial Experience and Aesthetic Appreciation*, New York and London: Routledge.

Phillips, D. M. (2009), 'Photography and Causation: Responding to Scruton's Scepticism', *British Journal of Aesthetics*, 49 (4): 327–40.

Piles, R. de (1993), *L'Idée du Peintre parfait*, ed. X. Carrère, Paris: Gallimard.

Pliny (1857), *The Natural History of Pliny*, trans. J. Bostock and H. T. Riley, London: Henry G. Bohn.

Plato (1989), *The Collected Dialogues*, ed. E. Hamilton and H. Cairns, Princeton: Princeton University Press.

Podro, M. (1982), *The Critical Historians of Art*, New Haven and London: Yale University Press.

Podro, M. (1987), 'Depiction and the Golden Calf', in A. Harrison (ed.), *Philosophy and the Visual Arts: Seeing and Abstracting*, 3–22, Dordrecht: D. Reidel.

Podro, M. (1993), 'Fiction and Reality in Painting', in S. Kemal and I. Gaskell (eds), *Explanation and Value in the Arts*, 43–54, Cambridge: Cambridge University Press.

Podro, M. (1998), *Depiction*, New Haven & London: Yale University Press.

Podro, M. (2004), 'On Richard Wollheim', *British Journal of Aesthetics*, 44 (3): 213–15.

Pollitt, J. J. (1974), *The Ancient View of Greek Art: Criticism, History, Terminology*, New Haven and London: Yale University Press.

Pollitt, J. J. (1990), *The Art of Ancient Greece: Sources and Documents*, Cambridge: Cambridge University Press.

Puttfarken, T. (2000), *The Discovery of Pictorial Composition: Theories of Visual Order in Painting, 1400–1800*, New Haven and London: Yale University Press.

Reynolds, J. (1997), *Discourses on Art*, ed. R. R. Wark, New Haven and London: Yale University Press.

Richter, G. (1995), *The Daily Practice of Painting: Writings and Interviews. 1962–1993*, trans. D. Britt, London: Thames & Hudson.

Robinson, J. (1981), 'Style and Significance in Art History and Criticism', *Journal of Aesthetics and Art Criticism* 40 (1): 5–14.

Robinson, J. (2000), '*Languages of Art* at the Turn of the Century', *Journal of Aesthetics and Art Criticism*, 58 (3): 213–18.

Robinson, J. (2005), *Deeper than Reason: Emotion and its Role in Literature, Music and Art*, Oxford: Oxford University Press.

Robinson, J. (2017), 'The Missing Person Found. Part I: Expressing Emotion in Pictures', *The British Journal of Aesthetics*, 57 (3): 249–67.

Rosenberg, H. (1959), *The Tradition of the New*, New York: Horizon Press.

Rudner R. and I. Sheffler, eds (1972), *Logic and Art: Essays in Honour of Nelson Goodman*, Indianapolis: Bobbs-Merrill.

Rugoff, R. (2007), *The Painting of Modern Life*, exh. cat., London: Hayward Publishing.

Salle, D. (2010), 'Amy Sillman and Tom McGrath', *The Paris Review*, 195. Available online at: https://www.theparisreview.org/art-photography/6067/amy-sillman-and-tom-mcgrath-david-salle.

Salz, J. (2012), Review of 'Wade Guyton OS', *New York Magazine*, 29 October. Available online at: https://www.vulture.com/2012/10/saltz-on-wade-guyton-os-at-the-whitney.html.

Sargent, A. (2020), 'Speaking Through Painting, Lynette Yiadom-Boakye interviewed by Antwaun Sargent', *Tate Etc.* 50: 33–43.

Saunders, M. (2010), 'Parts and Labour: Amy Sillman interviewed by Matt Saunders', *Frieze*, 133. Available online at: https://www.frieze.com/article/parts-labour.

Sauerländer, W. (1983), 'From Stilus to Style: Reflections on the Fate of a Notion', *Art History*, 6 (3): 253–70.

Savedoff, B. E. (2000), *Transforming Images: How Photography Complicates the Picture*, Ithaca and London: Cornell University Press.

Schapiro, M. (1994), *Theory and Philosophy of Art: Style, Artist and Society*, New York: Georges Brazillier.

Schier, F. (1986), *Deeper into Pictures*, Cambridge: Cambridge University Press.

Schjeldahl, P. (2015a), 'Take Your Time: New Painting at the Museum of Modern Art', *The New Yorker*, 5 January. Available online at: https://www.newyorker.com/magazine/2015/01/05/take-time.

Schjeldahl, P. (2015b), 'A Painting a Day: On Kawara's Extraordinary Project', *The New Yorker*, 16 Feb. Available online at: https://www.newyorker.com/magazine/2015/02/16/painting-day.

Schlieker, A. (2020), 'Quiet Fires: The Paintings of Lynette Yiadom-Boakye', in I. Maidment and A. Schlieker, *Lynette Yiadom-Boakye: Fly In League With The Night*, exh. cat., 9–25, London: Tate Publishing.

Searle, J. R. (1980), 'Las Meninas and the Paradoxes of Pictorial Representation', *Critical Inquiry*, 6 (3): 477–88.

Sheehan, J. J. (2000), *Museums in the German Art World: From the End of the Old Regime to the Rise of Modernism*, Oxford and New York: Oxford University Press.

Shiner, L. (2001), *The Invention of Art: A Cultural History*, Chicago and London: The University of Chicago Press.

Short, T. L. (2004), 'The Development of Peirce's Theory of Signs' in C. Misak (ed.), *The Cambridge Companion to Peirce*, 214–40, Cambridge: Cambridge University Press.

Sillman, A. (2020), *Faux Pas: Selected Writings and Drawings*, ed. C. Houette, F. Lancien-Guilberteau and B. Thorel, Paris: After 8 Books.

Smith, T. (2011), *Contemporary Art: World Currents*, London: Laurence King.

Smith, V. (2019), *Amy Sillman*, London: Lund Humphries.

Smith, Z. (2017), 'Lynette Yiadom-Boakye's Imaginary Portraits', *The New Yorker*, 12 June. Available online at: https://www.newyorker.com/ magazine/2017/06/19/lynette-yiadom-boakyes-imaginary-portraits.

Smythe, C. (2013), 'Deepest at its Surface', in *Limber: Spatial Painting Practices*, exh. cat., 8–20, Herbert Read Gallery, Canterbury, and Grandes Galleries de L'Erba, Rouen.

Smythe, L. (2014), 'Freedom and Exile in Gerhard Richter's Early Photopaintings', *Oxford Art Journal*, 37 (3): 305–25.

Sörbom, G. (1966), *Mimesis and Art: Studies in the Origin and Early Development of an Aesthetic Vocabulary*, Stockholm: Svenska Bokförlaget.

Spaid, S. (2020), *The Philosophy of Curatorial Practice: Between Work and World*, London: Bloomsbury.

Staff, C. (2013), *After Modernist Painting: The History of a Contemporary Practice*, London and New York: I.B. Tauris.

Steyerl, H. (2009), 'In Defence of the Poor Image', *E-flux Journal*, 10. Available online at: https://www.e-flux.com/journal/10/61362/in-defense-of-the-poor-image/.

Storr, R. (2002), *Gerhard Richter: Forty Years of Painting*, exh. cat., New York: Museum of Modern Art.

Swenson, I. (2016), 'In Conversation with Angela De La Cruz', exhibition booklet, Peer Gallery.

Trotter, D. (2020), 'Head in an Iron Safe', *London Review of Books*, 42 (24). Available online at: https://www.lrb.co.uk/the-paper/v42/n24/david-trotter/ head-in-an-iron-safe.

Valberg, A. (2005), *Light, Vision, Colour*, London: Wiley.

Vasari, G. (1987), *The Lives of the Artists*, trans. George Bull, 2 vols, London: Penguin.

Verwoert, J. (2005), 'Why are Conceptual Artists Painting Again?', *Afterall*, 12. Available online at: https://www.afterall.org/article/why.are.conceptual. artists.painting.again.because.

Volk, G. (2020), *Katharina Grosse*, London: Lund Humphries.

Weitz, M. (1956), 'The Role of Theory in Aesthetics', *Journal of Aesthetics and Art Criticism*, 15: 27–35.

Wiesing, L. (1997), *Die Sichtbarkeit des Bildes: Geschichte und Perspektiven der formalen Ästhetik*, Hamburg: Rowohlt.

Winckelmann, J. J. (1987), *Reflections on the Imitation of Greek Works in Painting and Sculpture*, trans. Elfriede Heyer and Roger C. Norton, La Salle, IL: Open Court.

Winckelmann, J. J. (2006), *History of the Art of Antiquity*, trans. H. F. Malgrave, Los Angeles: Getty Research Institute.

Wind, E. (1925), 'Zur Systematik der künstlerischen Probleme', in *Zeitschrift für Ästhetik und Allgemeine Kunstwissenschaft*, 18: 438–86.

Winters, E. (2015), 'Uncanny Absence and Imaginative Presence in Dalwood's Paintings', in D. Freeman and D. Matravers (eds), *Figuring Out Figurative Art: Contemporary Philosophers on Contemporary Paintings*, 37–53, London: Routledge.

Wittgenstein, L. (1958), *Philosophical Investigations*, trans. E. A. Anscombe, 2nd edn, Malden, MA and Oxford: Blackwell.

Wölfflin, H. (1888), *Renaissance und Barock: Eine Untersuchung über Wesen und Entstehung des Barockstils in Italien*, Munich: Theodor Ackermann.

Wölfflin, H. (1915), 'Vorwort', in H. Wölfflin, *Kunstgeschichtliche Grundbegriffe*, v–viii, Munich: F. Bruckmann.

Wölfflin, H. (1941), *Gedanken zur Kunstgeschichte: Gedrucktes und Ungedrucktes*, 2nd edn, Basel: Benno Schwabe.

Wölfflin, H. (1950), *Principles of Art History: The Problem of the Development of Style in Later Art*, trans. M. D. Hottinger, New York: Dover.

Wölfflin, H. (1986), *Classic Art: An Introduction to the High Renaissance*, trans. P. Murray and L. Murray, Oxford: Phaidon.

Wölfflin, H. (1991), *Kunstgeschichtliche Grundbegriffe. Das Problem der Stilentwicklung in der neueren Kunst*, 18th edn, Basel: Schwabe & Co.

Wollheim, R. (1973), *On Art and the Mind: Essays and Lectures*, London: Allen Lane.

Wollheim, R. (1979), 'Pictorial Style: Two Views', in B. Lang (ed.), *The Concept of Style*, 183–202, Cambridge: Cambridge University Press.

Wollheim, R. (1980), *Art and its Objects*, 2nd edn, Cambridge: Cambridge University Press.

Wollheim, R. (1987), *Painting as an Art*, London: Thames & Hudson.

Wollheim, R. (1995), 'Style in Painting' in C. Eck, J. McAllister and R. de Vall (eds), *The Question of Style in Philosophy and the Arts*, 37–49, Cambridge: Cambridge University Press.

Wollheim, R. (2001), 'A Reply to the Contributors', in R. van Gerwen (ed.), *Richard Wollheim on the Art of Painting: Art as Representation and Expression*, 241–61, Cambridge: Cambridge University Press.

Yau, J. (2012), 'Hidden in Plain Sight – Wade Guyton's Dirty Pictures', *Hyperallergic*, 28 October. Available online at: https://hyperallergic. com/59288/hidden-in-plain-sight-wade-guytons-dirty-pictures/.

Zangwill, N. (2001), *The Metaphysics of Beauty*, Ithaca and London: Cornell University Press.

Index